This book is due on the last date stamped below.
Failure to return books on the date due may result
in assessment of overdue fees.

Fines	$.50 per day	

The Indian Ocean Tsunami

THE

Indian Ocean Tsunami

*The Global Response
to a Natural Disaster*

Edited by
Pradyumna P. Karan and
Shanmugam P. Subbiah

Cartography by
Dick Gilbreath

THE UNIVERSITY PRESS OF KENTUCKY

Scholarly publisher for the Commonwealth,
serving Bellarmine University, Berea College, Centre College of Kentucky,
Eastern Kentucky University, The Filson Historical Society, Georgetown College,
Kentucky Historical Society, Kentucky State University, Morehead State University,
Murray State University, Northern Kentucky University, Transylvania University,
University of Kentucky, University of Louisville, and Western Kentucky University.
All rights reserved.

Editorial and Sales Offices: The University Press of Kentucky
663 South Limestone Street, Lexington, Kentucky 40508-4008
www.kentuckypress.com

15 14 13 12 11   5 4 3 2 1

Library of Congress Cataloging-in-Publication Data

The Indian Ocean tsunami : the global response to a natural disaster / edited by
Pradyumna P. Karan and Shanmugam P. Subbiah ; cartography by Dick Gilbreath.
    p. cm.
  Includes bibliographical references and index.
  ISBN 978-0-8131-2652-4 (hardcover : alk. paper)
  ISBN 978-0-8131-2653-1 (ebook)
  1. Indian Ocean Tsunami, 2004. 2. Tsunami relief—Asia. 3. Humanitarian
assistance—Asia 4. Emergency management—Asia. 5. Tsunami damage—Asia.
I. Karan, Pradyumna P. (Pradyumna Prasad) II. Subbiah, Shanmugam P.
III. Gilbreath, Dick.
  HV6032004.A78 I53 2011
  363.34'94091824090511—dc22   2010044406

Member of the Association of
American University Presses

Contents

List of Illustrations and Tables   vii

Preface   xi

Introduction: When Nature Turns Savage   1
    Pradyumna P. Karan

Part 1. Environmental and Ecological Impacts

1. The Tsunami Disaster on the Andaman Sea Coast of Thailand   35
    Masatomo Umitsu

2. The Geoenvironment and the Giant Tsunami Disaster in the Northern Part of Sumatra Island, Indonesia   51
    Masatomo Umitsu

3. Geological and Geomorphological Perspectives of the Tsunami on the Tamil Nadu Coast, India   65
    S. R. Singarasubramanian, M. V. Mukesh, K. Manoharan, P. Seralathan, and S. Srinivasalu

4. Tsunami Inundations and Their Impact in the Kaveri River Delta, Tamil Nadu, India   99
    S. Rani Senthamarai and J. Francis Lawrence

5. Impact of the Tsunami on the Coastal Ecosystems of the Andaman Islands, India   113
    Ramesh Ramchandran, Purvaja Ramachandran, Bojarajan Senthilkumar, and Brigitte Urban

6. Environmental Damage in the Maldives from the Indian Ocean Tsunami   127
    Koji Fujima

7. Tsunami Disasters in Seenigama Village, Sri Lanka, and Taro Town, Japan   135
   Kenji Yamazaki and Tomoko Yamazaki

Part 2. Socioeconomic Dimensions of Recovery, Reconstruction, and Response

8. Post-tsunami Recovery in South Thailand, with Special Reference to the Tourism Industry   163
   David Zurick

9. The Role of NGOs in Tsunami Relief and Reconstruction in Cuddalore District, South India   183
   Muthusami Kumaran and Tricia Torris

10. Sociocultural Frame, Religious Networks, Miracles: Experiences from Tsunami Disaster Management in South India   213
    Seiko Sugimoto, Antonysamy Sagayaraj, and Yoshio Sugimoto

11. Achievements and Weaknesses in Post-tsunami Reconstruction in Sri Lanka   237
    Martin Mulligan and Judith Shaw

12. Improving Governance Structures for Natural Disaster Response: Lessons from the Indian Ocean Tsunami   261
    Miranda A. Schreurs

Part 3. Geopolitical Perspective

13. Transnational Geopolitical Competition and Natural Disasters: Lessons from the Indian Ocean Tsunami   283
    Christopher Jasparro and Jonathan Taylor

List of Contributors   301
Index   305

Illustrations and Tables

Figures

I.1. Areas affected by the Indian Ocean Tsunami   2

1.1. Andaman Sea coast of south Thailand   36

1.2. Measured tsunami height in Khao Lak and Phuket   38

1.3. Tsunami flow in the northern part of the Nam Khem plain   43

1.4. Coastal change in the northern part of the Khao Lak plain   47

2.1. Location of Banda Aceh, Indonesia   52

2.2. Landform classification of the Banda Aceh coastal plain   53

2.3. Relationship between tsunami height and damages in the geoenvironment of the Banda Aceh coastal plain   55

2.4. Tsunami inundation in the Banda Aceh coastal plain   55

2.5. Direction and height of the tsunami flow in the Banda Aceh coastal plain   56

2.6. Casualties and missing people shown on a population map of Aceh province   60

3.1. Places affected by the tsunami along the Tamil Nadu coast   70

4.1. Methodology for tsunami water inundation mapping and groundwater quality   100

4.2. Seawater inundation along the Tamil Nadu coast   102

4.3. The study area: Kaveri delta   105

4.4. Location of surface and groundwater sample sites   109

5.1. Map of Andaman and Nicobar Islands   115

6.1. Location of atolls in the Maldives   129

7.1. Location of Seenigama village, Sri Lanka   137

7.2. Map of Seenigama and damages caused by the tsunami   139

7.3. Five types of house construction   147

7.4. Map of Taro Town, Iwate Prefecture, Japan   148

7.5. People's response to the tsunami in Taro Town   153

7.6. Taro reconstruction plan   154

7.7. Structure of how raw experiences are transformed into active experiences   158

7.8. Structure of vulnerability   158

7.9. Elements for mitigating the disastrous consequences of tsunamis   159

8.1. Map of tsunami-affected areas of south Thailand   166

8.2. Map of Phuket Island tourist resorts   167

9.1. South India location of Cuddalore district   189

10.1. Map of the Nagapattinam coast   217

Photographs

I.1. Fishing villages were damaged along the Andaman Sea coast of Thailand   3

I.2. Tsunami damage in the tourist resort of Phuket, Thailand   3

I.3. Tsunami damage in Aceh   14

I.4. Tsunami Nagar, a housing development in Chennai for tsunami victims, built with funding from the World Bank   25

1.1. Tsunami-damaged buildings in Patong Beach, Phuket   37

1.2. Destroyed resort cottages in south Khao Lak   40

1.3. Boulders carried by the tsunami on the coast of Pakarang Cape   40

1.4. Damaged buildings in Nam Khem   41

1.5. A fishing boat carried by the tsunami to the inner part of the Nam Khem coastal plain   44

1.6. Permanent rehabilitation houses in Nam Khem built by the Thai military   48

1.7. Recovered resort hotel and sign detailing evacuation route in Khao Lak   49

2.1. Temporary bridge on the main road on the west coast of Sumatra   58

2.2. Tents in the suburbs of Banda Aceh   61

2.3. Permanent rehabilitation houses in Ulee Lheue district   62

3.1a–f. Tsunami damages along the Tamil Nadu coast   72–73

3.2a–f. Tsunami damages and invasion of seawater   74–75

3.3. Satellite image of Karaikal before and after the tsunami, showing the inundation of villages   76

3.4. Satellite image of the Kodiyakarai region before and after the tsunami, showing landform changes   76

3.5a–f. Tsunami-induced erosion along the coast of Tamil Nadu   78–79

3.6a–f. Deposition of tsunami-borne sediments along the Tamil Nadu coast   81–82

4.1. Damaged home in Kaveri delta   103

4.2. Mapping the tsunami impact in Muthupet lagoon   107

4.3. Assessing water quality, Nagapattinam district   110

5.1. Mangrove area in Sippighat, South Andaman, destroyed by inundation
of seawater due to subduction of land   122

5.2. Seawater intrusion in agricultural fields adjacent to mangrove area in
Sippighat, South Andaman, due to subduction of land   123

5.3. Mangrove area in Kalighat Creek, North Andaman, exposed during
spring tides due to emergence of land   124

5.4. Coral reefs ecosystem of the North Reef, North Andaman, exposed
during spring tides due to emergence of land   125

6.1. Contaminated well and damaged water storage tank   130

6.2. Male International Airport inundated by the tsunami   131

6.3. Beach erosion in Muli   132

7.1. The temple as community center   141

7.2. Height the tsunami waves reached in Seenigama   142

7.3. Principal's house in Seenigama   143

7.4. Traditional-style house   143

7.5. Reconstruction area with government controls in Seenigama   144

7.6. Marks of the run-ups of the great tsunamis in Taro Town   150

7.7. Taro Town before the March 3, 1933, tsunami   151

7.8. Taro Town after the 1933 tsunami   151

7.9. Dikes of Taro Town   153

7.10. Mrs. Tabata presenting her picture story of her tsunami experience
155

7.11. Monument commemorating the victims of the 1933 tsunami   155

7.12. Wall painting of Kelaniya Temple   156

7.13. Another view of the wall painting   157

8.1. Entry point to Krabi province, August 2008   168

8.2. *Bangkok Post* front-page photo showing the destruction on Phi Phi
Don, December 27, 2005   170

8.3. The isthmus of Phi Phi Don, showing a recovered landscape, August
2008   170

8.4. Tsunami destruction in Patong Beach, December 27, 2005   174

8.5. Patong Beach fully recovered, August 2008   175

8.6. Tsunami destruction in Ton Sai, Phi Phi Don, December 28, 2005
180

8.7. Hotel construction in Ton Sai, Phi Phi Don, August 2008   180

9.1. Several NGOs, such as Missio Austria, focused on child welfare (health, nutrition, and education) in tsunami-affected areas of Cuddalore district   200

9.2. Inappropriate housing for tsunami victims built by the government in Cuddalore district   201

9.3. Appropriate temporary shelters built by NGOs   209

10.1. St. Thomas Mount   225

10.2. Santhome Cathedral, Mylapore, Chennai   225

10.3. St. Thomas Pole at Santhome Cathedral   229

10.4. Marker at the base of St. Thomas Pole, which Christians believe saved the area from the tsunami   229

Tables

3.1. Maximum inundation and run-up level of tsunami waves in some places along the Tamil Nadu coast   71

3.2. Pre- and post-tsunami sediment characteristic variation   92

4.1. Impact of the 2004 tsunami on the Indian coast   101

5.1. Sediment core sampling locations in South Andaman (August 2005)   116

5.2. Maximum run-up levels in Andaman and Nicobar Islands   118

5.3. Differences in physical and chemical parameters pre- and post-tsunami at Wright Myo, South Andaman   119

5.4. Average chemical index of alteration (CIA) for the surface and bottom sediments in tsunami-affected sites of South Andaman   121

7.1. Number of casualties and damaged houses in Sri Lanka   136

7.2. Location of houses and their damages   140

7.3. Villagers' responses to the tsunami   145

7.4. Tsunami chronology at Taro   149

7.5. The Sanriku Great Tsunamis   149

7.6. Relation between number of deaths in the family caused by the Meiji Sanriku Great Tsunami of 1896 and people's willingness to talk about the tsunami   152

9.1. Major relief, recovery, rehabilitation, and rebuilding activities provided by NGOs after the tsunami   186

9.2. Assistance provision during the first 48 hours after the tsunami   187

9.3. Satisfaction level in assistance received   188

9.4. NGOs' involvement in temporary housing in fisherfolk hamlets in Cuddalore district   191

9.5. Number of fishing units provided by NGOs in Cuddalore district   193

11.1. Estimated economic losses caused by the tsunami   240

Introduction

When Nature Turns Savage

Pradyumna P. Karan

Few natural disasters have captured the world's attention as did the Indian Ocean Tsunami of December 2004. *Tsunami,* a Japanese term, refers to earthquake-generated ocean waves associated with the sudden rise or fall of the seafloor that devastate coastal areas (Cartwright and Nakamura 2008). The emotional fascination with the tsunami was propelled by the mass media and live television images of the disaster (*Time Special Report,* January 10, 2005; *Newsweek,* January 10, 2005; *U.S. News & World Report,* January 10, 2005). It killed over 200,000 people and damaged the livelihoods and homes of over 1 million people around the Indian Ocean, from western Indonesia and southern Thailand to coastal Sri Lanka, southeastern India, and the Maldives. The tsunami produced an eerie, surreal landscape of destruction: huge ships and boats stranded miles inland, cars in the sea, lone two- or three-story buildings standing over vast open stretches of the flattened rubble of houses (Greenhough, Jazeel, and Massey 2005). Indonesia, Sri Lanka, India, and Thailand were the hardest hit. Citizens of forty other countries who were in the area were feared dead (Mottet 2005). Local officials and residents faced unprecedented challenges during the hours immediately following the tsunami. These included removing the debris that covered bodies, body identification, health and sanitation issues, and the necessity of creating mass graves. Prior experience with disasters, familiarity with the local area, the quality of preexisting networks among officials, a strong desire to rescue those yet living, and the presence of linkages between government and nongovernmental organizations were critical factors influencing the efficient management of mass fatality in areas impacted by the tsunami (Phillips et al. 2008). Over 9,000 foreign tourists in the area were among the dead or missing.

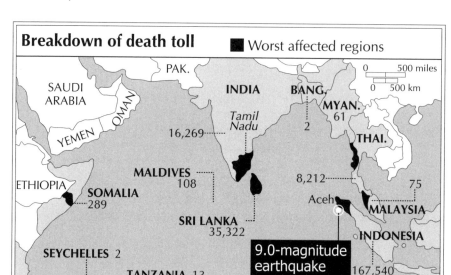

Fig. I.1. Areas affected by the Indian Ocean Tsunami. Death tolls based on the United Nations report. These figures vary because the estimate of numbers of people washed away by the tsunami waves varies.

Only 5,000–6,000 bodies were formally identified, most of them foreigners. The remaining bodies were buried in mass graves. This was especially true in Indonesia, where the resources and facilities were not available to identify the overwhelming number of victims. After the tsunami, the bodies were taken to public buildings such as temples and hospitals, where there were no records identifying the dead or where they came from. In Thailand and Sri Lanka, efforts were made to identify the many foreign dead. In Thailand, bodies were laid on the ground in temple courtyards. Only those who had been visually identified were buried or cremated. In Sri Lanka, most of those identified were foreigners and these were shipped to the morgue in Colombo. Cultural, religious, and legal factors are important considerations in the recovery and identification of the dead after a mass-death situation such as that produced by the Indian Ocean Tsunami. For many victims' families, emotional and legal complications continue years after the disaster.

Many areas, from coastal Sumatra to the Maldives, were out of reach when communication lines snapped. On Marina Beach in Chennai, India, women selling fish and children playing cricket, morning walkers and tourists all died as the tsunami waves came ashore. The waves struck tourist resorts from Phuket in Thailand to Bentos in Sri Lanka at the peak of the tourist and Christmas

Photo I.1. Fishing villages were damaged along the Andaman Sea coast of Thailand. (Photo by Masatomo Umitsu.)

Photo I.2. Tsunami damage in the tourist resort of Phuket, Thailand. (Photo by Masatomo Umitsu.)

holiday season. Fishing villages were washed away, and thousands of fishermen who put out to the sea on the morning of December 26, 2004, were engulfed by the huge waves. An Indian Air Force base on Car Nicobar Island was washed away, and the airport in Male, Maldives, was submerged.

The impact of the disaster was compounded by preexisting vulnerabilities such as socioeconomic, environmental, political, and age- and gender-based factors. In many areas poverty, environmental degradation such as overfishing and deforestation, displacement, inequalities, weak respect for human rights, and long-running armed conflict (north Sumatra and Sri Lanka) multiplied the impact of the disaster.

Natural Hazard Research in Geography

The study of natural disasters such as the Indian Ocean Tsunami provides insights into one of the major themes of geographic scholarship—the relationships of people and their natural environments. In the 1940s, following Gilbert F. White's first in-depth investigation of human response to natural hazards in the Mississippi River basin, the human dimension of disasters became a widely accepted focus of geographic research. The work of White inspired generations of geographers (Barton and Karan 1992; Mather and Karan 2000) and social scientists. The human response to natural hazards eventually became the dominant paradigm in disaster research. In line with White's work, this view acknowledges the responsibility of nature in explaining disaster occurrence. Individuals choose to adjust or not to the threat of natural hazards that are rare in time and magnitude. The choice of adjustment basically depends on how people perceive rare and extreme hazard threats and the risks associated with them. An individual or society with a low perception of risk is likely to adjust poorly to the threat. People with a higher perception of risk are likely to view the threats seriously and make efforts to adjust to natural hazard (Karan 1975). Burton, Kates, and White (1993) suggested a society-based classification of adaptations and adjustments to natural hazards depending on people's perception of nature's threat, contrasting traditional societies, allegedly having a poor capability of facing natural hazards, with the industrial Western societies, where adjustment is more effective but not perfect. Under the influence of the perception-adjustment paradigm, national governments and international agencies have adopted structural and technical solutions such as early warning systems, hazard mapping and evacuation plans, and information campaigns to manage natural hazards and raise people's perception of the hazardous phenomena.

Waddell (1977), Torry (1979), O'Keefe, Westgate, and Wisner (1976), and

Hewitt (1983) challenged the perception-adjustment paradigm, suggesting that people's behavior in the face of natural hazards is constrained by political-ecological factors beyond their control. Political neglect of the Acehnese in Indonesia and the Tamils in Sri Lanka, social marginalization of coastal fishing communities in the Indian Ocean countries, and the difficulty that powerless individuals face in accessing resources have contributed to their vulnerability to the tsunami hazards. The majority of the victims of the Indian Ocean Tsunami were marginal social groups such as women, children, the elderly, and the disabled. The low income, lack of knowledge of protection measures, poor housing conditions, and lack of savings of these groups further reduce their ability to protect themselves in the face of a natural disaster such as the Indian Ocean Tsunami. Inadequate social protections such as health services and limited social capital (networks) have also contributed to the vulnerability of coastal people affected by the tsunami. People's vulnerability and its root causes lie in the political ecology of the area and unique local contexts of the communities. A political ecology approach to the study of hazards should offer valuable insights into the relationships of people and their natural environments.

The focus of this book is on the environmental impact of the tsunami and practical policy issues of post-tsunami relief and reconstruction that are directed toward decision makers, managers, and the affected public as well as those concerned with the management of the human environment. Tsunami genesis, modeling of tsunami generation and propagation, tsunami detection and monitoring systems, and tsunami warning systems have been discussed in a recent book (Murty, Aswathanarayana, and Nirupana 2007). The present volume draws on the political ecology approach and takes forward the discussion of key environmental, social, political, and economic issues in the Indian Ocean disaster. The essays suggest culturally sensitive mitigation measures that consider the social, economic, and political context. Natural hazards cannot be prevented, but it is possible to reduce their impacts by reducing the vulnerability of people and their livelihoods.

The first seven chapters of this book highlight the contributions of geographers and geoscientists, and the next six deal with tsunami relief, reconstruction, sociocultural perspectives of disaster management, governance structures for natural disaster response, and geopolitical aspects of international disaster aid. While loss of human life and damage to infrastructure and economies have been recorded in numerous studies and reports by the World Bank and the Asian Development Bank, there are very few studies of the unprecedented environmental consequences of the tsunami on the fragile ecosystems of the coasts and islands in the Indian Ocean region. Scant attention has been paid to detailed research on the impact of the tsunami on natural marine and near-shore ecosystems. Understanding of coastal vulnerability and resilience in the face of natural disasters can help in the development of a sustainable coastal management plan as well as a comprehensive disaster management plan. Contributors to this volume undertook field surveys in Thailand, Indonesia, the Andaman Islands, Sri Lanka, the Maldives, and the Coromandel coast of India. They spent time inspecting the damages from both ground shaking and tsunami before the deposited sand and mud were cleared away or fenced off. They examine the role of physical, social, political, and economic factors as they interact with the local environment to understand the impact of the tsunami hazard. Many of these authors have served as advisors to state and local governments in attempts to solve the problems resulting from the disaster. This line of research builds on the work of Gilbert White (1945, 1964). In part 1, physical geographers and geoscientists Masatomo Umitsu, S. R. Singarasubramanian, M. V. Mukesh, K. Manoharan, P. Seralathan, S. Srinivasalu, S. Rani Senthamarai, J. Francis Lawrence, Ramesh Ramchandran, R. Purvaja, Brigitte Urban, Koji Fujima, Kenji Yamazaki, and Tomoko Yamazaki examine the nature of tsunami impacts on the landscape and local environment. In part 2, social scientists David Zurick, Muthusami Kumaran, Tricia Torris, Seiko Sugimoto, Antonysamy Sagayaraj, Yoshio Sugimoto, Martin Mulligan, Judith Shaw, and Miranda A. Schreurs investigate tsunami relief and reconstruction efforts and governance structures for disaster response, and in part 3, Christopher Jasparro and Jonathan Taylor look at the geopolitical aspects of transnational tsunami relief. Throughout the book, contributors point to the relationship between levels of development and intensity of damage from the tsunami disaster. The vulnerability of places and people to the Indian Ocean Tsunami varied with differences in wealth, power, and control over resources.

Social scientists have stressed the responsive capabilities of people. Human response to disaster in a region is influenced by a variety of factors, such as the frequency of natural hazards in the area, vulnerability to potential loss, and existing measures to prevent, avoid, or reduce loss. The post-tsunami relief efforts represent important responses to disaster: there is now greater emphasis on preparedness measures, such as the development of tsunami warning systems, and on loss-prevention measures, such as land use and development controls on seashore and coastal areas. International agencies and scientific organizations have begun to provide information and coordinate efforts for the development of an Indian Ocean Tsunami warning system. Although the volume of literature on natural disaster has grown rapidly, studies of the environmental and social dimensions of disasters in the non-Western world remain scarce. This book moves to plug this gap by bringing together contributions of an interdisciplinary group of scholars from Japan, India, the United States, Australia, and Germany in the first publication to address the problem of nature-society relationships in the areas affected by the Indian Ocean Tsunami. It contributes to increasing our understanding of the social dimensions of the catastrophe.

Geography of the Indian Ocean Tsunami

An undersea Sumatra-Andaman Earthquake along a plate boundary generated the mega-tsunami in the Indian Ocean on December 26, 2004 (Lay et al. 2005). The earthquake originated just north of Simeulue Island, off the western coast of northern Sumatra, Indonesia. The epicenter of the main earthquake was some 160 km (99.4 miles) west of Sumatra, at a depth of 30 km (18.6 miles) below mean sea level. The India plate, a part of the great Indo-Australian plate underlying the Indian Ocean and the Bay of Bengal, is drifting northeast at an average speed of 6 cm (2.4 inches) annually. The India plate meets the Eurasian plate at the Sunda trench. As a result of the movement between the plates, the seabed is estimated to have risen by several meters, displacing an estimated 30 km^3 of water and triggering the devastating tsunami waves. The energy released by the earthquake was estimated at 100 gigatons of TNT. In the open sea, tsunami waves barely ripple the surface. As they reach shallower water, however, these surging waves slow down, pile up, and become liquid mountains that crash onto land with furious force. The Indian Ocean Tsunami waves peaked at about 9 m (30 feet) as they reached shallow coastal waters. The tsunami waves crashed over Sumatra's Aceh province within 15 minutes of the initial tremors. The Andaman Islands were struck within 30 minutes, southern Thailand within 90 minutes, Sri Lanka and the eastern coast of India within 2 hours, and the Maldives within 3.5 hours.

As the 1,200 km (720 miles) of fault line affected by the earthquake was in a nearly north-south orientation, the greatest strength of the tsunami waves was in an east-west direction. Bangladesh, which lies at the northern end of the Bay of Bengal, had very few casualties despite being a low-lying country relatively near the epicenter. It benefited from the fact that the earthquake proceeded more slowly in the northern rupture zone, greatly reducing the energy along the western coast of India and Sri Lanka. If the north segment had experienced a normal earthquake, the estimated tsunami 5–6 m (16.5–19.8 feet) high waves along the Bangladesh coast would have killed more than 1 million people.

The tsunami transformed the coastal landscape of southeastern India. All houses and huts located along the frontal dunes were destroyed. In the worst-affected areas, stone-walled houses were also damaged. Identical scenes of shattered dwellings were reported from the Andaman Islands. Coastal geomorphic features displayed various degrees of damage. The high waves topped dune ridges, which were breached, eroded, or dissected. Saline waters occupied former flood-prone low beaches, and narrow inlets connected the lagoon to the sea. Before, the lagoons linked with the existing rivers inland. The roads perpendicular to the beach served as passageways for tsunami waves to travel inland, as at the Nagapattinam lighthouse and opposite the shrine at Velanganni. Opposite the Nagapattinam lighthouse, the tsunami followed the inlet and inundated a village over 1.6 km (a mile) inland. At Nagapattinam, the tsunami shattered the seawall of the fishing harbor, trawlers were tossed ashore, a communication tower was crushed, and oil storage tanks suffered erosive damage. High waves also damaged the seawall at Karaikal. A children's park and tourist facilities were washed away at Cuddalore.

In Sri Lanka, the tsunami devastated the eastern and southern coasts. With the nation having a population of 20 million and a land area of 65,780 km^2 (25,300 sq. miles), nearly everyone in the country was touched in some way. Severe damage occurred in densely packed, poorly constructed residential and commercial buildings along the coast. The physical infrastructure along the affected coastlines was destroyed. Tsunami impact varied by location; some areas were relatively unscathed while adjoining areas were completely devastated. Coral reef mining contributed to the impact of the tsunami through its effect on wave amplitude and energy, damage to buildings, and loss of life. In areas where sand dunes had been graded or mangroves cut, tsunami waves went further inland with greater force. Lack of information about the nature of the tsunami resulted in many deaths. When the first wave receded to expose the seafloor, large numbers of people in Sri Lanka (as well as in India) followed to collect seashells and fish. When the wave suddenly returned, they were too far out to reach safety. Some died when they climbed on buses or a train instead of taking shelter in nearby concrete buildings. Tsunami waves altered the natural and man-made canals and lagoons opening to the sea (Preuss 2005).

In the Maldives, with a population of about 300,000, the tsunami was felt across the country's numerous small islands. About a third of the population was severely affected. Damage was sustained on fifty-three islands, and the tsunami completely destroyed 10% of the islands. The islands are mainly coastal entities, and their ecosystem is among the world's most fragile. In April 1987, high waves covered two-thirds of Male; airport runway lights were washed away, and walls collapsed. If the worst-case projections of global warming become reality, rising waters could drown the nation within a hundred years.

The Maldives have no natural elevation higher than about 4.5 m (15 feet) above sea level, and the average altitude is 1.8 m (about 6 feet). The economic base is a narrow one, relying on tourism and fisheries. In the tourism sector, which is very important in the economy, out of eighty-seven resorts, nineteen were severely damaged and closed down, while fourteen others suffered major partial damage. Living conditions deteriorated on many inhabited islands, where the freshwater lens was affected by groundwater pollution and high salinity and increasing pollution of lagoons. The tsunami ravaged the infrastructure as the high waves and floods engulfed waste disposal sites and spread previously collected waste throughout the islands, endangering public health and putting groundwater at risk.

Impact of the Tsunami on Coastal Morphology

Major changes in the coastline after the tsunami have been studied by several scholars (Shaw 2008; Jaya Kumar et al. 2008; Pari et al. 2008). Using high-resolution satellite images, Baumann (2008) analyzed environmental changes in the Indonesian villages of Birek and Seungko Mulat between the pre- and post-tsunami periods. Baumann found that except for the mosque at Birek and a few homes located further inland and slightly higher in elevation at Seungko Mulat, both villages were completely destroyed by the tsunami. A year and a half after the tsunami disaster, the villages had been rebuilt and relocated at a higher elevation but still within the area that could be submerged by another large tsunami. The large beach area was pushed entirely inland by the tsunami surges, and the tree zone behind the beach was practically denuded of vegetation. The beach area has started to recover but is noticeably smaller than it was originally. A large part of the valley floor in this area was devoted to rice fields prior to the tsunami. After the tsunami the valley floor was covered with debris from uprooted vegetation and destroyed buildings, sand from the beach area, and marine sediment from the ocean. In recent years about one half of the rice fields have been recovered; the rest of the agricultural land is covered with noncultivated vegetation. The freshwater estuary near the mouth of the Krueng Kala River has now become a saltwater bay. The destruction of the sandbars separating the estuary from the open sea has allowed the saltwater tides to enter the area. Freshwater aquaculture along the edge of the estuary has been replaced with marine life.

The impact of the tsunami inundation and run-up level was influenced by the nature of coastal landform. The inundation was high along the coast adjoining river mouth and estuary. Shallow open coast also experienced high inundation. Beaches of elevated coast (medu) were relatively less affected by inundation as compared to estuarine coast. Coastal landforms were altered by direct tsunami run-up as well as by the vigorous backwash (Dawson 1994). The relationship between coastal landform and tsunami inundation along the southeastern coast of India has been pointed out in recent studies (Chandrasekar et al. 2005, 2006). A study of inundation characteristics and coastal landform by Kurian et al. (2006) along the Kerala Coast of India revealed that river inlets favored inundation, and devastation was severe because the tsunami coincided with the high tide. The severe damage along the coast of Nagapattinam in Tamil Nadu was also due to the physical features of the coast, which encouraged inundation (Raval 2005). Here the beaches along the coast were shallow and open. A close relationship between the morphology of the seashore and run-up level has also been reported by Narayan, Sharma, and Maheshwari (2005a, 2005b). Estuary and river inlets were most vulnerable to tsunami inundation (Jaya Kumar et al. 2005). The pattern of river inlets was also influenced by the deposition of the tsunami-borne sediments or by erosion and redistribution of sediments. The existence of elevated coastal dunes and beach ridges near the coastline in some parts of northern Tamil Nadu acted as barriers and reduced the extent of inundation (Mohan 2005). In the Maldives, the densely vegetated islands were less affected by the tsunami (Kench et al. 2006). Likewise, along the shallow coasts of the Kanyakumari district in southern India, areas that were encircled by coconut plantations and well-developed dunes suffered less damage (Reddy, Rao, and Rao 2005). In Sri Lanka, coral reef mining had a direct effect on wave amplitude and energy, damage to buildings, and loss of life. Tsunami waves were driven inland with greater force in areas where sand dunes had been graded or mangroves cut.

Mangrove Forest and Tsunami

The important role of mangrove forests in saving life and property from the tsunami has been analyzed by Giri et al. (2008) and Danielsen et al. (2005). Several studies (for example, Yanagisawa et al. 2009) have noted the protective role of healthy mangrove forests in reducing damage from the tsunami. The United Nations special envoy for tsunami recovery endorsed a program to allocate $62 million (U.S.) to preserve and reforest the mangrove as natural protective barriers. In his research, Andrew Baird (2006) of the Center for Coral Reef Biology at James Cook University found no relationship between the area of mangrove forest and damage by the tsunami. Although mangrove forests provide coastal communities with valuable resources and are important in preserving the ecosystem, their role in protecting against the tsunami was limited. Based on research in Aceh, Indonesia, Baird found "that neither reefs nor coastal forest reduced the damage caused by the tsunami." Mangrove forests, according to Baird, are effective in reducing the energy of wind-generated storm waves of lengths of a few yards. The earthquake-generated tsunamis have wavelengths of miles. The tsunami that hit the Acehnese coast was 12.9 km (8 miles) thick, and mangrove forests do not offer a meaningful protection against tsunami energy. A coastal buffer zone may offer protection from the tsunami, but enforcement of a buffer zone would be a difficult policy issue for local governments, involving social and economic costs. Luxury hotels in Thailand, Sri Lanka, and India have built on the waterfront on the coast and cannot relocate without economic loss.

Case Studies of Tsunami Impacts

Thailand: Nam Khem Coastal Plain

In Thailand, the entire Andaman coastal strip between the borders of Malaysia and Myanmar was affected (Rigg et al. 2008). Within this area, Krabi, Phanga, and Phuket provinces suffered the most damage. The tsunami affected 392 villages and nearly 54,500 people. Over 5,000 people lost their lives, and many more were missing. The area's two main sources of income—tourism and fishing—were severely affected (Henderson 2007; Lebel, Khrutmuang, and Manuta 2006). The natural environment of the region was also seriously damaged through the erosion of beaches and sedimentation of coastal ecosystems. Coral reefs and mangrove swamps along the Andaman coast suffered considerable damage.

Before the disaster this region of Thailand had experienced uncontrolled development of the tourism centers of Phuket and Phi Phi, and the newly emerging centers of Khao Lak and Krabi, which may have contributed to the large scale of deaths and destruction from the disaster. The increasing pressure on the natural environment from tourism, such as impacts on coral from marine sports, had already significantly affected the environment and ecology of the area. The ecosystem was already fragile when the tsunami hit. Additionally, the lack of coordination in the planning policies within the region in part contributed to enhance the damage from the tsunami. Moreover, research indicates that the religious affiliation, ethnicity, and place of residence of Thai citizens played a significant role in their capacity to confront and adapt to the consequences of the disaster (Paton et al. 2008).

Geographer Masatomo Umitsu of Nagoya University visited the area inundated by the tsunami shortly after December 26, 2004, and again several times between 2005 and 2009. In chapter 1 Umitsu discusses the landform changes resulting from the tsunami in the Nam Khem coastal plain of southern Thailand, located on the Andaman Sea coast of the Malay Peninsula. Landforms of the Nam Khem coastal lowland include distinct rows of beach ridges in its central part and artificial tin-mining mounds and ponds in the northern and southern parts of the plain. The lowland is generally about 3–4 m (9.8–13.1 feet) in elevation, although the tin-mining mounds in the northern part of the plain rise to over 10 m (32.8 feet). Nam Khem village is located in the northern end of the lowland, and grassland and plantations cover the other areas. Elevation of the upland located east of the coastal lowland is mostly above 10 m. Calculated high- and low-tide levels of the Ao Kaulak near Nam Khem on December 26, 2004, were 237 cm (93.3 inches) and 62 cm (24.4 inches), respectively, and the maximum tidal range of the region was about 2 m (6.6 feet) (based on data by Tsuji, Namegaya, and Ito 2005). Umitsu classified landforms through interpretation of aerial photographs and satellite images of the plains and field surveys. The 1:50,000 scale toposheets of the Nam Khem coastal plain, 1:25,000 scale aerial photographs taken on February 16, 2002, and an IKONOS satellite image taken on December 29, 2004, were used for the interpretation and classification of landforms. During the field surveys, heights and directions of flow indicators related to tsunami flow on the plains were measured by examining the orientation of snapped-off fence posts, fallen trees, and other indicators. The directions of grasses flattened by water were measured to determine tsunami backwash flow in the Nam Khem plain.

Geographer Umitsu's field research revealed that the most remarkable landform changes occurred in the lower parts of the small streams connecting with the Andaman Sea. Prior to the tsunami, small river channels flowing to the Andaman Sea coast on the Nam Khem plain and Khao Lak plain, 10 km (6.2 miles) south of the Nam Khem plain, were narrow and their mouths were usually blocked by the deposition of beach sand. Near the mouth of small channels, ponds had formed in several abandoned tin-mining pits. The channels changed their planar shape to a wedge-shape type and their river mouths opened to the width of 50–200 m (164–656 feet) after the tsunami event. Distinct tsunami deposits were not found either beside the channels or near the ends of eroded channels. Measured flow directions were mainly concentrated in or toward the channels, indicating backwash flow. Thus, the main widening of the channels was caused not by tsunami run-up, but by concentrated strong backwash flows from inland.

Evidence of erosion by the tsunami was seen on the northwestern tip of the Nam Khem plain, on the coast beside the small channel mouth, and on both sides of the Hua Krang Nui Cape in the central part of the Nam Khem plain.

Beaches in the most exposed part of the area, near the Hua Krang Nui Cape, retreated or vanished after tsunami inundation. The direction of the run-up tsunami flow was nearly perpendicular to the coastline, and that of the backwash flows in the Nam Khem plain concentrated close to the sea. Lower reaches of the rivers were eroded and changed their planar shape to wedge shape. Coastal erosion of the plains was caused by direct attack of the tsunami wave.

Indonesia: Banda Aceh Coastal Plain

In Indonesia, the tsunami caused heavy loss of life and great destruction in Aceh, with 130,400 dead, 36,800 missing, and 504,500 displaced. Activities directly related to the personal livelihoods of urban and rural communities, such as commerce, agriculture, and fishing, were severely impacted by the disaster. Environmental impacts included damage to coral reefs and mangrove swamps, loss of land, and physiographic changes in the coastal zone. Iverson and Prasad (2007) evaluated tsunami damage in Aceh and built an empirical vulnerability model of damage/no damage based on elevation, distance from shore, vegetation cover, and exposure. They found that highly predictive models are possible and that developed areas were far more likely to be damaged than forested zones. Baird and Kerr (2008) note that the modeling approach of Iverson and Prasad to predict areas susceptible to tsunami damage ignores important variables and their conclusion that tree belts provided an effective defense against the tsunami in Aceh is not justified.

In chapter 2 Umitsu discusses the impact of the tsunami on the northern part of Sumatra's Banda Aceh coastal plain, which is located along the lower reaches of the Aceh River. Deltaic lowland and beach ridges are occupied by houses, and the Banda Aceh urban area is located on the deltaic plain in the central part of the coastal plain. Calculated high- and low-tide levels of the Ulee Lheue near Banda Aceh on December 26, 2004, were 172 cm (67.7 inches) and 42 cm (16.5 inches), respectively, and the tidal range of the region was less than 1.5 m (4.9 feet) (based on data by Tsuji, Namegaya, and Ito 2005). The most extensive damage in Aceh city was from tsunami inundation. The tsunami inundation extended 4 km (2.5 miles) into the city proper. Almost all residential houses were destroyed. Inside Aceh city and inland, the tsunami destroyed or flooded everything and dumped all kinds of debris. Only brick-built mosques and a few two-story buildings survived. The small coastal villages were inundated by the high, floodlike tsunami wave, which left behind sand deposits at least 5 cm (about 2 inches) thick. In Ulee Lheue and Aceh Besar, the tsunami wave was more than 10 m (32.8 feet) high, and no houses and trees survived. Almost everything in its path was swept away, with tsunami waves

Photo I.3. Tsunami damage in Aceh. (Photo by Masatomo Umitsu.)

reaching the city heavily laden with all types of debris. The shorelines of Ulee Lheue and Aceh city were completely flattened. Large boulders transported by the waves were found in the Lhok Ngah area of Banda Aceh.

Flow indicators on the Banda Aceh coastal plain generally show inundation from the northwest. However, some areas show different directions of the flow. On the northeastern coast, flows spread out in a radial pattern from a gap in the sand dune along the coast. In the southwestern part of the plain, northeastward tsunami flow from the west coast penetrated the plain and the flow met in a gap of hills with the southward run-up tsunami flow. Indicators of tsunami flow in the western part of the coastal plain show southward flows deflected due to the existence of hills.

Tsunami flow extended inland in the central and western parts of the plain for about 4 km (2.5 miles) and for about 3 km (1.9 miles) in the eastern part. Remarkable invasion of the run-up tsunami flow along the Aceh, the Aceh drainage, and the Jreu rivers was recorded on the SPOT 2 image. The distances of the invasion of the flow from the coast into the rivers were 8 km (5 miles), 8.5 km (5.3 miles), and 6 km (3.7 miles), respectively. Inundation heights at similar distances from the coast were variable, with greater heights in the central and western part of the plain. The tsunami reached a height of about 9 m

(29.5 feet) on the ground near the port of the Banda Aceh and about 6–8 m (19.7–26.2 feet) in the western part of the plain about 2 km (1.2 miles) inland. In the eastern part of the plain about 2 km from the coast, however, tsunami heights were mostly lower than 3 m (9.8 feet).

Severe coastal erosion occurred in the parts of the tidal plain used for shrimp- or fishponds. The small narrow banks separating the ponds were easily eroded by the tsunami, returning these areas to former tidal flat conditions. The conversion of these areas to tidal flats was due to erosion by the tsunami rather than tectonic subsidence. Interviews with local people confirmed that tidal areas are now exposed at low tide to the same extent as they were before the tsunami, and tide levels marked on several bridges were almost similar to levels before the tsunami. It was difficult to reconstruct the flows of the tsunami backwash flow in the Banda Aceh plain because there are few indicators of backwash flow on the ground.

Erosion of channels was not violent and the linear erosion was not observed on the plain. In some areas of the plain, however, coastal landforms were greatly modified. Shrimp- and fishponds on the tidal plain were extremely damaged, and some of them disappeared after the tsunami. This indicates that the backwash flow was not concentrated linearly in the Banda Aceh plain, and sheet erosion of backwash flow dominated in the plain. This condition is shown on the SPOT image taken four hours after the tsunami intrusion.

Tsunami flow and inundation in the Banda Aceh plain are related to its landforms. The landforms of the Banda Aceh coastal plain are characterized as deltaic lowlands with tidal plains in the west and central parts and strand plains and beach ridges in the eastern part. Coastal erosion of the plains was caused by the direct attack of the tsunami wave in the Banda Aceh plain, and the broad tidal flat of the Banda Aceh coastal plain was severely damaged by the tsunami flow. Sheet erosion dominated in the Banda Aceh tidal plain. Microlandforms such as beach ridges and natural levees prevented the flow of the tsunami from penetrating further inland in the area near the margin of tsunami inundation.

India: Southeastern Coast and the Andaman Islands

The tsunami triggered by the earthquake off the coast of northern Sumatra struck the southeastern coast of India, as well as the Andaman and Nicobar islands, at about 08:00 on Sunday, December 26, 2004. The 10 m (32.8 feet) high tsunami waves traveled as far as 3 km (1.9 miles) inland. In India the tsunami killed at least 12,400 persons, and approximately 5,650 were missing and 6,900 were injured. Around 8,000 deaths occurred in the five districts—Chennai,

Kancheepuram, Cuddalore, Kanyakumari, and Nagapattinam—of Tamil Nadu state. A tsunami run-up survey was conducted along the east coast of India immediately after the disaster to study damages and inundation areas, and to obtain estimates of tsunami heights from perishable evidence like watermarks on houses and ocean debris transported inland. The results were reported by Chadha et al. (2005).

In chapter 3 Singarasubramanian and his colleagues provide a geological and geomorphological perspective of the tsunami impact along the coast of Tamil Nadu. Over 6,000 were killed in Nagapattinam during services at Velanganni Church, which was 200 m (656 feet) from the shore. Nagapattinam district was the worst-affected area, particularly regions adjoining the mouths of the rivers Vellar, Chinnavaikal (Pitchavaram), and Coleroon. Nearly 75% of those killed were women and children. Fishing villages located within 100 to 200 m (328 to 656 feet) of the coast bore the brunt of the losses, with the destruction of 190,000 homes and 52,638 boats in Tamil Nadu. Inland, thousands of acres of agricultural land were damaged by the saltwater (Government of India 2005).

Nagapattinam, the worst-affected area, comprises about 15% of the coastline of Tamil Nadu. It is the administrative capital of this district, with a population of 330,000 (2001). The rural population of the district is 1.15 million. The tsunami affected nearly 200,000 people in the coastal hamlets. The statistics available from the district administration indicate that among the affected, 87% were from fishermen communities. The rest were agricultural laborers, traders, and tourists/pilgrims. The tsunami affected thirty-eight villages and seventy-three habitations along the coastal zone. Among the confirmed human loss of 8,081 people in Tamil Nadu, the Nagapattinam coast alone accounted for 6,065 deaths, which is 76% of the state's total loss. The coastal zone was "Ground Zero" because of the fact that within a 10 km (6.2 mile) range 4,592 deaths were recorded, seventy-three habitations were affected, fifty-one fishing hamlets were devastated, there was a cut in total power and water supply, and the pilgrim towns of Nagore and Vailankanni were severely hit, with almost 450 deaths per square kilometer.

The tsunami also destroyed houses, boats and catamarans, fishing harbors, fishing landings, and auction centers in Nagapattinam. Ice plants, marine mechanic repair shops, and other traders on the coast were also destroyed. Damages were also reported due to the intrusion of saltwater into the aquifers and the inundation of sand over agriculture and aquaculture farms.

With increasing distance landward, the mean grain size of the sand sheets appeared to decrease. The graded sequence from coarse to fine upwards in each of two to three sand layers was observed at the 80 m (262.5 feet) positions at Devanampatnam. Maximum inundation distances along the profiles were established on the basis of most landward distribution of flotsam in debris lines or of anomalous articles, such as clothing, mats, fishing floats, and so on. Maximum inundation ranged between 140 and 800 m (459.3 and 2,624.7 feet) from the swash zone. Based on local topography, flow-direction indicators, and the orientation of debris lines, it was apparent that maximum landward inundation occurred by lateral flow at Devanampatnam, Parangipettai, and Tarangambadi. Lateral flows filled inter dune-ridge valleys that were landward of shore-parallel dune ridges at Devanampatnam and Parangipettai. The inter dune-ridge valleys at the landward ends of these two profiles were connected to tidal inlet channels. Lateral flow also filled shallow valleys in Pulicat and Tarangambadi, where breaches in shore-parallel dune ridges allowed the tsunami to inundate back-ridge areas. Flow features were recorded in most of the profiles that include vegetation flop-over, orientated beams, debris shields around tree trunks, and sand ripples. Loss of life and property was reported in the first 100 m (328 feet) from the shore, where several settlements were washed away.

Small differences in local run-up and coastal topography resulted in large differences in tsunami inundation and associated loss of life and damage within the Tamil Nadu coastal areas. The combination of local high run-up, low topography, and dense development apparently accounted for the large loss of life and property. The surge water elevations, together with surge water depths, appear to be important parameters in tsunami hazard analysis. Low valleys behind shore-parallel dune ridges claimed several lives due to lateral flows from tidal inlets or from breaches in the dune ridge.

Most of the population of the coastal areas depends upon fishing for survival. Fishing is one of the most important sectors that sustained severe loss. Fishing equipment and boats at the shore were destroyed. Large launchers and open board engine boats were also damaged by the tsunami. Next to human lives, potential loss in the fisheries sector was very high when compared to other sectors. The loss to the fishing industry was ten times larger if the destroyed fishing equipment was included. The amount of relief provided is based on the destroyed fishing equipment. There are no fewer than eleven ports on the coast of Nagapattinam district, of which eight are open to foreign trade. The coastline has a number of harbors, of which mention may be made of Nagore, Point Calimere, and Nagapattinam. The significant small ports are Kilvellore, Thirumulaivasal, Nagapattinam, Velanganni, Topputturai, Muthupet, and Adiramapatnam. The Nagapattinam district is made up of the six *taluks* (small administrative units): Nagapattinam, Kilvellore, Vedharanyam, Mayiladuthurai,

Sirkali, and Thrangampadi. The district is for the most part a flat plain, sloping very gently to the sea on the east.

As noted earlier, the state of Tamil Nadu experienced severe environmental devastation, such as erosion and deposition of sediments, disturbances in the environment of microbes, and water-quality deterioration in both surface and groundwater resources. In chapter 4 geographer S. Rani Senthamarai and geologist J. Francis Lawrence map the geographic extent of tsunami inundations in the Kaveri delta and evaluate the impact of inundations on both surface and groundwater quality. The area, with large mudflats, lagoons, swamps, and mangroves, suffered widespread inundation. Water sample collection and vertical electrical sounding (VES) were carried out in twenty-four predetermined locations, which were equally distributed throughout the study area. These water samples were analyzed for major cations and anions and processed by a computer program that classifies water with reference to several standard water-quality classifications. With the output of this computer program, various groundwater-quality maps were prepared in a geographic information system (GIS) environment. These output maps indicate the changes in the water quality along the coast due to the tsunami. The VES field data were processed both manually and digitally. With the geophysical output, isoapparent resistivity maps were prepared. Hydrogeochemical output matches the findings of the geophysical investigation. From this investigation it was concluded that in one or two monsoons the groundwater quality would return to normalcy. A similar study of the impact of the tsunami on the groundwater regime of an island in South Andaman was reported by Singh (2008).

In chapter 5 Ramesh Ramchandran and colleagues discuss the impact of the tsunami on the coastal ecosystem of the Andaman Islands. The islands were severely hit because of their proximity to the epicenter of the earthquake and the tectonic activity that led to the subsidence of the islands, causing the submergence of low-lying coastal areas. Great Nicobar, the southernmost island in the group, is only about 150 km (93.2 miles) from the epicenter near Banda Aceh in Sumatra. The lighthouse at Indira Point, the southernmost tip of Great Nicobar, now lies in the ocean. Before the tsunami, it was about 100 m (328 feet) inland from the high-tide line. The destruction in the central Nicobar group, comprising the inhabited islands of Nancowry, Camorra, Katchal, Trinket, Chowra, Teress, and Bompoka, was considerable. Trinket Island broke into three. Maximum destruction was recorded on the 126 km² (50.4 sq. mile) island of Car Nicobar, with a population of over 25,000 Nicobari tribals. Here huge waves topped over the relatively flat topography along the coast on which the tribal settlements as well as the Indian Air Force base were located. Most of the villages were flattened and washed away by the waves, leaving behind a desolate landscape. The survivors had lost not only relatives and property but also a major source of their livelihood, which is copra. Most of the coconut trees were destroyed, and the remaining trees were washed with seawater several times, rendering them infertile or dead. The Nicobarese, unlike the other indigenous peoples in the islands, are essentially a coastal-dwelling people, and consequently all their settlements were washed away. In areas where the original seacoast was submerged, sand deposits and beaches have formed along the new coast. Ecological processes are responding to restore a certain balance after the cataclysmic event. About a month after the disaster, the Indian Coast Guard reported that sea turtles were nesting on newly formed beaches near Indira Point on Great Nicobar Island.

The islands of the Andaman group did not experience as much destruction except on parts of South Andaman Island, where Port Blair is located. The Indian Council for Agricultural Research estimated that the cultivable area damaged by the tsunami inundation in the islands was about 4,500–5,000 ha spread over sixty-eight villages. Large areas under paddy cultivation, particularly in South Andaman (reclaimed for farming from mangroves), were destroyed by the seawater ingress.

The Andaman and Nicobar Environmental Team's rapid assessment of the environmental impact of the tsunami revealed that the worst-affected ecological system was the coral reefs (Brown 2005), particularly along the coast of the Middle and North Andaman. While there was substantial subsidence in the Nicobars, the northern part of the Andaman Islands experienced uplift, which exposed large area of coral reefs even at high tide.

The five indigenous communities in the islands—the Shompen of Great Nicobar (population about 300), the Sentinelese of North Sentinel Islands (about 100 people), the Onge, who live on Little Andaman (about 100 persons), the Great Andamanese, whose settlement of about 40 persons is on Strai Island, and the 260-odd Jarawas who live in the forests of the Jarawa Reserve on the western coast of South and Middle Andaman islands—were unscathed by the tsunami. These communities could sense the tsunami's coming from nature's signals and made their way to higher ground. The indigenous people have better and sharper knowledge of their environment and a heightened understanding of signals from natural processes occurring around them.

The Maldives

Koji Fujima of Japan's National Defense Academy has investigated the damage and characteristics of the tsunami in the Maldives. His findings are reported in chapter 6. The Maldives is a chain of low coral atolls no more than 128 km (80 miles) wide and stretching some 760 km (475 miles) from north to south. The country forms the central part of the Laccadive-Chagos ridge, a submerged mountain range that is mostly about 295 m (985 feet) deep, but increases to more than 984 m (3,280 feet) between the main part of the country and the two southernmost atolls. The total land area of the country is less than 299 km² (115 sq. miles). The Maldives consists of well over 1,000 islands—as many as 2,000 if all permanently exposed banks and reefs are included. Only nine islands are larger than 2.6 km² (1 sq. mile). The largest island, Fua Mulaku, is 4.8 km (3 miles) at its longest point. Most of the Maldives is less than 4.5 m (15 feet) above mean sea level, which makes the country vulnerable to inundation by tsunami waves. Male Island, on which the capital city of Male is located, is protected by solid seawalls. The tsunami was higher than the seawall and inundated Male, causing some damage. However, the damage was not very severe and the recovery was quick.

Sri Lanka

The tsunami struck a relatively thin but long coastal area stretching over 1,000 km (621 miles)—nearly two-thirds of the nation's coastline (Wijetunge 2005; Gunatilaka 2005). The damage stretched from Jaffna in the north down the entire eastern and southern coast, and covered the west coast as far north as Colombo and Chilaw. The tsunami claimed 35,300 lives, injured 121,440, displaced 443,000, and left 1,500 children without parents. About 88,000 homes and 24,000 boats were destroyed. Coastal infrastructure—roads, railway, power, telecommunication, water supply, and fishing ports—was severely damaged. The main victims were already-vulnerable groups, such as the fishermen living close to the shore in simple houses and shelters. In chapter 7 Kenji Yamazaki and Tomoko Yamazaki analyze the damage from the tsunami in Seenigama village, Galle province, Sri Lanka. The authors offer suggestions to mitigate the damages based on the experience of Taro Town in Iwate Prefecture, Japan.

The responses to the tsunami—the challenges of and attitudes toward relocation and post-tsunami livelihoods in Sri Lanka—were shaped by uneven development, social exclusion, and ethnic conflict. The responses were embedded in structures of gender, caste, class, and ethnicity. Ruwanpura (2008), based on studies in the southern and eastern provinces, has shown that gendered structures within the local political economy influenced the ways in which displaced communities and women initially devised livelihood strategies.

Sri Lanka's northeast region was the worst-affected area. The Asian Development Bank (Telford, Cosgrave, and Houghton 2006) estimated that the coastal population affected ranged from 35% in Kilinochi to 80% in Mullativu and 78% in Amparai. In the southern districts of Galle, Matara, and Hambantota, less than 20% of the coastal population was affected. The enormity of the tragedy has awakened Sri Lanka to the potential vulnerability of its coastal belt, which runs 2,092 km (1,300 miles) around the island and in varying amounts inland, depending on coastal features, past land-use practices, and susceptibility to natural hazards.

The tsunami crippled many of the livelihood assets (human, social, and physical) of the fishing communities in Sri Lanka. De Silva and Yamao (2007) have assessed the capacity to build livelihood assets in fishing communities in three villages in the southern districts of Sri Lanka in terms of the impact of the tsunami as well as the impact of the government policy on rebuilding. The fishing community in Tangalla was significantly ahead of the fishing communities in Hikkaduwa and Waligama. Experienced fishermen with better educational backgrounds were significantly better able to build livelihood assets.

Socioeconomic Dimensions of Recovery and Response

The Indian Ocean Tsunami had major societal and economic impacts (Rodriguez et al. 2006). A number of emerging issues, such as the impact of the tsunami disaster on tourism, the role of nongovernmental organizations (NGOs) in recovery and reconstruction, the importance of socioeconomic factors in local reconstruction programs, the achievements and weaknesses of post-tsunami reconstruction, the importance of governing structures for disaster response, and the political geography of transnational aid for tsunami victims, are discussed in this section. A better understanding of the societal impacts can protect populations residing in coastal regions.

Areas affected by the tsunami included many popular international tourist resorts in Thailand, Sri Lanka, and the Maldives. As the tsunami struck during the Christmas holiday period, people from foreign countries were directly affected, although the largest numbers of deaths were from the local population. The tsunami highlighted the vulnerability of coastal communities. The Andaman coast of Thailand, stretching from Ranong province bordering Myanmar (Burma) to Satun province flanking Malaysia, is dotted with hundreds of islands and numerous beaches. The entire coastline was affected by the tsunami, but some of the worst damage was in the major tourist destinations of Phuket, Phang Nga, and Krabi. The resort of Khao Lak, where the tidal flood topped more than 9 m (30 feet) and extended 2.4 km (1.5 miles) inland, suffered major destruction. Calgaro and Lloyd (2008) discuss the sociopolitical and environmental conditions that contributed to the vulnerability of this tourism community in the southern Phang Nga province of Thailand. The island of Phuket in Thailand, a top international tourist resort on the brilliant blue Andaman Sea seriously damaged by the tsunami, has been completely rebuilt (Dicum 2009).

Geographer David Zurick (chapter 8), based on his field observations in Thailand, discusses the reconstruction of tourism along the Andaman Sea coast. There are few signs of the tsunami in Khao Lak except for a few trees' exposed roots and stumps of twisted branches. Khao Lak now has more upscale luxury resort hotels than it did before the tsunami. The area's economy is dependent on tourism, and the government of Phuket has provided generous aid to rebuild the tourist infrastructure and facilities in the aftermath of the tsunami. However, due to the worldwide economic slump in 2009, international tourism on the Andaman coast is suffering nonetheless.

Muthusami Kumaran, a public policy scholar, and Tricia Torris, a professional health educator, provide information in chapter 9 on the role of NGOs in the rescue, relief, rehabilitation, and reconstruction of coastal communities after the devastating Indian Ocean Tsunami. They present a case study of tsunami relief and reconstruction provided by a network of NGOs in Cuddalore district, one of the worst-affected coastal communities in Tamil Nadu, South India. The essay has two parts. The first provides an overview of the extent of the devastation in Cuddalore and the responses of NGOs in providing assistance to the affected coastal communities. The second section presents the personal account and observations of coauthor Tricia Torris, who spent two months in the summer of 2005 working with a network of Cuddalore NGOs that provided various services to coastal villagers affected by the tsunami.

A network of twelve local NGOs—East Coast Development Forum (ECDF)—played an important role in responding to the tsunami on the east coast of India. Kilby (2008) examines how the ECDF sought to meet the needs of affected people through direct relief and rehabilitation programs focused on the restoration of livelihoods, and through advocacy to press for changes to government programs to make them more inclusive and to ensure that they satisfied the priority needs of the people most affected. The trust and capacity built up through past network activities involving the fishing, Dalit, and tribal communities enabled the ECDF to launch an effective response to the tsunami.

Anthropologists Seiko Sugimoto, Antonysamy Sagayaraj, and Yoshio Sugimoto, in chapter 10, discuss the important role of sociocultural factors in developing effective policy for rehabilitation in the tsunami-affected areas of South India. Their essay examines the role of religious organizations in the relief and rehabilitation work and discusses how the network of fishermen society worked in the rehabilitation of the fishing villages. Along the southeast coast of India, Muslims, Hindus, and Christians have lived together peacefully for centuries. The poor fishing communities worst hit by the tsunami were mostly Hindu. Caught up in disaster, they receive spiritual relief from their religious worldviews and practices. These Hindu fishing families tend to worship local deities with power to destroy as well as to create. The ocean itself is a god that eats people and boats but also provides fish as food. For the Muslims, the disasters are Allah's doing. Nature itself—wind, rain, storms—constitutes signs of his mercy and compassion. This built-in psychological cushion allows Muslims to absorb a disaster of this magnitude. Christians form a minority in the region, but the Christian communities also had to look at their faith to make sense of the sudden loss of life and property. Although the acceptance of suffering is deeply embedded in the Christian worldview, the massive destruction by the tsunami was a test of their belief.

Sugimoto, Sagayaraj, and Sugimoto's field research in the tsunami-affected areas revealed various problems in the recovery process. These emerged as a result of the gap between the aid agencies' perception of the need in affected regions and the demands of the people based on local social construction, local economic relations, and local culture. A better understanding of the local community would contribute to a successful implementation of recovery processes. The chapter's authors point out, for example, that aid agencies and government departments, unaware of the poor acceptance of assistance such as the distribution of used clothing, did not help the recovery and rehabilitation of the fisherfolk. A solar-powered fish-drier was donated to one rehabilitation village near Chennai, but the equipment was useless to the villagers. Plot allotment for building new houses for the affected households seems to be unduly delayed, remaining unaccomplished even five years after the disaster. Rendering aid without appreciating demand appears to have weakened the traditional local government and adversely affected the self-esteem of the fishing community.

The tsunami disaster provided an opportunity to see if decades of knowledge and experience of post-disaster settlement could and would be applied to post-tsunami reconstruction. Kennedy et al. (2008), using evidence from the study of settlement and shelter in post-tsunami Aceh and Sri Lanka, have examined safety, security, and maintenance of livelihoods, the connection between transitional shelter and permanent housing, and fairness and equity. The authors contend that focus on community involvement and integration of relief and development through long-term planning and disaster-risk education are essential for a successful post-disaster settlement and shelter program.

Martin Mulligan of RMIT University and Judith Shaw of Monash University provide an excellent assessment of the achievements and weaknesses of post-tsunami reconstruction in Sri Lanka in chapter 11. Wavering public policy, the weak coordination, management, and competence of actors, perturbed markets, a civil war, and the sheer size of the operation led to less than desirable outcomes of the recovery operations there. Recovery programs and projects require distinct approaches, resources, and competence (Koria 2008).

The task of responding to the tsunami disaster faced several constraints. Lack of viable local capacities, confusing and often complicated bureaucratic official policies and procedures, centralized decision making, and corruption (Asian Development Bank 2005) made the response difficult.

The Indian Ocean Tsunami forced our attention on the need to reevaluate national and international disaster preparedness, governance structures, and information tools to develop and implement effective response. In the aftermath of the disaster, over 5 million people lacked the bare necessities of life—clean water, food, shelter, sanitation, and health care (Sim and Makie 2005). The threat of disease spreading from decaying corpses and contaminated water made a speedy response critical. While millions of dollars of aid were pouring into the region, much of it was slow to reach the tsunami victims. In Sri Lanka there was a lack of full coordination between the government and aid agencies. In Indonesia aid supplies arriving at the airport could not reach the disaster victims in time. Aceh, on the island of Sumatra, was barely under the control of the Indonesian government. For years a rebellion had beens raging in Aceh. Crowded refugee shelters were beset by outbreaks of diseases.

Good governance and social capital are important elements for ensuring equitable recovery processes and for ensuring appropriate capacity building in marginalized and highly vulnerable coastal communities. Governance must be responsive to community systems, and communities need to tap their social capital to enhance their local coping capacities. Participation is a primary element in achieving these goals. Participation is crucial for governance to ensure that it is responsive, locally relevant, and accountable to the specific needs of less well-represented communities. Gupta and Sharma (2006) have highlighted the lack of recognition of the importance of local capacities in recovery processes, with little appreciation of the fact that rehabilitation needs to be based on local resources, determined by local capacities, and decided by local communities. Miranda A. Schreurs, a scholar of environmental politics, provides an insightful argument in chapter 12 on the need to improve governance structures to respond effectively to natural hazards.

The need to develop community resilience to threats of natural disasters is important in developing countries. Local and regional governments must

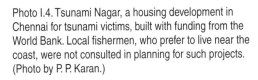

Photo I.4. Tsunami Nagar, a housing development in Chennai for tsunami victims, built with funding from the World Bank. Local fishermen, who prefer to live near the coast, were not consulted in planning for such projects. (Photo by P. P. Karan.)

develop structures that anticipate problems resulting from hazards, attempt to reduce vulnerabilities resulting from development policy, socioeconomic conditions, and sensibilities to potential threats, make efforts to respond effectively and fairly in the event of an emergency, and work to recover rapidly. This depends on knitting together local and regional authorities, first responders, grassroots nongovernmental and neighborhood organizations, the business community, the media, and state governments. GeoHazards International recently issued the *Tsunami Preparedness Guidebook* for community tsunami preparedness planning (GeoHazards International 2007), which contains information useful to coastal communities that are at risk from a tsunami. The tsunami has increased interest in replanting mangroves as natural storm barriers. Barbier (2008) has analyzed the household decision to replant mangroves in four villages in Thailand.

Geographic Perspectives on Tsunami Aid

The Indian Ocean Tsunami prompted rapid and generously funded aid. A massive media-fueled appeal for humanitarian assistance to the tsunami victims brought an estimated $14 billion in international aid from various countries, organizations, and agencies for rapid relief efforts as well as for long-term reconstruction and development. The losses from the tsunami were estimated at about $10 billion by the Tsunami Evaluation Coalition (Telford, Cosgrave, and Houghton 2006). The damage was most severe in Aceh, Indonesia, which was struck by tsunami waves within twenty minutes of the earthquake.

Geopolitical representations have shaped relief efforts. Mamadouh (2008) has examined how the Dutch geopolitical vision and national identity influenced the mobilization of tsunami relief effort in the Netherlands, citing such factors as water being a major threat to the Dutch national territory, the role of the nation as a development aid donor, and its relationship with Indonesia.

In chapter 13 Christopher Jasparro and Jonathan Taylor discuss geopolitical aspects of "competitive compassion," whereby legitimate states and international civil society are in competition with transnational criminals and terrorist/extremist groups in providing aid to the disaster victims. They describe how the complex web of extremist and terrorist-affiliated organizations began to appear in Aceh, Indonesia, to aid the victims. In addition to relief work, several of these organizations launched campaigns to counter what they believed were attempts by Western relief agencies to spread Christianity or establish military presence. In many cases they incited violence against foreign military and relief personnel.

In most of the affected areas substantial funding from national and international organizations allowed rapid relief and recovery. Within a few months there were visible signs of recovery in the landscape. Children were back in school and health facilities and services were partly restored within six months. Recovery and reconstruction were rapid in Thailand, where the entrepreneurial spirit of the Thai people played a major role in reconstruction of the tourist facilities in Phuket and along the Andaman coast. Tourism was on the rebound in 2008 in Thailand, but the global economic slump has impacted the tourist industry. In Sri Lanka most fishing communities were restored by 2007. In Aceh a large number of people were still living in tents in 2007. International aid was most effective when it enabled, facilitated, and supported local and national public institutions and was accountable to them. International aid was less successful in situations where locals and nationals were marginalized by an overwhelming flood of well-funded international agencies and private individuals and organizations. Among other weaknesses in the international aid identified by the Tsunami Evaluation Coalition (Telford, Cosgrave, and Houghton 2006) were inappropriate housing designs and livelihood solutions and poor understanding of the development process and livelihood options for women and men, small farmers, and small entrepreneurs, which led to greater inequities and gender-insensitive strategies and waste. The aid to affected areas has not enhanced local preparedness or significantly reduced longer-term vulnerability. How people conceptualize and organize to respond to risk remains to be addressed.

Principal Findings

The contributors to this volume discuss the geographic impacts of the tsunami and the monumental task of rebuilding schools, hospitals, government offices, businesses, and infrastructures—even entire villages—in areas devastated by the tsunami. The challenges were immense in the communities destroyed by the tsunami. Several lessons may be learned from the experiences discussed in the essays. After the tsunami one of the principal problems that emerged in most areas was the need to coordinate a multitude of local and international aid organizations to ensure the efficient, transparent, and corruption-free disbursement of relief and reconstruction funds. In the task of rebuilding, it would have been more desirable to consider more fully the needs and wishes of local communities in guiding the reconstruction programs of local governments, NGOs, and other donors. Reconstruction activities involving rebuilding villages and communities are by nature local, and generally a strong centralized authority impedes reconstruction. However, major infrastructure reconstruction projects in hard-hit areas such as roads, bridges, and ports are best planned and executed by the national or provincial government. As suggested in the several essays in this book, it is important to avoid layers of unnecessary bureaucracy in organizing relief and reconstruction efforts. An operational approach that balances thoughtful planning with speedy decision making can eliminate complexity and save time in implementing reconstruction projects.

Based on reconstruction experience in India, Indonesia, Sri Lanka, and Thailand, three principal activities are suggested for efficient implementation of reconstruction efforts after a disaster. First, create an integrated reconstruction blueprint through effective planning for the devastated communities to guide donors and for implementation of the projects. In addition to technical data, the plan should provide spatial, social, cultural, and economic data, including property boundaries and titles to avoid problems later on during the rebuilding of the area. Second, help local authorities and communities by providing skilled advisors, training, and technology to improve their ability to coordinate and make decisions through improved building capacity. Third, develop a system to monitor and evaluate projects by gathering data from donors and affected communities so that information from donors on progress of the projects may be compared with feedback from communities. This will help allocate resources more efficiently while monitoring the overall progress of reconstruction efforts.

These suggestions may appear academic, but they should be useful to government and private agencies involved in designing reconstruction efforts after a major disaster in the future similar to the Indian Ocean Tsunami or the Katrina hurricane along the U.S. Gulf Coast.

References

Asian Development Bank. 2005. *Corruption in tsunami relief operations*. Manila: Asian Development Bank.

Baird, Andrew. 2006. False hopes and natural disasters. *New York Times,* December 26.

Baird, A. H., and A. M. Kerr. 2008. Landscape analysis and tsunami damage in Aceh: Comment on Iverson and Prasad (2007). *Landscape Ecology* 23 (1): 3–5.

Barbier, E. B. 2008. In the wake of tsunami: Lessons learned from the household decision to replant mangroves in Thailand. *Resource and Energy Economics* 30 (2): 229–49.

Barton, Thomas F., and P. P. Karan.1992. *Geographic education.* Vol. 1 of *Leaders in American geography.* Mesilla: New Mexico Geographical Society, in association with Prestige Press.

Baumann, P. R. 2008. Tsunami 2004: The villages of Birek and Seungko Mulat, Indonesia. *Geocarto International* 23 (4): 327–35.

Bigalke, Terance W. 2006. *Aceh after the tsunami.* Honolulu: East-West Center Insights.

Brown, B. E. 2005. The fate of coral reefs in the Andaman Sea, eastern Indian Ocean following the Sumatran earthquake and tsunami, 26 December 2004. *Geographical Journal* 171 (4): 372–74.

Burton, I., R. W. Kates, and G. F. White. 1993. *The environment as hazard.* New York: Guilford.

Calgaro, E., and K. Lloyd. 2008. Sun, sea, sand and tsunami: Examining disaster vulnerability in the tourism community of Khao Lak, Thailand. *Singapore Journal of Tropical Geography* 29 (3): 288–306.

Cartwright, J. H. E., and H. Nakamura. 2008. Tsunami: A history of the term and of scientific understanding of the phenomenon in Japanese and Western culture. *Notes and Records of the Royal Society* 62 (2): 151–66.

Chadha, R. K., G. Latha, H. Yeh, C. Peterson, and T. Katada. 2005. The tsunami of the great Sumatra Earthquake of M 9.0 on 26 December 2004—Impact on the east coast of India. *Current Science* 88 (8): 1297–301.

Chandrasekar, N., J. L. Immanuel, M. Rajamanickam, D. S. H. Singh, J. D. Sahayam, and G. V. Rajamanickam. 2005. Geospatial assessment of tsunami (2004): Damages along the rocky coast of Kanya Kumari, India. In *Geomatics in tsunami,* ed. R. Ramasamy, 135–46. New Delhi: New India.

Chandrasekar, N., S. Saravanam, J. L. Immanuel, M. Rajamanickam, and G. V. Rajamanickam. 2006. Classification of tsunami hazard along the southern coast of India: An initiative to safeguard the coastal environment from similar debacle. *Science of Tsunami Hazards* 24 (1): 3–24.

Danielsen, F., M. K. Sorensen, M. F. Olwig, V. Selvam, N. D. Burgess, T. Hiraishi, and N. Suryadiputra. 2005. The Asian tsunami: A protective role for coastal vegetation. *Science* 310 (5748): 643.

Dawson, A. G. 1994. Geomorphological effects of tsunami run-up and backwash. *Geomorphology* 10 (1), 83–94.

De Silva, D. A. M., and M. Yamao. 2007. Effects of the tsunami on fisheries and coastal livelihood: A case study of tsunami-ravaged southern Sri Lanka. *Disasters* 31 (4): 386–404.

Dicum, Gregory. 2009. The rebirth of Phuket. *New York Times,* January 11.

GeoHazards International. 2007. *Tsunami preparedness guidebook.* www.geohaz.org/contents/projects/tsunamiguide.html.

Giri, C., Z. Zhu, L. L. Tieszen, A. Singh, S. Gillette, and J. A. Kelmelis. 2008. Mangrove forest distribution and dynamics (1975–2005) of the tsunami affected region of Asia. *Journal of Biogeography* 35 (3): 519–28.

Greenhough, Beth, Tariq Jazeel, and Doreen Massey. 2005. Indian Ocean Tsunami: Geographical commentaries one year on. *Geographical Journal* 171 (4): 369–86.

Government of India. 2005. *Tsunami—A report to the nation.* Delhi: Government of India.

Gunatilaka, A. 2005. The Indian Ocean megatsunami of December 2004: The scientific basis of the catastrophe. *Journal of the National Science Foundation of Sri Lanka* 33 (2): 69–80.

Gupta, M., and A. Sharma. 2006. Compounded loss: The post-tsunami recovery experience of Indian island communities. *Disaster Prevention and Management* 15 (1): 67–79.

Henderson, J. C. 2007. Corporate social responsibility and tourism: Hotel companies in Phuket, Thailand, after the Indian Ocean Tsunami. *International Journal of Hospitality Management* 26 (1): 228–39.

Hewitt, K. 1983. The idea of calamity in a technocratic age. In *The risks and hazards,* ed. K. Hewitt. Boston: Allen and Unwin.

Iverson, L. R., and A. M. Prasad. 2007. Using landscape analysis to assess and model tsunami damage in Aceh province, Sumatra. *Landscape Ecology* 22 (3): 323–31.

Jaya Kumar, S., K. A. Naik, M. V. Ramanamurthy, D. Ilangovan, R. Gowthaman, and B. K. Jena. 2008. Post tsunami changes in the littoral environment along the southeast coast of India. *Journal of Environmental Management* 89 (1): 35–44.

Jaya Kumar, S., D. Ilangovan, K. A. Naik, R. Gowthaman, G. Tirodkar, G. N. Naik, P. Ganeshan, and G. C. Bhattacharya. 2005. Run-up and inundation limits along southeast coast of India during the 26 December 2004 Indian Ocean Tsunami. *Current Science* 88 (11): 1741–43.

Karan, P. P. 1975. Perception of environmental problems in coal mining areas of India and the United States. *National Geographer* 10:1–8.

Kench, S. P., L. S. Nichol, F. R. Mclean, G. S. Smithers, and W. R. Brander. 2006. *Impact of the Sumatran tsunami on the geomorphology and sediments of reef islands: South Maalhosmadulu Atoll, Maldives.* www.tesag.jcu.edu.au/CDS/reports/impactSumatranTsunamiMaldives.pdf.

Kennedy, J., J. Ashmore, E. Babister, and I. Kelman. 2008. The meaning of "build back better": Evidence from post-tsunami Aceh and Sri Lanka. *Journal of Contingencies and Crisis Management* 16 (1): 24–36.

Kilby, P. 2008. The strength of networks: The local NGO response to the tsunami in India. *Disasters* 32 (1): 120–30.

Koria, M. 2008. Managing for innovation in large and complex recovery programmes: Tsunami lessons from Sri Lanka. *International Journal of Project Management.*

Kurian, N. P., A. P. Pillai, B. T. M. Krishnan, and P. Kalaiarasan. 2006. Inundation characteristics and geomorphological impacts of December 2004 tsunami on Kerala coast. *Current Science* 90 (2): 240–49.

Lay, T., H. Kanamori, C. J. Ammon, M. Nettles, S. N. Ward, R. C. Aster, S. L. Beck, and S. Sipkin. 2005. The great Sumatra-Andaman Earthquake of 26 December 2004. *Science* 308 (5725): 1127–33.

Lebel, L., S. Khrutmuang, and J. Manuta. 2006. Tales from the margins: Small fishers in post-tsunami Thailand. *Disaster Prevention and Management* 15 (1): 124–34.

Mamadouh, V. 2008. After Van Gogh: The geopolitics of the tsunami relief effort in the Netherlands. *Geopolitics* 13 (2): 205–31.

Mather, Cotton, and P. P. Karan. 2000. *Research.* Vol. 2 of *Leaders in American geography.* Mesilla: New Mexico Geographical Society, in association with Prestige Press.

Mohan, V. R. 2005. December 26, 2004 tsunami: A field assessment in Tamilnadu. In *Tsunami: The Indian context,* ed. R. Ramasamy and C. J. Kumanan. New Delhi: Allied.

Mottet, G. 2005. Le seisme et la tsunami du 26 decembre 2004 dans l'Ocean Indien: Localisation, mecanismes et consequences [The earthquake and the tsunami of 26th December 2004 in the Indian Ocean: Localization, mechanisms and consequences]. *Geographie* 176 (1516): 15–30.

Murty, Tad S., U. Aswathanarayana, and N. Nirupana, eds. *The Indian Ocean Tsunami.* New York: Taylor and Francis, 2007.

Narayan, J. P., M. L. Sharma, and B. K. Maheshwari. 2005a. Effects of medu and coastal topography on the damage pattern during the recent Indian Ocean Tsunami along the coast of Tamil Nadu. *Science of Tsunami Hazards* 23 (2): 9–18.

———. 2005b. Run-up and inundation pattern during the Indian Ocean Tsunami of December 26, 2004 along the coast of Tamil Nadu (India). *Gondwana Research* 8 (4): 611–16.

O'Keefe, P., K. Westgate, and B. Wisner. 1976. Taking the naturalness out of natural disasters. *Nature* 260 (5552): 5667.

Pari, Y., M. V. Ramamurthy, S. Jaya Kumar, B. R. Subramanian, and S. Ramachandran. 2008. Morphological changes at Vellar estuary, India—Impact of the December 2004 tsunami. *Journal of Environmental Management* 89 (1): 45–57.

Paton, D., C. E. Gregg, B. F. Houghton, R. Lachman, J. Lachman, D. M. Johnston, and S. Wongbusarakum. 2008. The impact of the 2004 tsunami on coastal Thai communities: Assessing adaptive capacity. *Disasters* 32 (1): 106–19.

Phillips, B., D. Neal, T. Wikle, A. Subanthore, and S. Hyrapiet. 2008. Mass fatality management after the Indian Ocean Tsunami. *Disaster Prevention and Management* 17 (5): 681–97.

Preuss, Jane. 2005. Why "tsunami" means "wake up call." *Planning* 71 (8): 4–7.

Raval, U. 2005. Some factors responsible for the devastation in Nagapattinam region due to tsunami of 26th December 2004. *Journal of the Geological Society of India* 65 (5): 647–49.

Reddy, K. M., A. N. Rao, and A. V. S. Rao. 2005. Recent tsunami and its impact on coastal areas of Andhra Pradesh. In *Tsunami: The Indian context,* ed. R. Ramasamy and C. J. Kumanan. New Delhi: Allied.

Rigg, J., C. Grundy-Warr, L. Law, and M. Tan-Mullins. 2008. Grounding a natural disaster: Thailand and the 2004 tsunami. *Asia Pacific Viewpoint* 49 (2): 137–54.

Rodriguez, H., T. Wachtendorf, J. Kendra, and J. Trainor. 2006. A snapshot of the 2004 Indian Ocean Tsunami: Societal impacts and consequences. *Disaster Prevention and Management* 15 (1): 163–77.

Ruwanpura, K. N. 2008. Temporality of disasters: The politics of women's livelihoods "after" the 2004 tsunami in Sri Lanka. *Singapore Journal of Tropical Geography* 29 (3): 325–40.

Shaw, R. 2008. Environmental aspects of the Indian Ocean Tsunami recovery. *Journal of Environmental Management* 89 (1): 1–3.

Sim, F., and P. Makie. 2005. The Asian tsunami remembered. *Public Health* 119 (5):345–46.

Singh, V. S. 2008. Impact of the earthquake and tsunami of December 26, 2004, on the groundwater regime at Neill Island (south Andaman). *Journal of Environmental Management* 89 (1): 58–62.

Telford, J., J. Cosgrave, and R. Houghton. 2006. *Joint evaluation of the international response to the Indian Ocean Tsunami: Synthesis report.* London: Tsunami Evaluation Coalition.

Torry, W. I. 1979. Hazards, hazes and notes: A critique of the environment as hazard and general reflections on disaster research. *Canadian Geographer* 23 (4): 368–83.

Tsuji, N., Y. Namegaya, and J. Ito. 2005. *Astronomical tide levels along the coasts of the Indian Ocean.* Tokyo: Earthquake Research Institute, University of Tokyo. http://www.eri.u-tokyo.ac.jp/namegaya/sumatera/tide/.

Waddell, E. 1977. The hazards of scientism: A review article. *Human Ecology* 5 (1): 69–76.

White, G. F. 1945. Human adjustment to floods: A geographical approach to the flood problem in the United States. Research Paper 29, Department of Geography, University of Chicago.

———. 1964. *Choice of adjustments to floods.* Department of Geography Research Paper 93. Chicago: University of Chicago.

Wijetunge, J. J. 2005. Indian Ocean Tsunami on 26 December 2004: Distribution of tsunami height and inundation along the coastline of Sri Lanka. *Journal of the National Science Foundation of Sri Lanka* 33 (2): 61–68.

Yanagisawa, H., B. V. Koshimura, K. Goto, F. Imamura, T. Miyagi, A. Ruangrassamee, and C. Tanavud. 2009 The reduction effects of mangrove forest on a tsunami based on field surveys at Pakarang Cape, Thailand and numerical analysis. *Estuarine, Coastal and Shelf Science,* 81 (1): 27–37.

Part 1

Environmental and Ecological Impacts

1

The Tsunami Disaster on the Andaman Sea Coast of Thailand

Masatomo Umitsu

The giant earthquake off Sumatra Island caused serious damage by tsunami along the Andaman Sea coast of southern Thailand. Narrow coastal plains are developing in a north-south direction along the Andaman Sea coast in Ranong, Phang Nga, Phuket, Krabi, Trang, and Satun provinces (see fig. 1.1). The tsunami flow spread over most parts of the coastal lowlands. Tsunami inundation height on the plains was about 3–5 m (11.5 feet) in general, and it exceeded more than 10 m (33 feet) in some places. Many famous resort beaches are located in the region, and most of them suffered from the tsunami disaster.

According to the Interior Department of Thailand, on January 20, 2005, 5,354 people in Thailand had been killed by the tsunami, and 3,113 were missing. The numbers of dead and missing persons in Phang Nga, Phuket, and Krabi provinces were 4,202 and 1,792, 260 and 646, and 721 and 663, respectively. There were also some damages in Ranong. Dead and missing persons in Ranong province were 160 and 11, respectively. In Trang and Satun provinces, located in the southern part of the Andaman Sea coast, however, there were very few casualties and missing persons and only very little physical damage. The reason is that these areas are located behind the Sumatra Island, away from the epicenter of the earthquake.

Tsunami Disaster on Phuket Island and Phi Phi Island

Phuket Island is located in the central part of the Andaman Sea coast of Thailand. The island is about 50 km (30 miles) long and 15–20 km (9–12 miles) wide. There is a narrow strait with a bridge connecting the island with the

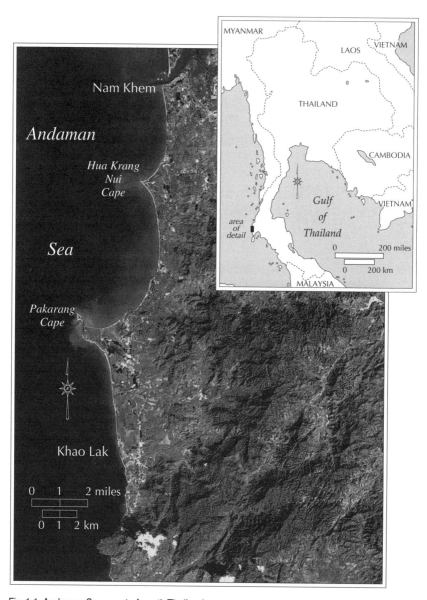

Fig. 1.1. Andaman Sea coast of south Thailand.

Photo 1.1. Tsunami-damaged buildings in Patong Beach, Phuket. (Photo by Masatomo Umitsu, January 22, 2005.)

mainland of Phang Nga province. Several pocket beaches developing along the west coast of the island, such as Patong, Kamara, and Ban Thao, were severely attacked by the tsunami.

The busiest beach on Phuket Island is Patong, located on the west coast. A large number of restaurants, hotels, and souvenir shops are close behind the beautiful sandy beach. The lowland behind the beach is approximately 3.5 km (2.7 miles) in length and 1 km (0.6 mile) in width, and its landforms are two rows of beach ridges and a wetland behind the ridges. Land use of the wetland was paddy field and swamp with mangrove forest in the 1970s, but the area became urbanized as the region developed economically (Hayashi et al. 2007). Ground elevation of the beach ridges is about 1–2 m (3.3–6.6 feet), and the relative height from the lowland behind is about 1 m (3.3 feet).

In Patong Beach, there is no distinct embankment between the present sandy beach and the area behind, and the height of a step between the beach and the ground behind is only about 1 m. The tsunami attacked the coastal zone directly and caused serious damage to the buildings, especially those facing the beach. Buildings in the inner area suffered less damage, and that was caused mainly by the tsunami flood inundation.

In general, how strong buildings are is related to their kind, their construc-

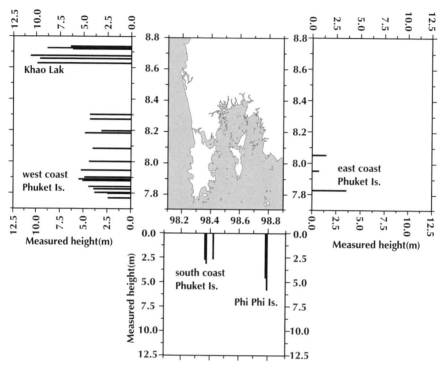

Fig. 1.2. Measured tsunami height in Khao Lak and Phuket. (Kawata et al. 2005)

tion, and their condition (Saatciglu, Ghobarah, and Nistor 2007). Additionally, the effect of a tsunami will have correlates to the density of the buildings. In Patong Beach, the density of the buildings facing the beach is very high, and the destructive power of the tsunami decreased rapidly due to the block formed by the buildings.

There are also several beaches and coastal lowlands on the west coast of Phuket Island, such as Kamara and Ban Thao beaches. Building density in the lowlands is not high, and the buildings in the inner part of the lowlands suffered greater damage in comparison with Patong Beach. Therefore, the tsunami flow in the lowlands could easily invade inland regions. There are also some beaches on the eastern coast of Phuket Island. Tsunami heights in these beaches were not high, measured from 0.7 to 3.6 m (2.3 to 11.8 feet) (Kawata et al. 2005).

There are many isolated limestone islands in and around the Gulf of Phang Nga, and many tourists visit the area to enjoy the beautiful landscapes, complete with coral reefs. One of the popular tourist sites is Phi Phi Island, which was also severely damaged by the tsunami. The island has two ranges of mountains with a narrow sandbar developing between them. Many resort hotels and cottages were located on the low and almost flat sandbar, and the tsunami waves attacked the bar from the north and south. The measured tsunami height from the north was 5.8 m (about 19 feet) and that from the south was 4.6 m (15 feet), and the flows met on the sandbar with an elevation of about 1–2 m (3.3–6.6 feet) (Kawata et al. 2005). Many buildings on the sandbar were washed away and destroyed by the tsunami, and large numbers of tourists, unable to escape the wave, lost their lives.

Tsunami on the Khao Lak Coastal Plain

Southern Phang Nga province is characterized by straight coastline extending about 50 km (30 miles), and landforms of the coastal zone are narrow beach and uplands behind the beach. As most people in the coastal zone live on the uplands and the population of the area is small, tsunami damage in the region was not severe. Only storages for fisheries and some boats were washed away or damaged by the tsunami.

To the contrary, damage in the central part of Phang Nga province, such as in Khao Lak and Nam Khem, was very severe. Khao Lak, located approximately 80 km (50 miles) north of Phuket, is one of the famous resort areas on the Andaman Sea coast. Landforms of the area are the narrow coastal plain and the upland behind. The Khao Lak coastal plain is 12–13 km (7.2–7.8 miles) long and 1–2 km (0.6–1.2 miles) wide, and its landforms are classified into beach ridges, swales, and back marsh behind the ridges. There are also several artificial mounds and ponds formed by the former tin mining. Elevation of the beach ridges is about 3 to 4 m (9.9 to 13.2 feet), and the height difference between the ridges and swales is less than 1 m (3.3 feet).

The tsunami flow spread out over almost the whole area of the Khao Lak coastal plain. Most of the inundation depths in the plain were measured at around 4–7 m (13.2–23.7 feet), but the tsunami heights in some places were higher than 10 m (33 feet) (Kawata et al. 2005; Umitsu et al., 2005). One patrol boat sailing about 200–300 m (660 to 990 feet) off the beach was carried to the east end of the plain due to the strong flow of the tsunami upstream.

The area was a newly developing tourist place; many hotels and cottages have been built in the last several years. Some of them were destroyed totally and some were broken up to the third floor. Seaward-facing walls of buildings especially were broken or severely damaged. Tsunami inundation depth could be recognized from many marks on the buildings, trees, and so on. Photo 1.2 shows the tsunami inundation depth from the destruction of a roof edge.

Photo 1.2. Destroyed resort cottages in south Khao Lak. (Photo by Masatomo Umitsu, January 21, 2005.)

Photo 1.3. Boulders carried by the tsunami on the coast of Pakarang Cape. (Photo by Masatomo Umitsu, August 2, 2005.)

The tsunami carried coral reef boulders to the coast. Distinct deposition of tsunami boulders is seen around the Pakarang Cape on the northwestern coast of the Khao Lak coastal plain. The maximum size of these boulders is about 4 m and the distribution pattern and the orientation of the long axis of boulders reflect the inundation pattern and behavior of the tsunami waves. According to Goto et al. (2007), most of the boulders were fragments of reef rocks, and the tsunami waves that were directed eastward struck the reef rocks and coral colonies, originally located on the shallow sea bottom near the reef edge, detaching and transporting the boulders shoreward.

Tsunami Event on the Nam Khem Coastal Plain

The most seriously damaged village in Thailand was Nam Khem in Phang Nga province. The village is located approximately 120 km (72 miles) north of Phuket and about 10 km (6 miles) west of the town of Takua Pa, which has developed tin mining. The village is in the northern part of the Nam Khem coastal plain, and the plain faces the Andaman Sea to the west and the Pak Ko River mouth (Laem Pom Sea) to the north.

Landforms of the coastal plain are characterized as the strand plain with sandbar and beach ridges, and the Pleistocene upland, about 10 m (33 feet) high, is located behind the lowland. The coastal plain is 1–2 km (0.6–1.2 miles)

Photo 1.4. Damaged buildings in Nam Khem. (Photo by Masatomo Umitsu, January 21, 2005.)

wide and 12–13 km (7.2–7.8 miles) long, and the ground level of the plain is generally about 3–5 m (9.9–16.5 feet). Rows of beach ridges with at least seven ridges and swales developed in the eastern part of the plain. Some tin-mining mounds with a maximum height of over 10 m (33 feet) are distributed in the plain, and several ponds derived from the tin mining are also in the lowland.

Tsunami waves attacked the coastal plain from the west and northwest, and the flow invaded the coastal plain toward the foot of Pleistocene upland located about 1–2 km (0.6–1.2 miles) inland from the coast. Nam Khem village is located in the northwestern part of the plain, and the tsunami wave attacked the village directly from the west and northwest. The second tsunami wave was observed as the largest in the area, and more than 2,000 people lost their lives. Many fishing boats around the fishery harbor of the village were also destroyed, and some boats were carried inland by the strong tsunami flow.

The orientation of snapped-off fence posts, fallen trees, and other indicators were measured to determine directions of run-up flows, and the directions of grasses flattened by water flow were measured to determine the flow of back-wash in the Nam Khem coastal plain (Umitsu, Tanavud, and Patanakanog 2007).

Based on field measurements on the ground, the general directions of the tsunami flows were clarified. Most of the tsunami run-up direction on the Nam Khem plain was eastward from the Andaman Sea and perpendicular to the coast. The directions of backwash tsunami flows on the ground, however, were various. Backwash flows from the eastern end of the lowland or slopes of tin-mining dumps were generally toward the sea, but the directions of backwash flow on the lowland were controlled by local topography. It was also concentrated in the lower parts of the plain, such as depressions and stream channels. Some run-up flows entered from the north through the Pak Ko River mouth (Laem Pom Sea) and met the flow from south of Nam Khem village. They reached inland, where a big fishing boat from the port of Nam Khem was deposited (fig. 1.3). Measured tsunami inundation height in the plain was generally 5–8 m (16.5–26.4 feet) (Kawata et al. 2005; Umitsu et al. 2005; Thailand Group 2005), and some flows went up the slope of a tin dump mound.

Figure 1.3 shows the distribution of tsunami deposits based on the classification of satellite image and measurement in the field. The color of the ground surface on the IKONOS satellite image provides a good indication of the thickness of tsunami deposits. In the image, bright white, dark brownish gray, and (greenish) gray areas can be distinguished, except in areas covered with trees or buildings. These differences in color were interpreted as differences in the thickness of tsunami deposits, and these interpretations were confirmed in more than fifty pits dug in the field.

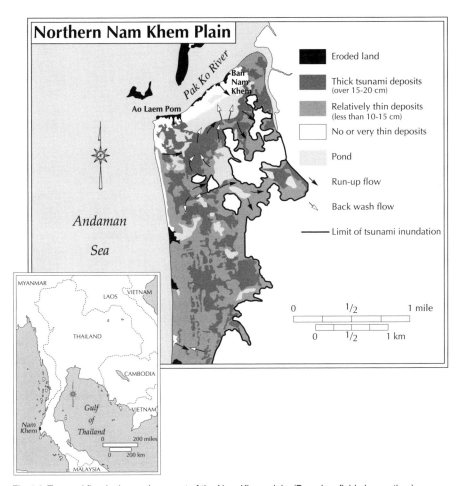

Fig. 1.3. Tsunami flow in the northern part of the Nam Khem plain. (Based on field observation.)

Thick tsunami deposits are distributed widely in the northern part of the Nam Khem plain. This distribution is closely related to the tsunami flow in the plain. The tsunami flows in the northern Nam Khem plain came as the flood flowed from both the Andaman Sea coast in the west and the Pak Ko River mouth (Laem Pom Sea) in the north, and they concentrated in the northern part of the plain. Moreover, some of the backwash caused by the artificial tin-mining mounds in the inner part of the plain also deposited materials in the northern part of the plain. Therefore, tsunami deposits accumulated in the region and thick tsunami deposits were distributed widely.

Landforms of the middle part of the Nam Khem coastal plain are rows

Photo 1.5. A fishing boat carried by the tsunami to the inner part of the Nam Khem coastal plain. (Photo by Masatomo Umitsu, January 21, 2005.)

of beach ridges and swales developed at the same direction of coastline. The width of each beach ridge is about 100 m (330 feet), and the relative height of the ridges from the swales is less than 1 m (3.3 feet). Run-up and backwash tsunami flows in the region had almost orthogonal orientation against the coastline, and the flow invaded about 1 km (0.6 mile) toward the boundary of lowland and upland. Tsunami inundation depths were about 7.5 m (25 feet) near the coast and about 5 m in the innermost part of the lowland (Umitsu et al. 2005). The village, located west of the ridges, was inundated at a level of 2.75 m (9 feet). Only one person died and one person was missing in this village, because the village people were able to escape to tin-mining mounds and the Pleistocene terrace behind the village.

In the central part of the Nam Khem coastal plain, thick tsunami deposits are distributed in parallel lines, and the orientation of them is almost north to south. This is caused by the microlandforms of the plain, and the distribution of the deposits is affected by the topography of the plain. Swales distributed between ridges also have the north-south orientation, and thick tsunami deposits are seen in the swales.

There is a difference in the thickness of tsunami deposits in the Nam Khem plain. In the plain, thick tsunami deposits are distributed widely in its northern part, and the reason is thought to be that the tsunami flow in Nam Khem invaded both from the west and northwest, and the confluence of the flows caused thick tsunami deposits. On the other hand, the tsunami deposits in the middle part of the plain derived only from the west, and most of these depositions are seen only in lower places, such as swales between the beach ridges (Umitsu, Tanavud, and Patanakanog 2007).

Landform Changes on the Nam Khem and Khao Lak Coastal Plains

Remarkable landform changes after the tsunami were seen along the coastlines of the Nam Khem and Khao Lak plains. On the north coastline of the Nam Khem coastal plain, the tidal flat near the mouth of the Bang Muang River, which flows east of Nam Khem village, and the beach on the western part of the coast were eroded. Especially, some small excavations in the coastal lowland near the jetty on the west coast were formed by the strong attack of the tsunami flow.

In the northernmost part of the Nam Khem coastal plain, the tsunami wave entered into the Pak Ko Estuary (Laem Pom Sea) and changed the landforms around the mouth of the estuary and the north coast of the Nam Khem coastal plain. A sand spit had been located in the northwestern tip of the Nam Khem coastal plain and a large sandbar with vegetation was distributed on the opposite bank of the Pak Ko Estuary (Laem Pom Sea) mouth. The sand spit and sandbar, however, disappeared after the attack of the tsunami, and the coastline of the area changed remarkably due to the event.

On the west coast of the Nam Khem coastal plain, the Hua Krang Nui Cape projects toward the Andaman Sea. The width of the beach on both the north and south coasts of the cape decreased after the attack of the tsunami. The south coast especially was eroded, not only the beach but also the ground behind the beach. The severer coastal retreat in the western part of the Andaman Sea coast of the Nam Khem coastal plain, however, was not seen in the coasts except around the cape.

There are some tin-mining pits very close to the beach on the Andaman Sea coast of the Nam Khem coastal plain. Some of the pits were separated from the beach by the deposition of sand and some were connected to the Andaman Sea by narrow streams. These pits and channels were widely opened to the sea after the tsunami hit. The mouths of them have been opened and expanded 50–100 m (165–330 feet) in width.

There was a distinct sandbar located around the northwestern tip of the Pakarang Cape in the northern part of the Khao Lak coastal plain. The bar, however, totally disappeared after the tsunami event. Remarkable landform changes were also seen around the lowest reaches of streams in the plain. The lowest reaches of the Phru Sei River, about 2.6 km (1.5 miles) south of the Pakarang Cape, changed shape from a narrow stream to a widely opened channel in a dendritic funnel shape. Similar situations can be seen around the river mouths in the Khao Lak coastal plain, especially in places about 4.5 km (2.7 miles), 6 km (3.6 miles), and 8 km (4.8 miles) south of the Pakarang Cape. Erosion in the lower reaches of streams not only occurred around the mouth of the channel but also extended to the inner part of the small valleys. Near Ban Thung Wa Nok, located about 8 km (4.8 miles) from the Pakarang Cape, two major streams meet and flow toward the Andaman Sea. The lower reaches of their valley plain were eroded and changed to a wedge-shaped inlet. The mouth of the channel opened widely, about 150–200 m (495–660 feet), and the neighboring coast at the south of the mouth retreated about 50 m (165 feet).

Coastal erosion extended to the area around Ban Bang Niang, located about 10 km (6 miles) south of the Pakarang Cape. Severe destruction of buildings is also seen in the southern part of the Khao Lak coastal plain, but there is little coastal erosion further south of the area around Ban Bang Niang.

The tsunami produced changes in the coastal landforms of Nam Khem and Khao Lak. There was a smoothing of the coastline in the northern part of the Nam Khem and Khao Lak coastal plains. Especially, projected sandbars and soft tidal flats were eroded or changed their shape. The beaches along places that projected out to the sea, like the Hua Krang Nui and Pakarang capes, were

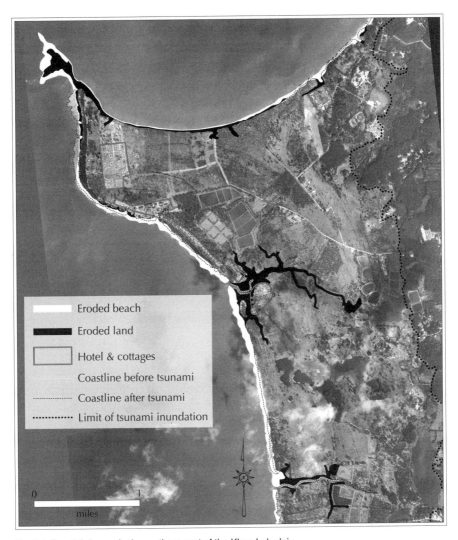

Fig. 1.4. Coastal change in the northern part of the Khao Lak plain.

also substantially eroded. The tsunami energy was concentrated on these places in the coastal zone.

Small river channels flowing to the Andaman Sea coast were usually narrow, and their mouths were blocked by the deposition of beach sand. The tsunami, however, opened the mouth of these streams and changed their form from a planar shape to a wedge shape. The mouths opened about 50–200 m (165–660

Photo 1.6. Permanent rehabilitation houses in Nam Khem built by the Thai military. (Photo by Masatomo Umitsu, August 2, 2005.)

feet) after the tsunami event. Because distinct tsunami deposits are not distributed either beside the channels or near the ends of eroded channels, and the directions of backwash flow were mainly concentrated toward the channels, it is thought that the main force responsible for the widening of the channels was not the tsunami run-up: rather, the change occurred due to erosion caused by concentrated strong backwash flows from inland. The ground level of the plains is generally 2–3 m (6.6–9.9 feet) higher than the stream channels, and the backwash flow easily concentrated on the lower parts of the plain; due to the concentration of the backwash of the tsunami, strong erosion occurred in lower parts of the plain, especially along channels.

Recovery from the Disaster

Already several years have passed since this extraordinary disaster, and tourists are again visiting places such as Phuket. In addition, reconstruction and recovery of some resort hotels and cottages proceeded well in Khao Lak, and many tourists also visit there again. Large numbers of rehabilitation houses have been constructed, and an excellent school building was reconstructed in

Photo 1.7. Recovered resort hotel and sign detailing evacuation route in Khao Lak. (Photo by Masatomo Umitsu, September 1, 2006.)

Nam Khem village. Furthermore, a monument and a museum of the tsunami disaster were constructed in Nam Khem village.

In this way, the life of the people in the tsunami-affected areas of Thailand is regaining vitality. However, the sorrow of people who were injured or lost loved ones cannot easily be overcome. Furthermore, daily life from the economic point of view has not yet recovered to the condition it was in before the disaster. Some people have lost their jobs and some have had to start a different kind of job. Fishermen whose houses were near the coast received rehabilitation houses inland, causing difficulties for them to reach their work. Moreover, some rehabilitation houses were without electricity and water, and some houses are still unfinished.

From the socioeconomic perspective, people's lives have not yet returned to normal. It may take several more years before complete recovery is achieved.

References

Goto, K., S. A. Chavanich, F. Imamura, P. Kunthasap, T. Matsui, K. Minoura, D. Sugawara, and H. Yanagisawa. 2007. Distribution, origin and transport process of boulders transported by the 2004 Indian Ocean Tsunami at Pakarang Cape, Thailand. *Sedimentary Geology* 202: 821–37.

Hayashi, K., S. Haruyama, C. Tanavud, and M. Miura. 2007. Coastal geomorphology of pocket beach in Thai Phuket and vulnerability for Tsunami hazards. [In Japanese with English abstract.] *Journal of Japan Society for Natural Disaster Science* 26:31–40.

Kawata, Y., Y. Tsuji, Y. Sugimoto, H. Hayashi, H. Matsutomi, Y. Okamura, I. Hayashi, H. Kayane, H. Tanioka, K. Fujima, F. Imamura, M. Matsuyama, T. Takahashi, N. Maki, and S. Koshimura. 2005. *Comprehensive analysis of the damage and its impact on coastal zones by the 2004 Indian Ocean Tsunami disaster.* http://www.tsunami.civil. tohoku.ac.jp/sumatra2004/report.html.

Saatciglu, M., A. Ghobarah, and I. Nistor. 2007. Performance of structure affected by 2004 Sumatra tsunami in Thailand and Indonesia. In *The Indian Ocean Tsunami,* ed. T. S. Murty, 297–321. London: Taylor and Francis.

Thailand Group. 2005. *The December 26, 2004 Sumatra Earthquake tsunami, tsunami field survey around Phuket, Thailand.* Report of International Tsunami Survey Team of the Indian Ocean Tsunami Disaster. Research Center for Disaster Reduction Systems, Disaster Research Institute, Kyoto University, Japan.

Umitsu, M., Y. Hirai, K. Kawase, C. Tanavud, and P. Boonrak. 2005. Land forms and tsunami inundation in the Andaman Sea coastal plain. [In Japanese.] In *Report on the coastal environmental change and tsunami deposits in the Andaman Sea Coast,* ed. M. Umitsu, 15–29. Nagoya: Graduate School of Environmental Studies, Nagoya University.

Umitsu, M., Charlchai Tanavud, and B. Patanakanog. 2007. Effects of landforms on tsunami flow in the plains of Banda Aceh, Indonesia, and Nam Khem, Thailand. *Marine Geology* 242:141–53.

2

The Geoenvironment and the Giant Tsunami Disaster in the Northern Part of Sumatra Island, Indonesia

Masatomo Umitsu

The catastrophic tsunami accompanied by the giant earthquake off Sumatra on December 26, 2004, inundated and caused severe disaster in the coastal lowlands of northern Sumatra, Indonesia. Remarkable tsunami damage occurred in the regions of the northwest and northeast coasts of Sumatra Island and the coastal area of Banda Aceh city, located in the northwestern end of Sumatra Island (fig. 2.1). The total number of victims of the tsunami in Indonesia, including missing persons, is about 170,000. Most of the victims are concentrated in the coastal regions of Banda Aceh city in the north; Aceh Besar, Aceh Jaya, and Aceh Barat districts in the northwest; and the Sigri district in the northeast part of Sumatra Island.

Banda Aceh Coastal Plain

Banda Aceh, the most seriously damaged city, is located in the Banda Aceh coastal plain, which is located along the lower reaches of the Aceh River. It is situated in a graben formed by movement of the Sumatra fault. The coastal plain is characterized by deltaic and tidal lowland in the central and western parts and by distinct rows of beach ridges in the eastern part (fig. 2.2). Elevation of the plain is 1–3 m (3.3–9.9 feet) above sea level in the central and western parts, except the higher parts of natural levees along the present and abandoned channels. The eastern coastal area is also low-lying, but there is a small sand dune along the coast, and rows of beach ridges, 1–2 m (3.3–6.6 feet)

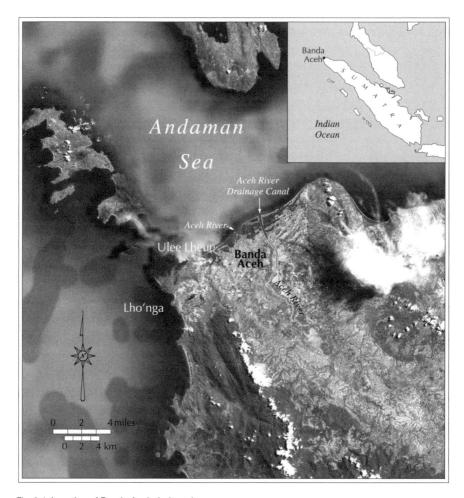

Fig. 2.1. Location of Banda Aceh, Indonesia.

above the swales, exist in the inner area. Shrimp- and fishponds are formed in tidal lowlands of the central and western parts of the plain. Deltaic lowland and beach ridges are occupied by houses, and the Banda Aceh urban area is located on the deltaic plain in the central part of the coastal plain. Calculated high- and low-tide levels of the Ulee Lheue (Oleelheue) near Banda Aceh on December 26, 2004, were 172 cm (5.7 feet) and 42 cm (1.4 feet), respectively, and the tidal range of the region was less than 1.5 m (4.9 feet) (based on data by Tsuji, Namegaya, and Ito 2005).

Generally speaking, the extent to which buildings on the Banda Aceh plain were destroyed was related to their distance from the coast. Distinct regional

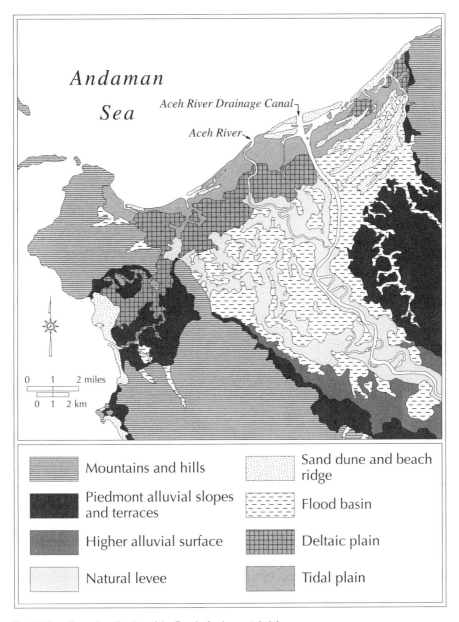

Andaman
Sea

Aceh River Drainage Canal

Aceh River

0   1   2 miles

0   1   2 km

Mountains and hills

Piedmont alluvial slopes
and terraces

Higher alluvial surface

Natural levee

Sand dune and beach
ridge

Flood basin

Deltaic plain

Tidal plain

Fig. 2.2. Landform classification of the Banda Aceh coastal plain.

differences regarding the destruction of buildings were also seen among the eastern and the central and western parts of the Banda Aceh coastal plain. The population of Banda Aceh city was about 264,000, and 71,000 are dead or missing. As for the buildings, about 14,000 units were totally destroyed and 7,000 were partially destroyed. According to Umitsu and Takahashi (2007), the spatial difference of damage and tsunami inundation can be classified into four zones and the relationship between them is as follows.

Assessing the damage to structures allows for a partitioning of the region into four areas: (I) a coastal area in which all buildings were almost or completely destroyed, and the land was eroded in some places; (II) an area just inland from the coast in which many buildings were destroyed, but most of the structures of the buildings remain; (III) an area that was inundated by tsunami flow without serious damage to buildings; and (IV) an area in which neither buildings nor humans were affected by the tsunami. The (I) and (II) areas of greatest damage correspond to the extended low-lying areas that had undergone sprawl-type urbanization, with tidal flats and mangrove forests converted to low-rise housing and shrimp ponds, in addition to fishing villages on coastal riverside areas.

The tsunami height for these areas can be surmised as approximately 3 m and over for the first area, approximately 1–3 m (3.3–9.9 feet) for the second, and less than 1 m for the third. In addition, the death rate in the coastal area (I) was over 80%, gradually decreasing inland: about 10–20% in area (II), with almost no death record collected for the other areas. The damages to humans and buildings are clearly differentiated between the first area (I) and the others, with a key height of the water being 3 m. Therefore, it should be noted that there are close relationships between the spatial configuration of area typology in terms of damage and the geoenvironmental conditions, including local-scale topographies and land uses, as schematically shown in figure 2.3.

Tsunami Flow on the Banda Aceh Coastal Plain

The tsunami flow extended inland in the central and western parts of the plain for about 4 km (2.4 miles) and for about 3 km (1.8 miles) in the eastern part (fig. 2.4). The remarkable invasion of the run-up tsunami flow along the rivers was recorded on the SPOT 2 image. The distances of the invasion of the flow from the coast into the Aceh River and the Aceh Drainage River were 8 and 8.5 km (2.28 and 5.1 miles), respectively.

Inundation heights at similar distances from the coast were variable, with greater heights in the central and western part of the plain. The tsunami reached a height of about 9 m (29.7 feet) on the ground near the port of Banda Aceh

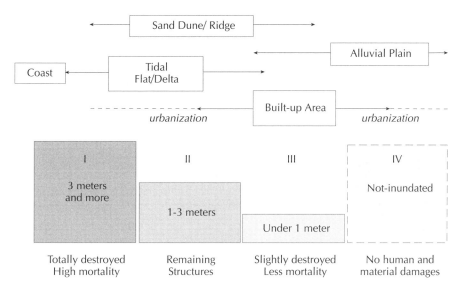

Fig. 2.3. Relationship between tsunami height and damages in the geoenvironment of the Banda Aceh coastal plain. (Umitsu and Takahashi 2007.)

Fig. 2.4. Tsunami inundation in the Banda Aceh coastal plain shown on the SPOT2 image. The image was taken about four hours after the earthquake. (Includes material (c) CNES2005, Distribution Spot Image S.A., France, all rights reserved. Umitsu, Tanarud, and Patanakanog 2007.)

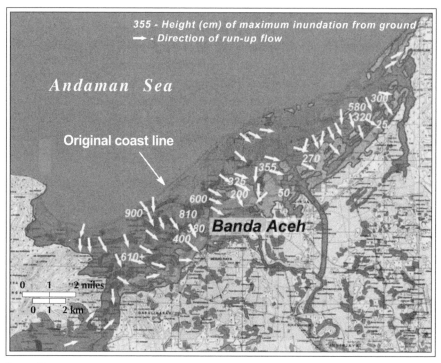

Fig. 2.5. Direction and height of the tsunami flow in the Banda Aceh coastal plain. (Based on field observation. Umitsu, Tanarud, and Patanakanog 2007.)

and about 6–8 m (19.8–26.4 feet) in the western part of the plain about 2 km (1.2 miles) inland. In the eastern part of the plain about 2 km (1.2 miles) from the coast, however, tsunami heights were mostly lower than 3 m (9.9 feet) (fig. 2.4). The orientation of fallen columns of destroyed buildings and the scratches on the floors of buildings are also good markers of run-up flow directions in the Banda Aceh coastal plain. During the field surveys, heights and directions were measured of flow indicators related to tsunami flow on the plains.

Flow indicators on the Banda Aceh coastal plain generally show inundation from the northwest. However, some areas show different directions of the flow (fig. 2.5). On the northeastern coast, flows spread out in a radial pattern from a gap in the sand dune along the coast. In the southwestern part of the plain, the northeastward tsunami flow from the west coast penetrated the plain and the flow met in a gap of hills with the southward run-up tsunami flow of the Banda Aceh coastal plain. We also mapped indicators in the western part of the coastal plain that show southward flows deflected due to the existence of hills.

Severe coastal erosion occurred in the parts of the tidal plain used for shrimp- or fishponds. The small narrow banks separating the ponds were easily eroded by the tsunami, returning these areas to their former condition of tidal flats. The conversion of these areas to tidal flats was due to erosion by the tsunami rather than tectonic subsidence. Interviews with local people confirmed that tidal areas are now exposed at low tide to the same extent as they were before the tsunami, and tide levels marked on several bridges are similar to levels before the tsunami. It was difficult to reconstruct the directions of the tsunami backwash flow in the Banda Aceh plain, because there are few indicators of backwash flow on the ground.

Effect of Landforms on Tsunami Flow in the Plain

Regional differences in tsunami flow patterns and tsunami height can be seen on the Banda Aceh coastal plain. The differences are related to the characteristics of the landforms of the plains. In the case of the Banda Aceh coastal plain, erosion of channels was not violent and linear erosion is not observed on the plain. In some areas of the plain, however, coastal landforms were greatly modified. Shrimp- and fishponds on the tidal plain were extremely damaged and some of them disappeared after the tsunami. This indicates that the backwash flow was not concentrated linearly in the Banda Aceh plain, and sheet erosion of backwash flow dominated in the plain.

The primary reason for the dominance of sheet erosion is that the ground level is related to the geoenvironment of the Banda Aceh coastal plain. There is a broad tidal plain in the central and western coastal area of the Banda Aceh plain, and the ground surface is low and flat. This environment did not produce the concentration of backwash, and linear-flow erosion was not remarkable.

Tsunami flow and inundation in the Banda Aceh coastal plain are related to its landforms. As mentioned earlier, the landforms of the Banda Aceh coastal plain are deltaic lowlands with tidal plains in the west and central parts and strand plain and beach ridges in the eastern part. Coastal erosion of the plains was caused by direct attack of the tsunami wave in the Banda Aceh plain, and the broad tidal flat of the Banda Aceh coastal plain was severely damaged by the tsunami flow.

The tsunami heights in the central and western parts of the Banda Aceh coastal plain at similar distances from the coast were higher than in the eastern parts. It is suggested that the existence of low-lying tidal and deltaic plains in the western and central parts of the plain facilitated the intrusion of the tsunami flow inland. The tsunami inundation height also did not decrease in the regions of the plain. In the eastern coastal region, relatively higher landforms such as dunes and beach ridges prevented the tsunami flow from penetrating inland. Microlandforms such as beach ridges and natural levees prevented the flow of the tsunami from penetrating further inland in the area near the limit of tsunami inundation.

West Coast

Remarkable damage along the west coast of Aceh province was seen in the regions of Lho'nga, Calang, and Meulaboh. These villages and towns are located about 10, 150, and 270 km (6.2, 93.2, and 167.8 miles) from Banda Aceh city, respectively.

The height of the tsunami at Lho'nga on the northwest coast of the Aceh province exceeded 15 m, and it was said that the tsunami reached to the rooftop of the mosque in the village. In some places near the area, the tsunami heights reached over 30 m. As a result, a whole area of the village was catastrophically destroyed, and a lot of inhabitants died.

The village is located on a small coastal plain connecting with the Banda Aceh coastal plain through a narrow segment. The tsunami flow washed the whole area of the plain, and it intruded toward the stenosis part between the Banda Aceh coastal plain. In addition, a cement factory located south of this village suffered severe damage from the tsunami, and large-scale cargo boats were grounded near the cement factory.

Photo 2.1. Temporary bridge on the main road on the west coast of Sumatra. (Photo by Masatomo Umitsu, August 30, 2005.)

In the area of the west coast near Calang, mountains ranging west of the Sumatra fault extend toward the coastline. Rocky coasts and small pocket beaches are located along the west coast, and alluvial lowlands along the rivers from the mountains are also distributed in the coastal region. This is the place where the Free Aceh Movement (GAM) has been fighting against the Indonesian military for the independence of Aceh, and there were few people living in the area. The only road running along the shoreline was severely damaged by the tsunami, contributing to the disruption in the transportation of goods and materials for recovery.

Calang and Meulaboh

Calang, located on the west coast, is a capital city of the Aceh Jaya district. According to data supplied by the United Nations in January 2005, the number of tsunami victims was 16,874 out of a district population of 98,000, with most of the victims inhabitants of Calang. The main part of the town of Calang is located on a sandbar, and the area was totally washed away by the tsunami. Previously verdant landscapes changed to desolate land, littered with the wreckage of buildings and scattered trees. A long coastal plain of around 2 km (1.2 miles) in width continues toward the south from Calang. Its length is more than 120 km (74.6 miles), and remarkable dunes and beach ridges have developed on the plain.

The tsunami inundation spread into the greater part of these coastal plains, invading about 2 km (1.2 miles) to the end of the hills and plateaus. In addition, a remarkable intrusion of tsunami flow was seen in the alluvial lowlands along the rivers flowing to the ocean. The distance from the coast was about 4 km (2.5 miles). Similarly to the lowland of Keudepate, located to the north of Calang, a sandy beach of the plain was eroded such that it presents a sawtooth appearance.

Tectonic movement occurred at the time of the giant earthquake, and coastal areas subsided in the region. The mouths of some rivers in this coastal plain were significantly broadened, and the swales between beach ridges in several parts changed to drowned water areas. There was a trunk road connecting Banda Aceh to the southern area, passing through Calang and Meulaboh, along which many villages were located—these villages were completely destroyed, together with the road.

Severe damage was also seen in the town of Meulaboh. Meulaboh, a capital of the Aceh Barat district, is located about 250 km (155.3 miles) south of Banda Aceh. Population of the district was 195,000, and the number of the casualties, including missing persons, was 13,785 people, of which a considerable number

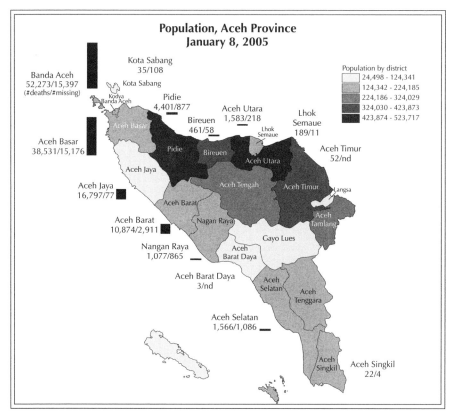

Fig. 2.6. Casualties and missing people shown on a population map of Aceh province.

were inhabitants of Meulaboh. The tsunami completely destroyed the buildings of the town from the coast to an area approximately 200 m (656 feet) inland. The height of the tsunami reached to the third floor of buildings.

A highway (Aceh West Coast Road) connecting Meulaboh and Banda Aceh on the northern tip of Sumatra Island is of strategic importance for conveying recovery aid after the tsunami. However, restoration of this road did not proceed after its temporary repair in early 2005 (see photo 2.1). Repairs on about 120 km of the highway (of the 270 km between Aceh and Meulaboh), connecting Calang and Meulaboh, were finally completed thanks to Japanese aid on December 27, 2006.

Recovery from the Disaster

Several years have passed since the severe tsunami disaster occurred in late 2004, and active recovery and rehabilitation are still in progress in the affected

Photo 2.2. Tents in the suburbs of Banda Aceh.
(Photo by Masatomo Umitsu, August 29, 2005.)

areas. By December 2005, one year after the disaster, temporary houses had been constructed in many places, but the number of the new houses and those still under construction was only about one-fourth of the necessary number. Many damaged buildings still remained in the region, and there were also many people still living in tents, an arrangement meant to be only temporary. The life of the inhabitants was not stable; people who had lost their jobs and homes were being supported by various organizations, including domestic and international governments, aid organizations, NGOs, and so on.

By December 2006, two years after the disaster, many rehabilitation permanent houses had been built, but their number was still only about half of those needed. The houses are one-story, compact houses consisting of two or three small rooms, a kitchen, and a bathroom. The houses for the most part were built through the aid of governments and NGOs of many countries. In the area 1 or 2 km (0.6 to 1.2 miles) from the coast, many people were living in partially destroyed buildings, and the newly built permanent houses and repaired houses were poorly built.

In the coastal areas, where the buildings were completely destroyed, many residential estates of rehabilitation permanent houses were constructed. However, the occupancy rate of these permanent houses was not high in December 2006; there were a considerable number of unoccupied houses. The reason for this was the inadequacy of the infrastructure, such as a lack of electricity and water service for the residential estates (Takahashi et al. 2007). In addition, problems arose over the location of the houses and the way they were distributed. On the other hand, recovery was considerably advanced in the central part of the city where the damage wrought by the tsunami was not so serious. In those areas, some damaged buildings were still left, but most had already been restored as stores or office buildings.

By December 2008, four years after the disaster, the life of people in Banda Aceh had calmed down considerably. Recovery of the region in and around

Photo 2.3. Permanent rehabilitation houses in Ulee Lheue district. (Photo by Masatomo Umitsu.)

Banda Aceh city had shifted from the rehabilitation of inhabitants to the recovery of public facilities such as a city hall, a police station, and so on. The port of Ulee Lheue, once a center of marine transportation for Banda Aceh, had been eroded and destroyed by the tsunami, together with the ground on which it stood. Harbor facilities, including the rebuilding of the Ulee Lheue port, were newly constructed after the landfill of the area, and port services had already started. Furthermore, four-story buildings with tsunami shelters were built in and around the Ulee Lheue district, to be used as refuges for the local people. A beautiful graveyard park was also constructed near the port of Ulee Lheue, where many victims were buried just after the disaster. A fishing boat stuck on the second floor of a private house in Lampulo district in the northern part of Banda Aceh city has been preserved and a monument was built adjacent to the house. In the Ounge Blan Cut district of southwestern Banda Aceh city, a memorial park was constructed beside a large-scale generator ship that moved about 2 km (1.2 miles) inland from the Ulee Lheue port. Furthermore, a large tsunami museum is under construction now in the central part of the city.

In this way recovery from the damage caused by the tsunami is progressing steadily in and around Banda Aceh city. The recovery of the city and neighboring areas seems to have advanced in stages. At the time of the tsunami attack, for people merely to survive was the most important consideration. Next came the need to ensure that the basic requirements for day-to-day living were available, including the recovery of infrastructure required for life to go smoothly. Then, the focus of recovery efforts shifted to the construction of public facilities not indispensable for the support of life. And finally, as of late 2008, recovery came to include memorializing the disaster.

The speed of the recovery, however, has been slow. Takahashi et al. (2007) have pointed out the obstacles encountered in housing reconstruction, the lack of established adjustment mechanisms for aid groups, the slow pace of the reconstruction in society overall, and the failure of market functions.

The change in focus of the recovery efforts is also seen in the regions of the west coast of Aceh province. As noted above, the Aceh West Coast Road was partially reconstructed in December 2006. The construction of rehabilitation permanent houses in the western coast region was completed by late 2008. But other infrastructure projects, such as rebuilding the road between Banda Aceh and Calang, are still to be completed, and the slower recovery of the western coastal region is clear in comparison with Banda Aceh city and the surrounding areas. It may take several years to complete the physical recovery from the damage caused by the disaster, and the mental and emotional recovery of the inhabitants may take even longer.

References

Takahashi, M., S. Tanaka, R. Kimura, M. Umitsu, R. Tabuchi, T. Kuroda, M. Ando, and F. Kimata. 2007. Restoration after the Sumatra Earthquake tsunami in Banda Aceh: Based on the results of interdisciplinary researches by Nagoya University. *Journal of Natural Disaster Science* 29:53–61.

Tsuji, N., Y. Namegaya, and J. Ito. 2005. *Astronomical tide levels along the coasts of the Indian Ocean.* Tokyo: Earthquake Research Institute, University of Tokyo. http://www.eri.u-tokyo.ac.jp/namegaya/sumatera/tide/.

Umitsu, M., and M. Takahashi. 2007. Geo-environmental features in the damages of the 2004 Indian Ocean Tsunami in/around Banda Aceh, Indonesia. [In Japanese with English abstract.] *E-journal GEO* 2 (3): 142–52.

Umitsu, M., Charlchai Tanarud, and B. Patanakanog. 2007. Effects of landforms on tsunami flow in the plains of Banda Aceh, Indonesia, and Nam Khem, Thailand. *Marine Geology* 242: 141–53.

United Nations. 2005. *Map of population Aceh Province.* 8 January. HIC Sumatra. United Nations Banda Aceh, Sumatra.

3
—

Geological and Geomorphological Perspectives of the Tsunami on the Tamil Nadu Coast, India

S. R. Singarasubramanian, M. V. Mukesh, K. Manoharan, P. Seralathan, and S. Srinivasalu

Eastern Continental Margin of South India

The Tamil Nadu coast of India extends to a length of about 1,026 km (615.6 miles). The coastal zone—the transition between the land and the sea—is a fragile, complex, and productive ecosystem. The southern part of the coast is tectonically more stable than the northern part (Rao and Rao 1985). The width of the continental shelf varies from about 10 to 45 km (6 to 27 miles) in nondeltaic areas. During the last glaciation, as a result of the lowering of the sea level, the entire continental shelf was exposed to subaerial erosion and fluvial deposition. The rivers cut across the shelf up to the edge, depositing sediments directly onto the continental slope or into the submarine valleys.

During the mid-Holocene, the sea level rose rapidly, the carbonate reef growth was truncated, and submarine valleys were delinked from river sources, as they could not keep pace with the rapid sea level rise. More sediment deposit on the inner shelf created barriers and ridges. The Holocene delta progradation of the Palar and Kaveri rivers of Tamil Nadu into the offshore regime is limited, unlike other rivers of India's east coast such as the Mahanadi, Godavari, and Krishna.

Bathymetric Distribution

The width of the continental shelf varies from between 20 km (12 miles) near Pazhaverkkadu (Pulicat) lagoon and 50 km (30 miles) at Chennai. The average width of the shelf is 25 km (15 miles) in the Puducherry-Parangipettai (Pondicherry–Porto Novo) sector, while it narrows to 15 km (9 miles) at the head of the submarine valleys. Further south, the shelf gradually widens from 35 km (21 miles) near Karaikal to 80 km (48 miles) at Kodiyakarai (Point Calimere). The average width of the near-shore zone up to a 20 m (66 feet) depth contour is 5–8 km (3–4.8 miles), but widens from Karaikal toward the south.

The shelf is wider off Pulicat-Palar and Karaikal–Point Calimere, and the shelf break occurs at a deeper depth. The shelf has two distinct morphological units separated by ridge or terrace. The inner shelf has an average gradient of 1:400. Terraces occur at 54 m (178 feet), 75 m (247 feet), 85 m (280 feet), and 115 m (379 feet) depths. The outer shelf beyond 120 m (396 feet) has a relatively steeper gradient, in the order of 1:80, and the seafloor is regular at 185 m (610.5 feet), 270–360 m (891–1,188 feet), and 465 m (1,534 feet) depths due to the exposure of hard substratum.

The shelf break occurs at unequal depths: at 100 m (330 feet) off Pulicat lagoon, 350 m (1,155 feet) off Chennai, 100 m (330 feet) off Pondicherry–Porto Novo, and 110–465 m (363–1,534 feet) off Karaikal–Point Calimere. The shelf edge truncates against the head of the submarine valleys off Pondicherry– Porto Novo. The edge invariably exhibits a convex shape and is characterized by a dome-shaped substratum.

The shallow Palk Bay, with a water depth of <20 m (66 feet), is designated as a wave-sheltered coast. The 5 m (16.5 feet) depth contour in Palk Bay runs at a distance of 6–10 km (3.6–6 miles) from the coast, except off Manalmelkudi, where it runs at a distance of about 30 km (18 miles). The 10 m (33 feet) depth contour south of Point Calimere and Kodiyakarai is seen at a distance of 50–55 km (30–33 miles), but toward the west it narrows down marginally. Off Manalmelkudi, a 10 m (33 feet) depth contour is located about 45 km (27 miles) from the coast. Manalmelkudi is a cuspate foreland and so both 5 and 10 m (16.5 and 33 feet) depth contours are projected offshore. But south of Manalmelkudi and up to Thanushkodi, the 10 m (33 feet) depth contour runs at a distance of 2,530 km (1,518 miles) from the coast. The coastal land and the adjoining seafloor on the Western Palk Bay, falling between the WNW-ESW trending Vedharanyam fault and the NW-SE trending Vaigai fault, have been also uplifted (Loveson, Rajamanickam, and Chandrasekar 1990).

Geomorphic Features

The coastal zone of Tamil Nadu is endowed with varied landscape, such as sandy beaches, beach ridges, backwaters, estuaries, intertidal mud and sand flats, dunes, cliffs, beach rocks, deltas, lagoons, mangrove forests, and coral reef ecosystems. The coast has constantly undergone physical changes, from the geological past to the present. Many rivers bring considerable sediments, which affect shore processes significantly.

The Palar River delta occupies an area of about 4,000 km^2 (1,600 sq. miles). The mature stage of the Palar River is characterized by vast flood plains and lateral accretion deposits. The old stage of the river occurs in the coastal region, where it debouches into the Bay of Bengal, 5 km (3 miles) east of Sadras. The river drains an area of 17,871 km^2 (7,148 sq. miles), of which 10,856 km^2 (4,342 sq. miles) are in Tamil Nadu and the rest in Karnataka. The geomorphic features along the river course include mounds, dissected pediplains, flood plains, and coastal plains.

The coast between Chennai and Pondicherry through Muttukadu, Mamallapuram, and Marakkanam is a narrow sandy belt. The major geomorphic features include tidal flats, estuary, beaches, dunes, and beach ridges. The dunes are stable at their base and mobile on their crest. The coastal dune field, which is stabilized by vegetation, occurs in a very high-energy wind regime. Linear dunes along the shoreline, which are stabilized to a large extent, represent the major geomorphic features. A spit protects the low-lying marshy land at Muttukadu. Four major zones within the tidal flat were recognized at Mamallapuram, Muttukadu, and Marakkanam: (1) an outer sand flat merging with the beach dune complex and rock exposures; (2) middle sand flat; (3) sandy to silty inner flats; and (4) salt marsh (Achyuthan 2002).

The coastal area between Pondicherry and Nagapattinam is occupied by various geomorphic features: beach ridges, swales, sand dunes, deltaic plain, chenniers, palaeo-tidal flats, palaeo-lagoons, salt marshes, palaeo-channels, and lagoons (Anbarasu and Rajamanickam 1997).

The coastal features in and around Point Calimere include beaches, beach ridges, swales, dunes, tidal flats, palaeo-tidal flats, barrier islands, alluvial plain, chenniers, palaeo-lagoons, flood plains, mud flats, salt pans, and mangroves (Shanthi Devi and Rajamanickam 2000).

The coastal landforms between Devipattinam and Mandapam were classified into depositional and erosional features and others (Chockalingam, Suresh Gandhi, and Rajamanickam 2000). Series of beach ridges are distinctly noticed. Sandy beaches are more prominent. Rocky beaches are characteristic of Mandapam to Rameshwaram. The important features in these areas include spits, swales, sand dunes, shoals, deltaic plains, sand sheets, mud flats, chennier plains, cliffs, beach rocks, sea caves, sea cliffs, and marine terraces.

The coastal landforms between Mandapam and Kanyakumari are classified into fluvial, coastal/marine, and aeolian (Rajamanickam and Loveson 1998). Fluvial landforms include pediplains, floodplains, deltaic plains, and palaeo-channels. Marine landforms include beach ridges, swales, backwaters, marine terraces, wave-cut platforms, sea caves, beaches, spits, tidal flats, mud flats, and cuspate forelands. The aeolian landforms are stable sand dunes and teri complexes.

Apart from the coastal geomorphic features, the Tamil Nadu coast is protected with a coral ecosystem in the Gulf of Mannar region. Coral reefs act as a barrier against wave action and prevent coastal erosion. There are twenty-one islands, situated at an average distance of about 8 km (4.8 miles) from the coast and running parallel to the coastline. Along this coastline both erosion and accretion takes place. Island erosion and accretion are caused mainly by the action of waves, wave-induced currents, and long shore currents along the shore.

Tsunami

Tsunamis are a less known coastal hazard in this part of the globe, in comparison to more commonly occurring hazards such as coastal floods, cyclones, coastal erosion, storm surges, oil spills, coastal pollution, and algal bloom. Tsunamis are associated with earthquakes that are always related to crustal movements or deformation leading to displacement of a water body from an equilibrium state. When large areas of the seafloor elevate or subduct suddenly, a tsunami can be generated. Its destruction capability is enormous, as it can crush homes and other coastal structures and can inundate or flood hundreds of meters of coastal lands with a run-up height of around 10 m (33 feet) or at times even up to 30 m (99 feet). Sometimes it can strip a waste beach that may have taken years to build.

Tsunamis have long wavelengths (up to 500 km [300 miles]) and can travel across the open ocean with speed ranging from 500 to 1,000 km (300 to 600 miles) per hour, depending upon the water depth. As tsunamis are characterized by shallow water waves, the energy of a tsunami wave passes through the entire water column up to the seabed even in deep ocean water. When the wave approaches shallow seas and finally the coast, the wave no longer travels with the same speed as in open water; but it begins to pile up due to wave transformation, and the wave front becomes steeper and taller with less wavelength. Unlike meteorologically induced waves, tsunamis are capable of affecting deep shelf and ocean floor. Hence, tsunamis transport sizable amounts of sediments landward, and when they finally cross the shore they dump considerable off-shore sediments on the coast. They also alter geomorphic features considerably. Sometimes the tsunami waves cause the near-shore water to recede, exposing the ocean floor, as in Kanyakumari and Tiruchendur on the coast of Tamil Nadu.

The mega-earthquake occurred on December 26, 2004, off the west coast of northern Sumatra (3.2760N, 95.821E), close to Sunda Trench at a water depth of about 1,300 m (4,290 feet). Its epicenter, located at a shallow depth of 10 km (6 miles) below the ocean floor, triggered a tsunami in the Indian Ocean. The tsunami hit most of the Tamil Nadu coast, with wave height varying from 3 to 10 m (9.9–33 feet). This catastrophic wave devastated the coastal regimes in eleven Asian countries. The tsunami left considerable sedimentary signatures along the coast of Tamil Nadu, either opening or closing estuaries, breaching the coastal sand dune ridges, developing long erosional channels across the beach, and dumping large quantities of sediments beyond the backshore.

Inundation of Tsunami Waves in Tamil Nadu

A tsunami turns into a killer wave when it crosses land, destroying life, land, and property. As the wave strikes the shore, it may inundate low-lying coastal areas, resulting in mass destruction of land and life (see fig. 3.1). The behavior of tsunami waves in the coastal area is dependent on several factors. The most important are the topography of the seafloor and the actual geomorphic condition of the coastal land.

The maximum vertical height of a tsunami in the coastal area to which water is observed to rise with reference to sea level (spring tide or mean sea level) is referred to as "run-up." The maximum horizontal distance reached by a tsunami is referred to as "inundation." The run-up and inundation of a tsunami will vary depending upon local geomorphic features, submarine topography, orientation of the oncoming waves, tide level, and magnitude of the tsunami.

Field observations were made to identify the inundation and run-up level of the December 26, 2004, tsunami along the Tamil Nadu coast by various workers. The inundation and run-up levels of some villages along the coast of Tamil Nadu are given in table 3.1.

Maximum devastation was recorded in the fishing hamlets located nearer to the coast. The settlements and beach resorts located near the coast were badly affected. Some of the villages were protected by back dune ridges, as their settlements were located to the west of dunes. The wide variation noticed in the run-up and inundation within small areas was due to variation in onshore topography but also a consequence of offshore bathymetry. Concave-shaped

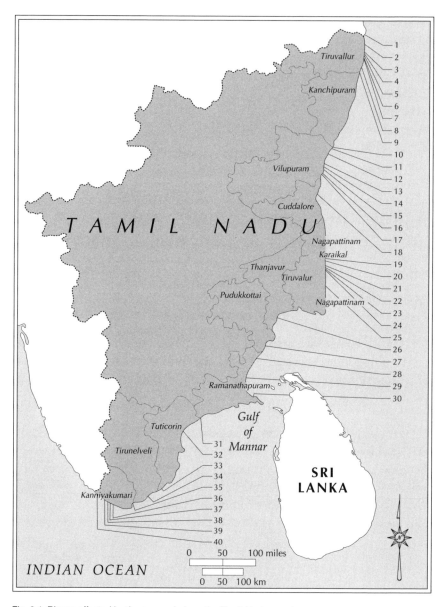

Fig. 3.1. Places affected by the tsunami along the Tamil Nadu coast.

1 Cherian Nagar, Ennore	11 Kotakuppam	21 Nagapattinam Beach	31 Vembar
2 Royapuram	12 Puducherry	22 Namiyar Nagar	32 Thoothukudi Port
3 M.G.R. and Anna Square	13 Nallwarkuppam	23 Vellipalayam	33 Arogyapuram Village
4 Marina Beach	14 Manjakuppam	24 Nagapattinam Port	34 Librahmkuppam Village
5 Srinivasapuri	15 Tazhanguda	25 Velanganni Beach	35 Chinnamuttam
6 Elliot's Beach	16 Devanampattibnam	26 Alatikut Village	36 Kanyakumari
7 Basat Nagar	17 Kuddukullam	27 Arupudapattinam	37 Keelmanakudi
8 New Beach	18 Kuddupattinam	28 Thondi	38 Chinnavilai Village
9 Kudukuppam	19 Kilinjal Village	29 Navapasanam	39 Pattupetta Village
10 Chinnapattam	20 Amman Kerapattu	30 Dhanushkodi	40 Colachal Harbor

Table 3.1. Maximum inundation and run-up level of tsunami waves in some places along the Tamil Nadu coast

Place	Maximum inundation (m)	Run-up height (m)
Pulicat	405	1
Kattupalli	600	2.5
Chepauk	600	3.5
Marina Beach Road	500	4
Besant Nagar	150	2.5
Palavakkam	335	3
Injambakkam	300	4
Shozhinganallur	550	4
Muthukadu	300	3
Pattipulam	500	4.5
Mamallapuram	650	6
Pudupattinam	650	4.3
Kadalur	770	4.7
Mogaiyur	450	4.5
Paramankeni	650	5.5
Cuddalore Old Town	1,190	2.5
Kudikadu	370	3.1
Parangipettai	1,700	2.9
Nagapattinam	1,100	4.5
Akaraipettai	3,000	4
Vedharanyam	1,400	2.3
Kodiyakarai	900	2.1
Colachel	1,500	6
Melmanakudi	1,500	6
Keezhamanakudi	1,000	5

coastline in some areas appears to have amplified the run-up and inundation. Sand dune ridges protected the coast but many dune ridge breaks have led to tsunami inundation (see photos 3.1a–f and 3.2a–f) through the saddle in between ridges or breaching of the stable ridges. When stable dune ridges protect the coasts, swales, creeks, and other inlets permit the free flow of water inland. The maximum inundations recorded were through waterways like the Vellar River, the Vedharanyam canal, and the Coleroon and Gadillam rivers. The high death toll in certain villages was due to the successive wave propagations through backwaters. Satellite images show tsunami inundation in some villages in Karaikal and Kodiyakarai (photos 3.3 and 3.4).

Photos 3.1a–c.
Tsunami damages
along the Tamil Nadu
coast. (Photos by S. R.
Singarasubramanian.)

Photos 3.1d–f. Tsunami damages
along the Tamil Nadu coast. (Photos
by S. R. Singarasubramanian.)

Photos 3.2a–c. Tsunami damages and invasion of seawater. (Photos by S. R. Singarasubramanian.)

Photos 3.2d–f. Tsunami damages and invasion of seawater. (Photos by S. R. Singarasubramanian.)

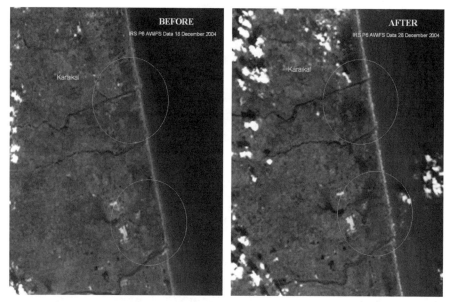

Photo 3.3. Satellite image of Karaikal before and after the tsunami, showing the inundation of villages.

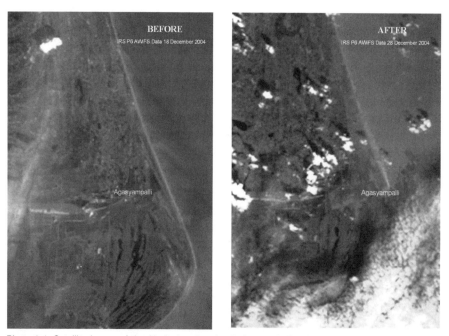

Photo 3.4. Satellite image of the Kodiyakarai region before and after the tsunami, showing landform changes.

Overlaying land-use patterns and the extent of tsunami inundation indicates that barren lands with lower elevation permitted the free flow of the tsunami while areas covered by vegetation and coastal dunes restricted the inundation process (Senthilnathan 2006). Beach ridges occurring at the berm crest were breached at many places through which inundation took place. Mangroves, rasaporis, fulifera, and casurina acted as barriers that restrained the force of the tsunami waves and hence it is presumed that the energy of the tsunami was dissipated. Though Pitchavaram lagoon connects tidal channels from both the Vellar and the Coleroon, the expansion of the lagoon during the tsunami was limited to a few meters only. This was due to the fact that the mangrove plants absorbed the tsunami wave energy significantly.

Nagapattinam district in central coastal Tamil Nadu was the worst-affected district, with the highest death toll of 6,065 people. The death toll reported in Cuddalore district was more than 500 people. The areas adjoining the river mouths of the Vellar, Chinnavaikal (Pitchavaram), and Coleroon were severely damaged; more than 1,000 lives were claimed.

Sedimentological Observations

The tsunami deposits are characterized by a sequence of fine sediments upward and thinning landward. This is indicative of decreasing wave energy away from the coast. Tsunami deposition is a very complicated process involving turbulent currents that cause deposition as well as erosion. It is hard to conclude that distinct sedimentary units represent separate waves or periods of run-up and backwash. However, evidence for bidirectional currents has been found from tsunami deposits in Tamil Nadu, shown by sedimentary structures. In many places the deposits have followed the maximum landward inundation of individual tsunami waves. This has caused additional erosion and sediment redeposition. But in some places back flow has taken different ways. The lower contact was unconformable or erosional and contains intraclasts of reworked material. Loading structures could be identified at the base of the deposits. This indicates a rapid sedimentation. Particle and grain size ranges from sand to fine mud, depending upon the availability of source materials—barrier, beach or dune sand, soil materials, and so on. Individual shells and shell-rich units were often present (photos 3.6a–f). Based on the sediment characteristics of the December 26, 2004, tsunami, three waves were recorded in many places along the Tamil Nadu coast. But in some places, due to the backwash, the wave signatures were not preserved. Apparently, each wave that struck the coast did not deposit a sandy layer. Alternatively, the sandy layer deposited by a wave might have been resus-

Photos 3.5a–c. Tsunami-induced erosion along the coast of Tamil Nadu. (Photos by S. R. Singarasubramanian.)

Photos 3.5d–f. Tsunami-induced erosion along the coast of Tamil Nadu. (Photos by S. R. Singarasubramanian.)

pended with the passage of the next wave. Hence, there does not appear to be a one-to-one relationship between the number of waves inundating the coast and the number of sandy layers in a deposit. The base of each layer was characterized by darker sand and abundant heavy mineral content, although in no instance did the heavy minerals exceed 3%.

Quartz sand is one of the most common components of the coastal sand and occurs in a variety of clear colors, including white, rose, and purple. If the surface texture of a quartz grain is not clear and glasslike, it indicates that the grain has undergone minor abrasion. Many of the surface features were induced by grinding during transportation. The grains that have been transported farthest have a more rounded shape. Some of the surface textures of quartz sand from the tsunami deposits show strong grooves of mechanical abrasion, indicating a high-energy environment of deposition. A rise in the percentage of silt and clay content after the tsunami was appreciable in certain coasts such as Nagapattinam and the central part of the Tamil Nadu coast. Such enhancement is likely due to the admixture of the fine sediments brought forward by the receding tsunami waves from the hinterland. A rise in carbonate content from 3.12 to 6.90% in tsunami deposits is attributed to the contribution of fresh debris brought forward by the onward movement of the tsunami waves. The tsunami deposits could be easily differentiated, with the presence of mudslips and beach rock fragments along the Tamil Nadu coast depending upon the offshore and onshore sediments.

The coasts nearer to Chennai, Mahabalipuram, Pondicherry, Cuddalore, and Nagapattinam were affected by direct tsunami waves from a southeast direction, whereas the coastal regions in Palk Bay and the Gulf of Mannar were affected partly by direct waves, but mainly by the diffracted waves after they crossed the Sri Lankan island. Hence, the impact of the waves over the coastal settlements varied from place to place.

In Vedharanyam about 18 cm (7.2 inches) of thick fresh fine sediments brought by the tsunami were deposited. Fine fresh sediments were spread along the coast and inland. In some places the water entered through erosional and older channels. Point Calimere has encountered widespread sedimentation and the formation of eroded channels due to the tsunami. The newly created channel is about 120 cm (48 inches) deep near the shore and extends up to 1 km (0.6 mile) inland. Here the beach was eroded and occupied by the sea to the extent of about 20 m (66 feet) after the tsunami. It can be evidenced by the current position of the Chola lighthouse, at present in the sea. South of Point Calimere, the erosion was less but the depositions of fine clayey fractions were more from the shore. About 15 cm (6 inches) of fine sand were

Photos 3.6a–c. Deposition of tsunami-borne sediments along the Tamil Nadu coast. (Photos by S. R. Singarasubramanian.)

Photos 3.6d–f. Deposition of tsunami-borne sediments along the Tamil Nadu coast. (Photos by S. R. Singarasubramanian.)

deposited over the 5 cm (2 inches) thick clayey sand. In Kodiyakarai, a layer of sediments about 30 cm (12 inches) thick was deposited near the shore, thinning as it led inland. Clayey sand was spread up to 700 m (2,310 feet) from the shore. The sediments were deposited over the medium to coarse sand along the coast. Here the new deposits were easily identifiable by the presence of shell and old clothing under them. Destruction by the tsunami waves of boats and the deposition of sediments over them indicate that the waves brought the sediments. Parallel to the shoreline in the beach, erosion is prominent and filled with water bodies. The stable dunes in these areas were breached at places or eroded.

From eyewitness accounts as well as from field evidence, it is understood that the Point Calimere coast was struck by tsunami waves from both the northeast and the southeast, which means that the Palk Bay coast was affected by the refracted tsunami waves from the Bay of Bengal and the diffracted waves that came from the northern Sri Lankan island (Ramanamurthy et al. 2005). The 10 m (33 feet) bottom contour that runs between Point Calimere and Kankesanthurai in Sri Lanka across Palk Strait would have certainly played a major role in arresting the tsunami propagation into Palk Bay.

Mallipattinam, Manora, Kalamangudi, Manthiripattinam, Prathabharamapattinam, Adhipattinam, Palakudi, Pudupattinam, and Vattanam encountered sedimentation in the fishing harbors. Muddy sediments from offshore transported by the tsunami waves were spread along the near shore and beaches. In some areas, like Prathabharamapattinam and Manora, the coastal fishing areas became clayey. Up to 30 cm (12 inches) of thick clay were deposited over the coarse sand on the shore and up to 20 m (66 feet) into the sea. In all these areas the beaches are shallow and wave domination is less. In the Manthiripattinam, Palakudi, Adhipattinam, Kalamangudi, Pudupattinam, and Vattanam areas, the sediments brought by the tsunami waves came 50–200 m (165–660 feet) inland. The tsunami sediments were fresh, loosely packed, medium- to fine-grained, and gray in color, with some shell fragments lying over the dark-colored medium to coarse sand. The tsunami sediments were deposited as thin layers, with some dark bands of heavy minerals in most places.

Along the Thondi-Uchipuli segment, the tsunami inundation was about 30 m (99 feet). In Thondi, the waves entered up to 30 m (99 feet) inland but no sedimentation was observed. But the tsunami waves brought considerable fine sediments in some areas, depositing them on the beach, and the areas became clayey up to 22 m (72.6 feet). From Thondi to Uchipuli, less inundation and sediments were observed. This may be due to the shallowness of the near shore.

From information gathered from the local communities, it was understood that the tsunami propagation was very slow and was from the southeast. Due to the reduction in velocity, the inundation may have been less and deposition was also meager.

The coastal stretch between Rajamadam and Devipattinam, about 80 km (48 miles), has only one or occasionally two beach ridges with an elevation of 1–2 m (3.3–6.6 feet). The low coastal elevations, small number of beach ridges, and low sand dunes along the western and northern sides of Palk Bay is attributable to small fluctuations in sea level. The coastal dune heights vary between 1 and 2 m (3.3 and 6.6 feet) only. However, along the Devipattinam and Mandapam coastal belt, three to four series of beach ridges are observed. The Mandapam coast of Palk Bay is also characterized by 2–3 m (6.6 –9.9 feet) high coralline terraces. The northeastern part of the Rameshwaram coast in Palk Bay is occupied by shallow lagoons. Sand dunes with heights varying from 3 to 6 m (9.9 to 19.8 feet) are well developed along the southeastern tail portion of the island.

The coastal regions between Rameshwaram and Vembar in the Gulf of Mannar were not affected much by the tsunami waves. Only swelling of the sea was seen by the local communities, and therefore the inundation and resultant sedimentation were very much less compared with that of other northern and central coastal regions of Tamil Nadu.

However, the coastal stretch between Vaippar and Thoothukudi was affected considerably by tsunami waves. In Taruvakulam, very thick sedimentation, up to 120 cm (48 inches), was recorded, though inundation was only 150 m (495 feet) inland. The coastal geomorphology was completely altered. Thick sedimentation in the northern part of Taruvakulam led to the seaward expansion of beach. The sediments were fresh, medium to fine, loosely packed, and layered. Here rich, heavy minerals were deposited as thin bands over the pre-tsunami sediments by tsunami waves. The segregation of heavy minerals into fine and coarse was observed. The coarse heavy minerals were deposited away from the coast, while the fine ones were found near the coast (5 to 20 m [16.5 to 66 feet] from the coast).

Vellapatty, near Thoothukudi, was also affected by sedimentation due to the tsunami waves. The inundation was up to 75 m (247.5 feet) inland. A thin layer of tsunami sediments (10–15 cm [4–6 inches]) was deposited over the pre-tsunami coarser beach sediments. The layering was prominent, with thin, dark-colored bands of sediments. The fresh sediments brought by the tsunami were identified based on their freshness, color, and textural differences from the older sediments. Oxidation of fresh sediments was observed.

South of Thoothukudi harbor, sedimentation was recorded up to 500 m (1,650 feet) inland. Tsunami waves moved inland by eroding a channel, 15 m (49.5 feet) wide near the coast and becoming narrower inland. Sedimentation took place in and around the channel. Fresh, fine, and loose layering of sediments was noticed inland. The thickness is about 50 cm (20 inches). Dark banding of sediments is prominent.

In Pulavali, the tsunami waves moved inland into dense scrubs. The inundation was up to 60 m (198 feet) inland. Erosion along the shoreline is prominent. Fine sediments (30 cm [12 inches] thick) layered with dark colors were observed over the eroded surface along the coast.

The southern sector of the Tamil Nadu coast includes Palayakayal, Punnakayal, Kayalpattinam, Virapandipattinam, and Tiruchendur. The Tamiraparani River joins the sea through two inlets, Palayakayal and Punnakayal. Erosion caused by tsunami waves was prominent in the backwater channels. Tsunami waves entered up to 2,100 m (6,930 feet) inland through the channels. A fresh fining-up sequence about 23 cm (9.2 inches) thick was observed in the estuarine region. The deposition of coarse sand thins toward the northwest in the areas running almost perpendicular to the estuaries. Widespread deposition of fine sediments with some coral and broken shell fragments was observed in these regions. Along the estuarine bank rip-up clasts could be recorded, with some shell debris.

In Kayalpattinam, the tsunami inundation was up to 1,100 m (3,630 feet) from the shore. A backwater channel about 15 m (49.5 feet) in width was filled with tsunami sediments. The thickness of the sediments' fining-up sequence was about 70 cm (28 inches), at a distance of 100 m (330 feet) from the shoreline. After the tsunami event, the near shore became shallow. Due to the filling of the channel, the fishing communities find it difficult to operate their powerboats in the near-shore area.

In Virapandipattinam, the tsunami waves eroded 20 to 25 m (8 to 10 inches) of the beach. Due to the erosion, the beach became steep. The fresh tsunami sediments were deposited over the prominent older coarse sediments with shell fragments. About 56 cm (22.4 inches) of sediments were deposited by the tsunami wave. Even after the tsunami, erosion of the coastline continued in the region. In Tiruchendur, the effect of tsunami waves was less. Tsunami waves eroded the coastline in some localities but not all. The steep height of the coast in Tiruchendur prevented the waves' inundation inland. Here the retreat of waves up to 20 m (66 feet) was observed by the local communities during the tsunami.

Tsunami Effect on Coral Islands

The shelf width off Pamban in the Gulf of Mannar is about 25 km (15 miles) (Hari Narain, Kaila, and Verma 1968) and the shelf break occurs at about 200 m (660 feet) depth. The shelf is very wide off the coast between Sippikulam and Tuticorin. The 20 m (66 feet) depth contour lies at a distance of 30 km (18 miles) between Rameshwaram Island and Valinokkam and about 40–45 km (25–28 miles) between Valinokkam and Tuticorin. The Rameshwaram and Tuticorin coast is characterized by the presence of twenty-one coral islands of varying sizes arranged in an en echelon manner within the 20 m depth contour. Between Tuticorin and Tiruchendur, the 20 m depth contour runs about 25–30 km (15–18 miles) from the coast, but from Tiruchendur to Kanyakumari, the 20 m depth contour is aligned very close to the coast. On the other hand, the 50 m (165 feet) depth contour east of Tiruchendur lies at a distance of about 30 km (18 miles). The shelf is very wide between Tiruchendur and Kanyakumari. Off Chinnamuttom and eastern Kanyaku-mari, the shelf width is nearly 80 km (48 miles), and the shelf break occurs at about 60 m (198 feet) depth.

The tsunami inundation between Kanyakumari and Arokkiapuram ranged between 150 and 210 m (495 and 693 feet), as the coast is moderately elevated and consists of a number of pocket beaches and low cliffs, as at Vattakotai and Idinthakarai. The Panchal, Periyathalai, Perumanel, and Kulasekharapattinam segments are low-lying coastal plains and so tsunami inundation reached up to 500 m (1,650 feet). The coast is raised coast consisting of coralline terraces. Similar to what happened on the Mannar coast, both diffracted tsunami waves from the southern Sri Lankan coast and waves traveling westward in the Indian Ocean affected the southwestern coast of India. Kizhmanakudi and Melma-nakudi, coastal settlements located on the southern and northern banks of the Palayar River, respectively, were inundated for ten hours, and seawater entered up to 1,500 m (4,950 feet) inland. The bridge connecting the two coastal villages was thrown nearly 50 m (165 feet) up the estuary. Even the coastal settlements behind the 4–6 m (13.2–19.8 feet) high cliffs and elevated beaches were not spared. As the tsunami wave approach was from the south and southwest, the coastal settlements located north of the rocky promontories or groins were affected only partially. But settlements south of the rocky promontories, such as Azhikkal, Pillaithoppu, Muttom, Kottilpadu, and Colachal, were severely affected.

Four coral islands situated off Thoothukudi were studied for post-tsunami sedimentological aspects. On Pandian Island, the tsunami deposited some debris and scrubs along the coast and inland. Sediments ranging from medium to coarse size were deposited as layers over the very coarse sand with coral debris. About 8 cm (32 inches) of thick, gray, medium sand brought by tsunami waves were deposited over the dirty, yellow, compact older sediments inland (about 12 m [39.6 feet] from the shoreline). The medium sand was transported and deposited even in the fly ash pond near the island. Koswari, Van, and Kariyashuli islands also experienced sedimentation. On Van Island, the deposition of medium-sized sediments over the coarser fractions was observed. About 30 cm (12 inches) of fresh, medium-sized sand was deposited with thin dark bands of sediments over the coarse to very coarse sand. On Koswari Island, fine clayey material was deposited along the shore. A thick layer of fine- to medium-sized heavy mineral deposits parallel to the shore was prominent on Kariyashuli Island. About 30 cm thick alternate medium and coarse sediments were deposited with shell and coral fragments on Kariyashuli Island.

Sediment Characteristics

Large tsunamis may significantly disturb the permanent sedimentation regimes of coastal areas, and landward-tapering units of sand extending far inland constitute the commonest signature of tsunamigenic flooding in intermediate to slightly reflective coastal environments. A tsunamigenic event will most probably be locally sourced, and the associated disturbance will likely leave signatures related to changes in the composition of sediment rather than texture and with physical and chemical properties translated to geochemical proxies of salinity or unusual plankton contribution to the total fossil content. Tsunami waves produced by any processes will vertically displace the sea surface. Tsunamis are capable of affecting deep shelf and even oceanic floors. Most open-ocean tsunami waves have the required wavelengths (up to 100 km [60 miles]) but not the amplitude (a few meters maximum) to significantly move sediment in deep water. Tsunami deposits can be recognized primarily as rapidly deposited, tabular, and extensive unusually coarse layers laid down (or at least reworked) by traction currents within fine-grained sections, but it is very difficult to differentiate them from storm and hurricane deposits. Very rapid deposition was indicated by plants found bent over and buried by the sand or removed by the tsunami, leaving an erosive base to the deposit: the lower part of the tsunami included rip-up clasts of the underlying muddy layer (depending upon the coastal sediments). Few internal structures were found, although in a few places some faint horizontal stratification could be observed.

The sedimentological investigation of tsunami deposits is a fairly new field of research (Dawson 1999). The impact of tsunami waves on coastlines is unlike that of storm waves, because tsunami waves have greater wavelengths and wave periods. If there is a sufficient sediment supply, tsunami waves are constructive as they move inland and transport a variety of grain sizes, ranging from silt to boulders. The retreating waves can remobilize and erode sediments (Keating, Whelan, and Brock 2004). Literature on tsunami deposits may be organized into three primary categories (Whelan and Kelletat 2003): large clasts (e.g., boulders), coarse and fine sediments (e.g., gravel, sand, silt), and other, fairly obscure deposits such as washover fans. The nature of tsunami deposits is largely determined by sediment supply. The most commonly investigated tsunami deposits are fine sediments that occur as sediment sheets.

Grain-size parameters are widely used as indicators of environment differentiation (Friedman 1961; Duane 1964) and depend on factors such as availability of source material, medium of transport, physiography and geomorphology of the area, winds, waves, climate, and long shore currents (King 1972; Swift 1976). Textural attributes like mean, standard deviation, skewness, and kurtosis of sediments are used to reconstruct the depositional environment (Amaral 1977). The physical process assumption was that these different statistical parameters reflect differences in the transporting and depositing mechanisms of fluid flow (Sahu 1964; Greenwood 1969).

Identification of tsunami deposits was based on several criteria, including differences in grain size and color. Sedimentary deposits from the tsunami were found in most places where significant inundation occurred. For tsunami deposits that were overlying a known preexisting surface that was texturally distinct, such as from soils, identification was fairly simple, whereas if the underlying material was beach sand that was similar both texturally and visually, identification was more difficult. In tsunami deposits, grain size generally fines upward and rip-up clasts may be present. The base of the deposits erodes the underlying structures, and a heavy mineral layer may be present at the base. Underlying sands were often trampled, while tsunami sands were relatively undisturbed. Many of the deposits had multiple layers. It was very difficult to differentiate the tsunami sediments from the normal beach sand, since the tsunami deposits did not show much difference from the beach sand. The mud content was also very low except in the low-lying zones, where the tsunami water column was trapped for a considerable time. In some transects the heavy mineral accumulation was considerable.

Field investigation to study the sedimentary signatures left by the December 26, 2004, Indian Ocean Tsunami was carried out on certain shores with normal profiles along the coast of Tamil Nadu between Injambakkam and Cuddalore.

Tsunami deposits were identified in three different coastal settings: (1) muddy; (2) fluvial; and (3) sandy beach along the coastal tract from south of Chennai. Tsunamigenic sediments (2–40 cm [0.8–16 inches] thick) were found deposited up to 620 m (2,046 feet) inland. Thickness of the deposits varied from site to site, generally thinning out within 15 m (49.5 feet) of the limit of inundation. The tsunami deposits were identified away from the coastal zone above the agricultural soil, where the demarcation is very distinct.

The typical thickness was 40 cm (16 inches) at 100 m (330 feet) from the shoreline and thinning landward. The beach face and berm showed no evidence of deposition from the tsunami. On the berm the exposed roots of some shrubs indicated the erosion of sediments up to a height of 30 to 40 cm (12 to 18 inches). The zone of erosion extended up to 50 m (165 feet) from the shore. The tsunami sand deposits often contained two or more similar layers. The thicknesses of the layers were not uniform.

The thickness of tsunamigenic sediments varied from place to place depending upon the coastal morphology. Near Cuddalore the thickness varied from 30 to 80 cm (12 to 32 inches) in the open foreshore beaches. In estuaries the thickness went up to 90 cm (36 inches), as in Devanampattinam, and 25–65 cm (10–26 inches) at Pitchavaram. In the foreshore beaches of small embayed/coast areas, the thickness was higher (45 cm [18 inches] at Sothikuppam and 55 cm [22 inches] at Mulukkuthurai) than on open beaches. In the central part of the Tamil Nadu coast, the thickness of tsunamigenic sediments varied from 1 to 60 cm (0.4 to 24 inches). Very fine clay layers deposited over the paddy fields as high saline soils could be observed near Nagapattinam and Point Calimere away from the coast. The sediment thickness was less along the coast between south of Point Calimere and Thoothukudi. In these regions the impact of the tsunami was less, since they were shadowed by Sri Lanka. The coasts along these regions had maximum water inundation of about 150–200 m (495–660 feet), with fine clay sediments occupying the shallow coast. Near Thoothukudi, in the Taruvakulam, Pulavali, and Harbour region, the inundation was greater, up to 500–700 m (1,650–2,310 feet), and the sediments were deposited by tsunami waves. Sedimentation and erosion were prominent along the projecting coasts in this region. The inundation of sediments was up to 500 m (1,650 feet) in the southern part, i.e., along Tiruchendur, Kanyakumari and Colachel.

The sediments were fine to medium or even coarser than the normal tidal sediments. The tsunami sediment characteristics differ from coast to coast depending upon the offshore and near-shore sediments. In Tamil Nadu the sediments were finer in the northern and central part, clayey between the central and southern, and coarser in the southern part.

From the examination of tsunamigenic sediments from several cores, it is seen that textural parameters vary with depth: the tsunami deposits are coarser than pre- and post-tsunami deposits. The coarser nature of the tsunamigenic sediments is due to the fact that the powerful tsunami waves, with heights varying from 1 to 5 m (3.3 to 16.5 feet) while striking the coast, winnowed the finer fractions either landward (in the case of low-lying coasts, estuaries, and tidal inlets) or seaward, if the coast was steep. Hence the tsunami deposits are in a sense lag deposits. Tsunamigenic sediments are usually larger in grain size than surrounding sediments, indicating higher-energy conditions.

The pre- and post-tsunami sediments show more or less uniform textural characteristics. In many cores, the pre- and post-tsunami sediments reveal the variations of regular spring and neap tidal cycles. But the tsunamigenic sediments, though coarser than pre- and post-tsunami, show only marginal variation in mean grain size with depth without any grading due to rapid sedimentation. One of the main reasons for the coarser nature of the tsunamigenic sediment may be that sediments would have been derived from the plunge point and near shore and added to the existing beach sediments.

Analyses of vertical core sediments reveal the difference between the tsunami and seasonal sediments. Statistical parameters of vertical core give the approximate thickness of the tsunamigenic sediments. The mean values range between 1 ø to 2 ø, indicating the medium-sand category, in part of north and central Tamil Nadu, and 2 ø to 3 ø (fine sand) in the south of central Tamil Nadu, and 0 ø to 1 ø (coarse sand) on the southern part of the Tamil Nadu coast. The mean size revealed the fluctuation in energy conditions. The mean size indicates that the fine sand was deposited in moderately low-energy conditions and the medium sand was deposited in moderate-energy conditions. The mean size hence revealed that different energy conditions led to the deposition of these kinds of sediments in different locations. The coarser fractions deposited by the tidal cycle might have been carried back by the high-energy tsunami waves in the northern and central part of the coast (Singarasubramanian, Mukesh, and Manoharan 2005; Singarasubramanian et al. 2006). But in the southern part, the diffracted tsunami waves eroded the rocky surfaces of the beach and deposited them along the coast.

Standard deviation (1 ø) measures the sorting of sediments and indicates the fluctuations in the kinetic energy or velocity conditions of the depositing agent (Sahu 1964). The sediments ranged from very well sorted to poorly sorted in nature. The sorting character of sediments indicates the type of wave and energy condition in the depositing medium. This kind of sorting nature of the sediments may be due to the intermixing and influx of the sediments from the sea as well as the river. The presence of fine sand of a well-sorted nature suggests effective wave action. Down core variations clearly demarcate the tsunamigenic and tidal sediments along the coast. This infers that, depending upon the coastal morphology and available offshore sediments, the deposits will vary from place to place along the Tamil Nadu coast.

Skewness measures the asymmetry of a frequency distribution. The symmetry of the samples varies from strongly fine skewed to strongly coarse skewed. The strongly fine-skewed and fine-skewed sediments generally imply the introduction of fine material or removal of coarser fraction (Friedman 1961) or the winnowing of sediments (Duane 1964). The fine-skewed nature of sediments indicates excessive riverine input. The positive skewness of sediments indicates the unidirectional transport (channel) or the deposition of sediments in a sheltered low-energy environment (Brambati 1969).

Friedman (1962) suggested that extreme high or low values of kurtosis imply that part of the sediment achieved its sorting elsewhere in a high-energy environment. The tsunami sediments range from leptokurtic to mesokurtic, depending upon the energy flow and sediment load of the wave. The variation in the kurtosis values is a reflection of the flow characteristics of the depositing medium (Seralathan and Padmalal 1994; Baruah, Kotoky, and Sarma 1997). Finer size and dominant leptokurtic sediments reflect maturity of the sand, and variation in the sorting values is likely due to the continuous addition of finer/coarser materials in varying proportions (Prabhakara Reo et al. 2001). The mesokurtic nature of sediments indicates that the original characters of sediments existed during the deposition without any mixing of populations or that a single supply of sediments was maintained (Mohan and Rajamanickam 2001).

The frequency curves of the sediments collected from different parts of the coast show some similarities. In some cases the frequency curves of tsunamigenic sediments show a bimodal nature with coarse tail. The bimodal nature of the sediments is an indication that the sediments have more than one source. Similarly, the frequency curves of the tsunamigenic sediments show distinct traction population. In tsunamigenic sediments fine populations are considerably less prevalent along the southern Tamil Nadu coast. On the other hand, the pre- and post-tsunami sediments show considerable fine population. This clearly shows that during the tsunami wave attack the fines were deflated and would have been transported either landward or seaward. In the northern and central coast of Tamil Nadu the coarser fractions are smaller. Hence, this reveals that the size characteristics of tsunamigenic sediments depend upon the available source materials.

A rise in the percentage of silt and clay (2.34–6.70%) after the tsunami was

Table 3.2. Pre- and post-tsunami sediment characteristic variation						
Location	Clay content (%)		Organic material (%)		Calcareous fragments (%)	
	Pre-tsunami	Post-tsunami	Pre-tsunami	Post-tsunami	Pre-tsunami	Post-tsunami
Poompuhar	0.6–4.3	1.17–3.74	0.2–0.29	1–1.18	0.59–3.44	0.58–6.9
Chinnankudi	0.59–1.18	1.15–1.29	0.29–0.3	0.38–0.5	1.38–1.78	0.7–4.28
Kuttiyandavar	0.3–0.8	0.5–4.3	0.2–0.22	0.1–0.2	2–2.5	1.5–2
Chandirapadi	0.3–0.9	0.2–0.9	0.1–0.2	0.1–0.4	0.7–1.5	0.8–0.9
Kottucherimedu	0.5–0.6	0.5–0.8	0.1–0.2	0.1–0.2	0.9–2.2	0.8–2
Vadakkuvanjiyur	0.2–1.2	0.4–1.4	0.1–0.2	0.1–0.2	0.7–2.4	1.3–2.5
Nagore Beach	0.59–2.34	0–2.66	0–1.08	0.1–0.61	0.68–1.48	0.5–0.79
Source: Rajamanickam 2006.						

observed in some coastal transects. Such enhancement is likely to be due to the admixture of fine sediments brought forward by the receding tsunami waves from the hinterland or from the prograding tsunami waves from offshore. A rise in the percentage of carbonate content from 3.12 to 6.90% in tsunami deposits, particularly along the Poompuhar coast, is attributed to fresh debris brought forward by the onward tsunami waves. In the case of organic matter, one could find no appreciable rise among the pre- and post-tsunami sediments (table 3.2).

The December 2004 tsunami altered not only the sediment texture along the coast, but also the heavy mineral concentrations. Depending upon the available sources along the coast/offshore, tsunami waves either enhanced the heavy mineral concentrations or totally eroded them. They deposited more etched, angular, or pitted heavy minerals with overgrowth texture along the coast compared to the normal seasonal deposits in certain localities like Poompuhar and Karaikal. The concentration of certain heavy minerals enriched in particular grain size compared to seasonal deposits may be due to the high-energy waves. The concentration of ilmenites along the coast clearly points out that these heavies are from offshore sediments. This enrichment of heavies in certain localities must have been from the offshore sediments brought by tsunami waves. The assemblage of heavy minerals was not significant to the study of tsunamigenic deposits except for interpretation based on the textural attribute rather than concentration along the east coast.

As quartz sand is one of the most common components of coastal sand, it is appropriate to discuss some of the surface characteristics of the quartz mineral from tsunami deposits. Quartz can demonstrate such surface morphology as conchoidal fractures, microfractures, crystalline nodes, quartz overgrowths, microblocks, abrasion textures, and weathering textures. Many of these features were induced by grinding during transportation. The grains that were transported the furthest have a more rounded shape. Some of the surface textures of quartz sand from the tsunami deposits of the study area show strong grooves of mechanical action. This indicates that this feature is formed as a result of a high-energy environment. The quartz grains carry either straight or slightly curved grooves caused probably by the collision of sharp-edged sand grains, indicating that these textures are of littoral origin. Surface features of mechanical processes are also seen in the sand grain of tsunami deposits. Some grains exhibit intense chemical dissolution. The grains have a series of subparallel indentations probably produced by a portion of one grain slipping across another. The quartz grains illustrate a clear, strong groove of mechanical action modified by chemical action. Grains with a blocky conchoidal breakage pattern are of littoral origin. Some rounded quartz grains exhibit mechanical "V" pits subsequently modified by chemical weathering.

Changes in Faunal Assemblages

The study of microfossils within tsunami deposits is relatively new (Dawson and Shi 2000). Hemphill-Haley (1995, 1996) demonstrated the value of diatom analysis in identifying tsunami deposits on the coasts of Washington, Oregon, and Vancouver Island. Intertidal and marine diatoms in far-inland tsunami deposits indicate that sand was transported landward from a marine source rather than downstream as a fluvial deposit. Diatom analysis can also be used to determine the landward extent of tsunami flooding beyond the range of stratigraphic markers (Hemphill-Haley 1995, 1996). Unusually well-preserved diatoms in tsunami deposits relative to the underlying and overlying strata indicate rapid burial. However, Hemphill-Haley warns that diatoms alone cannot differentiate tsunami deposits from storm or seiche deposits, and they should be used in combination with other evidence for earthquakes.

The presence of *Ammonia beccarii* really does not give any clues as to the provenance of the tsunami sediments along the coast. It is unambiguously considered a cosmopolitan species worldwide, with its living specimens having been recovered from hyposaline to hypersaline environments. Records from the Indian regions also point to its adaptability in a variety of habitats. *Ammonia dentata* is known to occur in the shelf areas, ranging from near-shore regions to relatively deeper waters in the Bay of Bengal. Sediments from the inner shelf, however, yielded specimens of the same species with long and slender spines at relatively greater water depths and with higher mud content in the substrate. This could be attributed to the adaptability of this species to a wide range of environmental conditions, i.e., the turbulent near shore to the relative calm of the inner-shelf region.

Asterorotalia trispinosa (Thalmann) specimens recovered from the tsunami sediments have only short and blunt spines, thus indicating that the sediments have been derived from the inner-shelf region. *Amphistegina radiata* is typically an inner-shelf species that flourishes on sandy substrates at depths ranging from 15 to 40 m (49.5 to 132 feet) (Rajeshwara Rao 1998). Fresh specimens of this species in the subsamples are indicative of derivation of sediments from water depths of at least 15 m. Bathymetry of the area shows that the 15 m (49.5 feet) depth contour runs at about 3–4 km (1.8–2.4 miles), suggesting that the sediments might have been derived from the inner shelf.

The presence of species such as the *elphidiids* and *Pararotalia nipponica* (Asano) indicate that the sediments were derived from the near-shore region, as these taxa are typically near-shore-dwelling ones. Sediments along the Ennore, Kalpakkam, Mamallapuram to Cuddalore, Nagapattinam, Karaikal, and Vedh-aranyam regions of the east coast of Tamil Nadu were comprised of 50% or more reworked foraminiferal specimens, indicating that the tsunami sediments could have been derived from a water depth of at least 55 m (181 feet).

According to Hussain (2006), the following species are distributed in the estuarine/creek (brackish water) tsunami sediments of Ennore to Cuddalore: *Bairdoppilata alcyonicola, Bairdoppilata* sp.cf. *cushmani, Basslerites liebaui, Callistocythere flavidofusca intricatoides, Caudites javana, Mutilus pentoeken-sis, Neocytheromorpha* sp., *Neomonoceratina iniqua, N. jaini, N. porocostata, Paradoxostoma bhatiai, Paranesidea fracticorallicola, Spinoceratina spinosa, Stigmatocythere indica, S.kingmai,* and *Tanella gracilis.*

He also indicates the presence of composite fauna of foraminifera of benthic nature. Among them, Milliolina occupies the dominant place followed by Rota-lina and others. Among the genera, *Ammonia, Quinqueloculina,* and *Elphidium* are dominant, followed by *Pararotalia, Nonion,* etc. The living species are rare and cosmopolitan in nature. The genera *Ammonia* and *Quinqueloculina* are distributed in all the stations. All the foraminifers recorded are benthic forms and preferably thrive in the inner-shelf environment, except *Globigerina,* which is planktonic and generally occurs in relatively deeper environments.

All the ostracodes recorded are benthic forms and occur in neritic and upper bathyl zones. Most of the forms are less ornamented, and few are moderately ornamented. Both foraminifera and ostracoda are less prevalent in living condition. Predated forms are almost absent in these tsunami samples. However, the samples collected were from beaches, creeks, and river-mouth upstreams. This supports the fact that the tsunami sediments have been deposited in these marginal marine water bodies. When compared to pre-tsunami samples, the offshore samples yield less organic matter, and in turn the living populations are found to be low in most of the post-tsunami deposits.

Three waves struck the coast of Tamil Nadu. In general, the tsunami sedimentation along the east coast indicates that it was deposited at different times and at different inundation distances. The deposits were thinning landward. In some localities along the Tamil Nadu coast, multiple grading of sediment deposition was prominent, indicating that the deposition took place by successive waves. In the central part of the east coast of Tamil Nadu, where the wave was not dominant, the deposition of sediments was less prevalent, and the tsunami waves deposited mostly on the shore itself and made the coast clayey. The thickness of tsunamigenic deposits along the coast varied, depending upon the morphological setting. Thick deposition was noticed in the northern and southern parts of the Tamil Nadu coastal area. The south-central part was shadowed by Sri Lanka; hence, only reduced-velocity diffracted waves hit the shore, and sedimentation was less. The tsunamigenic sediments can be classified based on their texture, faunal content, and, to a certain extent, their heavy mineral assemblages.

Note

The authors thank the Department of Science and Technology, New Delhi, for financial assistance in carrying out this study.

References

Achyuthan, H. 2002. Coastal response to changes in sea level since the last 4500 BP on the east coast of Tamilnadu, India. *Radiocarbon* 44 (1): 137–44.

Amaral, E. J. 1977. Depositional environment of the St. Peter sandstone deduced by textural analysis. *Journal of Sedimentary Petrology* 47:32–52.

Anbarasu, K., and G. V. Rajamanickam. 1997. Abandoned channels of rivers—An evidence for neotectonism. *Indian Journal of Geomorphology* 2:209–17.

Baruah, J., P. Kotoky, and J. N. Sarma. 1997. Textural and geochemical study on river sediments: A case study on the Jhanji River, Assam. *Journal of the Indian Association of Sedimentologists* 16:195–206.

Brambati, A. 1969. Stratigraphy and sedimentation of Siwaliks of north eastern India. *Proceedings of the international seminar on intermontane basins: Geology and resources,* 427–39. Chiang Mai, Thailand: International Seminar on Intermontane Basins.

Chockalingam, M., M. Suresh Gandhi, and G. V. Rajamanickam. 2000. A study on the evolution of coastal landforms between Mandapam and Devipattinam, east coast of India. *Indian Journal of Geomorphology* 5:81–90.

Dawson, A. G. 1999. Linking tsunami deposits, submarine slides and offshore earthquakes. *Quaternary International* 60:119–26.

Dawson, A. G., and S. Z. Shi. 2000. Tsunami deposits. *Pure Applied Geophysics* 157:875–97.

Duane, D. B. 1964. Significance of skewness in recent sediments, western Pamlico Sound, North Carolina. *Journal of Sedimentary Petrology* 34:864–74.

Friedman, G. M. 1961. Distinction between dune, beach, and river sands from their textural characteristics. *Journal of Sedimentary Petrology* 31:514–29.

————. 1962. On sorting, sorting coefficients and the log normality of the grain-size distributions of sandstones. *Journal of Geology* 70:737–53.

Greenwood, B. 1969. Sediment parameters and environment discrimination: An application of multivariate statistics. *Canadian Journal of Earth Sciences* 6:1347–58.

Hari Narain, K. L. Kaila, and R. K. Verma. 1968. Continental margins of India. *Canadian Journal of Earth Sciences* 5:613–27.

Hemphill-Haley, E. 1995. Diatom evidence for earthquake induced subsidence and tsunami 300 yr ago in southern coastal Washington. *Geological Society of America Bulletin* 107:367–78.

————. 1996. Diatoms as an arid aid in identifying late Holocene tsunami deposits. *Holocene* 6 (4): 439–48.

Hussain, S. M. 2006. *26th tsunami causes, effects, remedial measures pre and post tsunami disaster management: A geoscientific perspective,* ed. G. V. Rajamanickam, 83–115. New Delhi: New Academic.

Keating, B., F. Whelan, and J. B. Brock. 2004. Tsunami deposits at Queen's beach, Oahu, Hawaii—Initial results and wave modeling. *Science of Tsunami Hazards* 22 (1): 23–43.

King, C. A. M. 1972. *Beaches and coasts.* 2nd ed. New York: St. Martins.

Loveson, V. J., G. V. Rajamanickam, and N. Chandrasekar. 1990. Environmental impact on microdeltas and swamp along the coast of Palk Bay, Tamil Nadu: Several variation and its impacts on coastal environment. Tamil University, Thanjavur, Tamil Nadu, India.

Mohan, P. M., and G. V. Rajamanickam. 2001. Depositional environment inferred from the core samples of beach ridge, Mahabalipuram, east coast, Tamilnadu. *Journal of the Indian Association of Sedimentologists* 20 (1): 59–74.

Prabhakara Rao, A., V. Anilkumar, A. Yugandhar Rao, G. S. Ravi, and S. Krishnan. 2001. Grain size parameters in the interpretation of depositional environments of coastal sediments between Bendi Creek and Vamsadhara River, east coast, India. *Journal of the Indian Association of Sedimentologists* 20 (1): 106–16.

Rajamanickam, G. V. 2006. *26th tsunami causes, effects, remedial measures pre and post tsunami disaster management: A geoscientific perspective,* ed. G. V. Rajamanickam, 68–77. New Delhi: New Academic.

Rajamanickam, G. V., and V. J. Loveson. 1998. Geomorphology and evolution of the east coast from Kanyakumari to Mandapam, Tamilnadu. *Indian Journal of Geomorphology* 3 (2): 233–44.

Rajeschwara Rao, N. 1998. Recent foraminifera in the inner shelf of the Bay of Bengal, off Karikattukuppam. Ph.D. diss., University of Madras.

Ramanamurthy, M. V., S. Sundaramoorthy, Y. Pari, P. Rangarao, P. Mishra, M. Bhat, Usha Tune, R. Venkatesan, and B. R. Subramaniyan. 2005. Inundation of sea water in Andaman Nicobar Islands and parts of Tamil Nadu coast during 2004 Sumatra tsunami. *Current Science* 88:1736–43.

Rao, T. C. S., and B. Rao. 1985. Geophysical studies over the continental margins of east coast of India. *Marine Geology* 67:151–61.

Sahu, B. K. 1964. Depositional mechanisms from the size analysis of clastic sediments. *Journal of Sedimentary Petrology* 34:73–83.

Senthilnathan, D. 2006. *26th tsunami causes, effects, remedial measures pre and post tsunami disaster management: A geoscientific perspective,* ed. G. V. Rajamanickam, 10–44. New Delhi: New Academic.

Seralathan, P., and D. Padmalal. 1994. Textural studies of the surficial sediments of Muvattupuzha River and central Vembanad estuary, Kerala. *Journal of the Geological Society of India* 43:179–90.

Shanthi Devi, R., and G. V. Rajamanickam. 2000. Distribution of coastal landforms between the coast of Adirampattinam and Nagapattinam, Tamilnadu. *Indian Journal of Geomorphology* 5:137–60.

Singarasubramanian, S. R., M. V. Mukesh, and K. Manoharan. 2005. A preliminary report on coastal sediment characteristics after M 9 tsunami event along the central Tamil Nadu, east coast of India. In *Sumatra tsunami on 26th December, 2004,* ed. Byung Ho Choi and Fumihiko Imamura. Proceedings of Special Asia Tsunami Session at Asian and Pacific Coasts. Seoul: Hanriwon.

Singarasubramanian, S. R., M. V. Mukesh, K. Manoharan, S. Murugan, D. Bakkiaraj, A. John Peter, and P. Seralathan. 2006. Sediment characteristics of the M 9 tsunami event between Rameswaram and Thoothukudi, Gulf of Mannar, southeast coast of India. *International Journal of the Science of Tsunami Hazards* 25 (3): 160–73.

Swift, D. L. P. 1976. *Coastal sedimentation: Marine sediment transport and environment management.* New York: John Wiley and Sons.

Whelan, F., and D. Kelletat. 2003. Analysis of tsunami deposits at Trafalgar, Spain, using GIS and GPS technology. *Essener Geographische Arbeiten* 35:25.

4
–

Tsunami Inundations and Their Impact in the Kaveri River Delta, Tamil Nadu, India

S. Rani Senthamarai and J. Francis Lawrence

The Indian Ocean Tsunami inundated large areas along the southeast coast of India. This chapter discusses the mapping of tsunami inundations and the impact of seawater intrusions on the groundwater of the area. Inundation distance, run-up level, and post-tsunami water quality of groundwater were measured and assessed. The methodology for these measurements was developed by the Department of Science and Technology, government of India, to record and document the run-up, inundation, and infiltration along the tsunami-affected areas on the Tamil Nadu coast. The methodology is schematically described in figure 4.1 using the geospatial technologies of remote sensing, global positioning system (GPS), and geographic information system (GIS). The study is restricted to two areas as case studies: (1) the coastal stretch running westward from Kodiyakarai (Vedharanyam) and (2) the area southward from Karaikal of Puducherry (Pondicherry) state. These stretches are located in the delta districts of Thanjavur, Nagapattinam, and Tiruvalur of Tamil Nadu and the Karaikal region of the Union territory of Puducherry.

Tsunami Inundation

When tsunami waves approach the shore, their speed declines as they begin to "feel" the bottom, and their height drastically increases. As the waves strike shore, they may inundate low-lying coastal areas, resulting in mass destruction and loss of life. When the waves of a tsunami approach the land, their appearance and behavior depends on the topography of the seafloor, the shape of the shoreline, and the nature of the land topography. When a tsunami wave encoun-

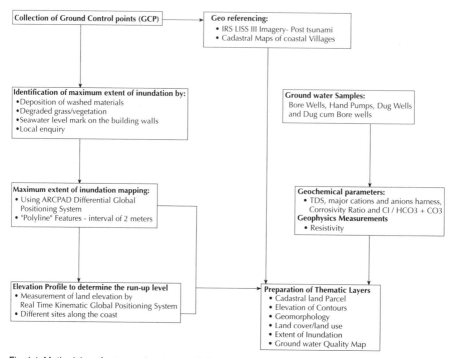

Fig. 4.1. Methodology for tsunami water inundation mapping and groundwater quality.

ters shallow waters surrounding the shoreline, its height can increase from 1 m (3.3 feet) or less to over 20 m (66 feet). Wave heights may increase when concentrated on headlands or when traveling into bays having wide entrances that become progressively very narrow. Geomorphic features of the near shore and coastal land of an area may alter the inundation pattern of tsunami waves. For instance, the presence of an offshore coral reef or shoal in the near shore and sand dunes or coastal forestry on the land may dissipate the energy of a tsunami, decreasing the impact on the shoreline (Subramaniam 2006).

During the tsunami, the maximum vertical height to which the water is observed with reference to sea level (spring tide or mean sea level) is referred to as run-up. The maximum horizontal distance that is reached by a tsunami is referred to as inundation. The run-up and horizontal inundation during a tsunami may be highly variable in a local area depending on the underwater topography, orientation to the oncoming wave, tide level, and the magnitude of the tsunami.

The most common method for determining tsunami wave height is measuring the run-up, the highest vertical point reached by the wave. Run-up heights are measured by looking at the distance and extent of salt-killed vegetation and the debris left once the wave has receded. Measurements of run-up level are useful in determining the extent of an area's vulnerability to tsunami waves and delineating areas vulnerable to coastal hazards to manage the coastal ecology and environment. Vulnerability maps are prepared, using spatial data for the area on land use, geomorphology, land elevation, bathymetry, extent of inundation, and socioeconomics. Mathematical models may be applied to define vulnerability from multiple and complex parameters, and remote sensing and GIS may be adopted to manipulate the data for vulnerability mapping.

Inundation and Run-ups along the Coasts of Tamil Nadu

The damage survey revealed large variations in the tsunami run-up and inundation. Table 4.1 indicates the severe damage caused by the tsunami of 2004 on the coast of India.

Tamil Nadu has a coastline of about 910 km, and there are thirteen coastal districts (fig. 4.2), of which Nagapattinam in the Kaveri delta was the worst affected, with a death toll of 5,525 persons. It was followed by Kanyakumari district (808 deaths), Cuddalore district (599 deaths), the state capital, Chennai city (206), and Kancheepuram district (124). Other districts recorded a total death toll of 135 persons. In the Union territory of Puducherry (Pondicherry), about 30,000 people were rendered homeless, and about 560 were killed. Karaikal, a minor port town in the Kaveri delta, was the most devastated area in the Union territory of Puducherry.

Table 4.1. Impact of the 2004 tsunami on the Indian coast					
	Andhra Pradesh	Kerala	Tamil Nadu	Puducherry	Total
Population affected	211,000	2,470,000	691,000	43,000	3,415,000
Area affected (ha)	790	Unknown	2,487	790	4,067
Length of coast affected (km)	985	250	1,000	25	2,260
Extent of penetration (km)	0.5–2	2	1–1.5	0.30–3	
Reported height of tsunami (m)	5	5	10	10	
Villages affected	301	187	362	26	876
Dwelling units	1,557	11,832	91,037	6,403	110,829
Cattle lost	195	Unknown	5,476	3,445	9,116
Source: Disaster Management and Research Foundation, India, 2005.					

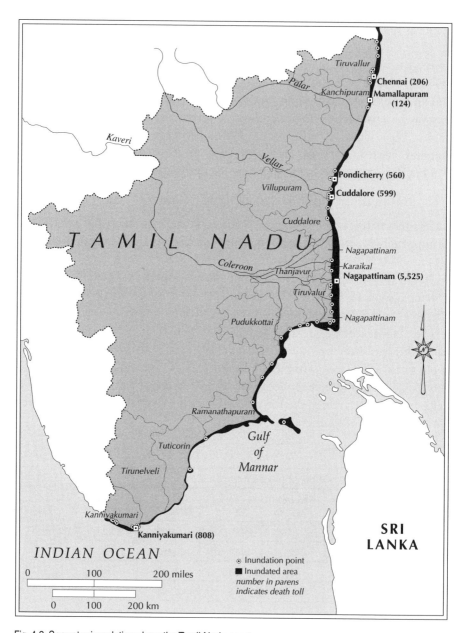

Fig. 4.2. Seawater inundation along the Tamil Nadu coast.

The impact of the tsunami was not significant in Tiruvalur district due to natural features like shoals and man-made protection measures like an array of boulders and a seawall. The inundation of tsunami waves ranged from 100 to 600 m (330 to 1,980 feet) and run-up varied from 0.5 to 2.5 m (1.65 to 8.25 feet). But to the north of Chennai city, near the mouth area of Pazhaverkkadu Lake (Pulicat Lake), the tsunami water inundated up to 450 m (1,485 feet) and washed out an area of about 1.23 km^2 (0.49 sq. miles). Here the surge went to a height of 2.5 m (8.25 feet). Marina beach, south of Chennai port, a few centimeters above mean sea level, reported maximum inundation. An area of about 2 km^2 (0.8 sq. miles) on the coast between the Adyar and Coovum rivers was inundated. The run-up level ranged from 1 to 5 m (3.3 to 16.5 feet).

While the run-up ranged from 2 to 6 m (6.6 to 19.8 feet) in Kancheepuram district, inundation varied between 106 to 778 m (349.8 to 2,567 feet). The highest run-up was recorded in Mamallapuram (Mahabalipuram), and the highest inundation was reported where the river Palar joins the sea. This district was declared a badly affected district, because a number of settlements and beach resorts were damaged.

In Villupuram district, the inundation of tsunami water ranged from 160

Photo 4.1. Damaged home in Kaveri delta. (Photo by S. Rani Senthamarai.)

to 380 m (528 to 1,254 feet). The impact of the tsunami was very much less in the northern coastal part of this district, as the shores here are marked by high relief with a series of sand dunes and casuarinas plantations. But the southern part was affected largely because of the gently sloping nature of the coast, the presence of many river mouths, creeks, and estuaries, and the absence of sand dunes.

The coastal area of Cuddalore district witnessed maximum inundation, ranging from 200 m to 2 km (660 feet to 1.2 miles), as the initial terrain slope (from the coast) is very gentle and a large expanse of landward areas is low-lying. The run-up level ranged from 2.5 to 3.5 m (8.25 to 11.55 feet). Successive propagations of tsunami waves were able to travel through backwaters for long distances landward, resulting in more damages. The areas adjoining the river mouths of Vellar and Kollidam were severely damaged, claiming more than 1,000 lives.

The southern part of Tamil Nadu, consisting of Pudukkottai, Ramanathapuram, Tuticorin, and Tirunelveli, suffered the least damage mainly because of its location behind Sri Lanka. But the district of Kanyakumari witnessed severe damage during the second attack of the tsunami. This may have been due to the lesser width of the continental shelf and the interference of receded first waves with the reflected waves from the Maldives Islands. It was also noticed that river mouth areas were much affected by the refraction of tsunami waves. The run-up elevation varied from less than 2 to 10 m (6.6 to 33 feet), and the inundation varied from 100 to 1,500 m (330 to 4,950 feet) from the shore.

The Study Area

The case study on mapping inundation and run-up was taken up in a stretch extending for a distance of about 80 km (48 miles) from Rajamadam in Than-javur district to Vedharanyam in Nagapattinam district, including the wetlands of Muthupet in Tiruvalur district. The study area covers 5 km (3 miles) on the seaward part of the delta developed by the river, Kaveri, and it is characterized by a multitude of channels, paleo-channels, canals, and streams along with inter-tidal salt marshes, forested wetlands, mangroves, and brackish to saline lagoons.

The study on groundwater quality was carried out on the northern coastal stretch of Nagapattinam district and Karaikal region. This area is composed of recent to subrecent alluvium and beach sands. Older Tertiary and Creta-ceous sediments are encountered only at deeper levels. The 5 km buffer from the shoreline was marked as the western boundary for this part of the study (fig. 4.3).

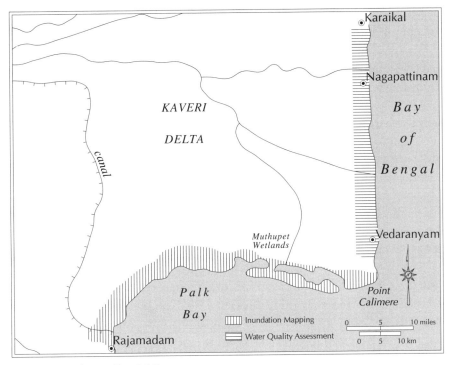

Fig. 4.3. The study area: Kaveri delta.

Extent of Inundation on the Southern Coastal Stretch of Kaveri Delta

The dual wave effects from the Sri Lankan coast, the gentle slope of the continental shelf and hinterland, coupled with the presence of the Uppanar River and Vedharanyam canal in the southern side, triggered the deadliest impact of tsunami waves along the Nagapattinam coast. A coastal stretch of 28 km (168 miles) along the Vedharanyam coast in Nagapattinam with an elevation ranging between 0 and 6 m (0 to 19.8 feet) above mean sea level (MSL) was considered for a detailed study.

In this coastal stretch, the maximum tsunami inundation recorded was 1.96 km (1.17 miles), and the minimum was 0.4 km (0.24 mile). The inundation extent is farther inland than the coastal regulation zone (CRZ) line, drawn at a distance of 500 m (1,650 feet) from the high tide line. The run-up level was estimated based on the watermarks on the walls of buildings. The watermarks were very clearly observed on the walls of the mosque, lighthouse, compound wall, and other buildings. The height was recorded using a measuring tape from ground level. The run-up levels varied from 0.5 to 2.4 m (1.65 to 7.92 feet).

Severe damage to infrastructure lifelines such as roads, railway lines, bridges, and telephone service was reported in this stretch. Extensive ground erosion and uprooting of trees were observed everywhere during the field study. Many big boats/vessels had been thrown violently toward the coast. Tsunami sediments were located along the coast, on the banks of the canal as well as at some interior parts of the coast. Changes were also noticed in the reserve forest. Few patches of forests were surrounded by new sandbars developed by inundations. A new channel was found formed near the coast, aided by tsunami-brought mud deposits. A lighthouse located in Kodiyakarai, the southeastern tip of Kaveri delta, and established by the Chola dynasty about 1,000 years ago was totally destroyed by the tsunami waves, its top portion pulled down to a distance of 200 m from the base (Usha Natesan 2006).

Thanjavur and Tiruvalur coasts, known for their estuarine environment, with large mudflats, lagoons, swamps, and mangroves, witnessed widespread devastation. These wetlands are associated with the coastal wetlands of Vedharanyam's swampy area. A curious thing about this near-shore zone is that continuous wave action causes clay and silt-sized particles to flocculate into loose, relatively large aggregates in seawater. Often this material is moved from the shore zone into lagoons by wave or tidal action. When the wave or tidal action ceases or becomes slack, the flocculated material is deposited in the shore zone. These deposited materials scrub the water column, depositing the more coarse sand and gravel-sized material on the beach and preparing the clay and silt-sized particles for deposition elsewhere.

The field observation to a distance of 52 km (31.2 miles) along the coast of Thanjavur and Tiruvalur districts revealed that tsunami inundation in this zone varied from 5 to 3 km (3 to 1.8 miles). The impact of the tsunami was the least in this zone mainly because of the presence of thick mangrove forests. The luxuriant growth of Muthupet (16.22 km² [6.48 sq. miles]) and Marvakkadu mangroves (13.58 km² [5.43 sq. miles]) acted as a restraining force, and thus the energy of the tsunami waves was dissipated when the water flooded through the mangroves. Though the two lagoons, Mullipallum (18.79 km² [7.51 sq. miles]) and Serttalikkadu (33.27 km² [13.3 sq. miles]), have connecting tidal channels from both Vellar and Vettar, the expansion of the lagoon during the tsunami was limited to a few meters only. This is due to the fact that the mangrove plants absorbed the energy of the tsunami, preventing the waves from moving further. Environmental experts are of the opinion that mangroves forming a natural buffer between land and sea could prove to be a dependable

Photo 4.2. Mapping the tsunami impact in Muthupet lagoon. (Photo by S. Rani Senthamarai.)

defense against the ravages of nature. The present study, too, indicates that the Thanjavur-Tiruvalur-Vedharanyam coastal wetlands served to break the speed of the tsunami waves. Further, thanks to the fact that the coastal population is very sparse in these areas due to the hostile terrain of swampy and low-lying mudflats, human casualty was limited.

Finally, village-wide inundation maps were prepared for each village, incorporating the information on maximum extent of inundation, elevation contours, and cadastral land parcels with survey numbers, high tide line, CRZ corridors, and infrastructure and cultural features.

Impact of the Tsunami on the Groundwater Regime along the Coastal Regions of Karaikal (Puducherry) and Nagapattinam

A stretch of about 5 km (3 miles) landward from the shoreline from the mouth of the river Kollidam in the north to Nagapatinam district in the south is the specific study area for looking into saltwater intrusions due to the tsunami. Post-tsunami water quality of both surface and groundwater sources was assessed by measuring the geochemical parameters, such as total dissolved solids (TDS), major cations and anions, hardness, corrosivity ratio, and $Cl/HCO_3 + CO_3$, from the samples. Salinity and freshwater horizons are described with microlevel resistivity survey, mainly to classify the types of water and the nature and extent of aquifers in the study area.

Cations and Anions

Calcium (Ca), magnesium (Mg), sodium (Na), and potassium (K) are the major cations present in groundwater. Sodium and potassium are highly mobile, and nearly all sodium compounds are readily soluble. The dissolution of clays, gravel, and feldspar enhances the concentration of alkalies. The presence of these alkalies in groundwater may lead to corrosion and acceleration of scale formation. The major anions present in groundwater are carbonate (CO_3), bicarbonate (HCO_3), chloride (Cl), sulphate (SO_4), and nitrate (NO_3). The carbonates and bicarbonates represent the major sum of alkalinity. Alkalinity of water is the measure of its capacity of neutralization. An excess of these anions in groundwater may lead to quality deterioration.

Analysis of Water Samples

The collected water samples were analyzed for major cations and anions, viz., pH, Ec/TDS, Ca, Mg, Na, K, CO_3, HCO_3, Cl, SO_4 using the APHA, AWWA, and WPCF (1984) standard procedure. The analytical output was processed through HYCH program, which classifies the water without adopting a cumbersome manual procedure. From the results, the existing ground/surface waters were classified, adopting standard water classification procedure and based on the parameters of TDS, total hardness, and corrosivity ratio (CR).

Classification of Groundwater

The classification of groundwater is made based on its quality and usage (Todd 1980). TDS, total hardness (TH), CR, and $Cl/HCO_3 + CO_3$ are the parameters mainly used in this classification. Water with high TDS has more ionic concentration, which causes physiological disorders to its users. TDS is one of the basic factors that determine the suitability of water for various uses, and this helps to classify groundwater as fresh, brackish, saline, or brine. Freshwater is that which has TDS less than 1,000 mg/l. The geochemical characteristics of groundwaters pre- and post-tsunami (2003–2004) were compared. In the Karaikal coastal area, Ec of the groundwater ranges from 840 to 20,500 mmho/

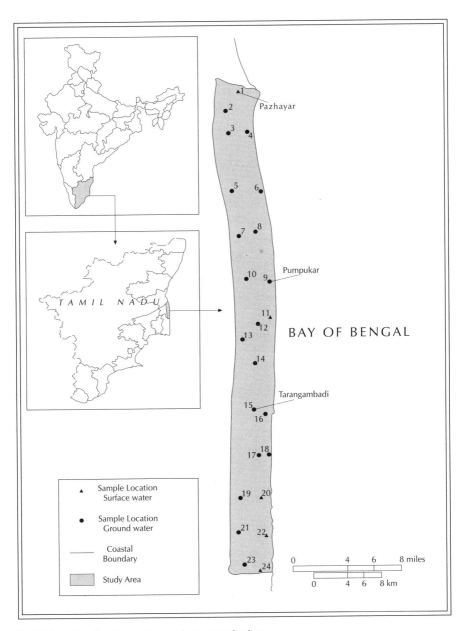

Fig. 4.4. Location of surface and groundwater sample sites.

Photo 4.3. Assessing water quality, Nagapattinam district. (Photo by J. Francis Lawrence.)

cm, and the highest Ec value was recorded at Achalapuram in Sirkali taluk. The TDS of groundwater ranges from 200 mg/1 (Pillai Perumal Nallur) to 24,550 mg/1 (Melvanjiyur), and that of the surface water ranges from 9,410 mg/1 (Mariamman Pettai) to 36,350 mg/1 (Pazhayar). As per Freeze and Cherry's (1979) classification, in the study area, water quality ranges from fresh to saline.

Total hardness results from the presence of divalent metallic cations, of which calcium and magnesium are most abundant in groundwater. Hardness may be temporary due to the presence of carbonates of calcium or magnesium, and calcium sulphate or chloride makes the water permanently hard water. Total hardness denotes the concentration of calcium and magnesium in water and is usually expressed as the equivalents of $CaCO_3$. Water is classified as soft or hard, based on this parameter. Total hardness of groundwater ranges from 69.7 mg/1 (Sannamangalam) to 2,861 mg/1 (Melvanjiyur). As per the classification followed by Sawyer and McCarty (1967), in the study area, groundwater is found from soft to very hard. Total hardness of surface water ranges from 1,740 mg/1 (Mariamman Pettai) to 4,262 mg/1 (Pazhayar).

Corrosion is basically an electrolytic process, which severely attacks and corrodes away the metal surfaces. The rate at which corrosion proceeds depends upon a variety of chemical equilibrium reactions as well as upon certain physical factors like the temperature, pressure, and velocity of flow. If the CR < 1, then the water is noncorrosive, and if the CR > 1, then the water is corrosive (Ryzner 1944). Mostly corrosive water existed, except in the southern region, during the first fieldwork.

The chlorinity of the groundwater ranges from 26 mg/1 (Pillai Perumal Nallur) to 13,799 mg/1 (Melvanjiyur), and the surface water ranges from 3,678 mg/1 (Mariamman Pettai) to 40,768 mg/1 (Pazhayar). As per Stuyfzand's (1989) classification, groundwater is oligohaline to brackish. From the above study, it could be seen that there is water-quality deterioration due to the tsunami. Freshwater exists in a few locations.

Geophysics Measurements

Resistivity measures help to get the details of subsurface geology, and electrical resistivity technique is widely used in groundwater studies and hydrogeological investigations. However, an integrated use of hydrochemical and geophysical methods is often recommended. A groundwater table may be located from resistivity soundings. The resistivity of rock is directly proportional to the compactness of the rock. The interpretation depends on knowledge of the subsurface and the experience of the interpreter. Units saturated with freshwater exhibit high resistivities, if primary porosity is low. In coastal areas, the delineation of interface between the freshwater and saline water may be established through the electrical resistivity method (Zohdy, Eaton, and Mobey 1974).

During the first and last fieldwork, vertical electrical soundings were conducted in the same locations; water samples were collected with an electrode spread of 100 m (330 feet). From the sounding data, isoapparent resistivity maps were prepared. The water-quality change with reference to time was reflected in isoapparent maps. The geophysical findings confirm the geochemical investigation.

Conclusion

The geomorphology of an area was a very important factor in influencing the extent of inundation in the study area. Geomorphic features such as sand dunes, mudflats, lagoons, and spits acted as shields, assimilating the energy of the tsunami waves and thereby protecting the areas just behind them. Examining land-use patterns vis-à-vis the extent of tsunami inundation indicates that barren lands with low elevation permitted free flow of the tsunami while mangrove vegetation in other areas restricted the inundation process. The Thanjavur-Tiruvalur coastal wetlands served as a speed-breaker and protected the villages situated behind them.

This integrated study also shows that the tsunami water stayed for some time and infiltrated into the aquifers. The aquifers became contaminated and recovered only slowly. The ionic concentration increased dramatically immediately after the tsunami, and then it was found to be decreasing gradually. This is clearly seen in the isoapparent resistivity maps prepared for the two scenarios. The rate of recovery depends on rainfall. In the study area, the subsurface lithology may not favor faster infiltration. Therefore, it may take a few more monsoon seasons to get back to normal. In 2005, the study area received good rains during monsoons, and the measurement of geochemical parameters undertaken in December 2005 indicated a significant recovery. Good monsoons in the coming years may quickly put the situation back to normal in the study area.

References

APHA, AWWA, and WPCF. 1984. *Standard methods for the examination of water and wastewater.* 16th ed. Washington, DC: APHA.

Freeze, R. A., and J. A. Cherry. 1979. *Groundwater.* Englewood Cliffs, NJ: Prentice-Hall.

Ryzner, J. W. 1944. A new index for determining amount of calcium carbonate scale formed by water. *Journal of American Water Association* 36:472–86.

Sawyer, C. N., and P. L. McCarty. 1967. *Chemistry for sanitary engineers.* 2nd ed. New York: McGraw-Hill.

Stuyfzand, P. J. 1989. A new hydrochemical classification of water types, with examples of application. *International Association of Hydro Sciences* 184:89–98.

Subramaniam, B. R. 2006. *Inundation of seawater due to the Indian Ocean Tsunami along the Indian coast.* New Delhi: New Academic.

Todd, D. K. 1980. *Groundwater hydrology.* New York: John Wiley and Sons.

Usha Natesan. 2006. Mapping of areas of inundation—Vedaranyum, Nagai District. In *Indian Ocean Tsunami: The impact of assessment and lessons for the future,* ed. B. R. Subramaniam et al. New Delhi: New Academic.

Zohdy, A. A. R., G. P. Eaton, and D. R. Mobey. 1974. *Applications of surface geophysics to groundwater investigation technology: Water resources investigation.* Washington, DC: U.S. Geological Survey.

5

Impact of the Tsunami on the Coastal Ecosystems of the Andaman Islands, India

Ramesh Ramchandran, Purvaja Ramachandran,
Bojarajan Senthilkumar, and Brigitte Urban

Any event that causes a significant displacement of the seafloor also causes the displacement of an equivalent volume of water. This is the basic mechanism governing the generation of tsunamis. Although most tsunamis are produced from earthquakes, they can also be caused by volcanic activity, submarine landslides, slumps, meteor impacts, and occasionally by human activity. The primary cause of wave generation is the release of energy and associated crustal deformation resulting from the earthquake. Thus, any earthquake that produces a tsunami is known as a tsunamigenic earthquake. The magnitude of the earthquake does not dictate whether or not a tsunami will be produced or its size; these issues are decided by the type of fault from which the earthquake is generated. The Mw 9.0 December 2004 earthquake is the largest to have occurred in the Andaman-Sumatra subduction zone. This chapter summarizes the findings of various scientific groups that investigated the immediate impacts of the December 26, 2004, tsunami along the coasts of the Andaman and Nicobar Islands, the Indian state in the Bay of Bengal, from field-based and remote-sensing studies. Wherever available, data prior to the December 2004 tsunami were compared to the changes after the event.

Study Area: Andaman Islands

The Andaman and Nicobar Islands are a group of about 572 islands and islets located off the eastern cost of India in a junction with the Bay of Bengal and the Indian Ocean on one side and the Andaman Sea on the other. The islands lie approximately 1,200 km (720 miles) from mainland India and are in close proximity to Myanmar, Thailand, Malaysia, and Indonesia. The Andaman and Nicobar Islands are located in the Bay of Bengal between 6°–14° N and 92°–94° E.

They are part of a submerged mountain range related to the Arakan Yoma range of Myanmar. Andaman islands where inhabitation is found are South Andaman, Middle Andaman, and North Andaman (fig. 5.1). Fringing reef and barrier reefs dominate the coasts of the Andaman Islands (960 km² [(384 sq. miles]), forming a natural barrier to dissipate the wave energy from the Bay of Bengal. Coral reefs form the dominant ecosystem, creating habitats for sea grasses and mangroves in the lagoons and creeks protected by the reef. In the Nicobar Islands there are twelve large and small islands, of which only the large islands are inhabited.

The Andaman–Sunda section of the subduction zone has produced many earthquakes in the past, some of which resulted in destructive tsunami surges. The largest among the historical earthquakes occurred in 1833 (Mw 8.7), 1860 (Mw 8.5), 1881 (Mw 7.9), and 1941 (Mw 7.7). They, though large, ruptured only a few hundreds of kilometers (200–300 km [120–80 miles]) of the plate boundary. The 2004 earthquake ruptured more than a 1,200 km (720 miles) length of the arc, stripping the regions that had ruptured in the past (Gupta 2003).

Methodology

We made detailed physical surveys in addition to monitoring the changes in surface water characteristics after the tsunami. Soil and sediment cores with lengths ranging from 0.4 to 0.7 m (1.32 to 2.31 feet) were sampled from agricultural, mangrove, and coral reef sites of South Andaman. Coring was achieved using a stainless steel 50 mm (2.2 inches) diameter gauge auger. Sediment samples were extruded in the field, wrapped in plastic foils, and transferred into dry ice for laboratory analysis. The cores from Sippighat (11°36'25.6" N; 92°41'30.5" E) and Wright Myo (11°47'26.1"N; 92°42'30.8" E) were sectioned at 2 cm (0.8 inch), while those from Redskin Island (11°34'17.3" N; 92°39'03.2" E) were sectioned at a 1 cm (0.4 inch) interval. As a preliminary investigation, geochemical and trace metal analyses were performed in the core sections using X-ray fluorescence spectroscopy (XRF). Bulk chemistry carried out on sediment cores using XRF gives the overall distribution of major and trace elements in a sediment profile. Assessments using X-ray fluorescence were critical in characterizing the changes in the

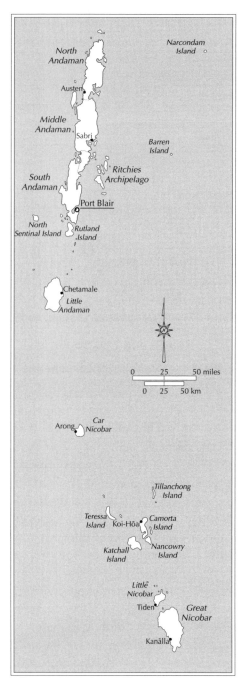

Fig. 5.1. Map of Andaman and Nicobar Islands.

Table 5.1. Sediment core sampling locations in South Andaman (August 2005)			
Location	Land use	Distance from the sea (m)	Length of core (cm)
Sippighat	Agricultural land adjacent to mangroves	200	38
Sippighat	Mangroves	100	40
Wright Myo	Mangroves	700	70
Redskin Island	Coral reefs	0	48

nature of major and trace metal distribution in sediment profiles. Soil samples were analyzed for pH, salinity, and organic carbon (Page, Miller, and Keeney 1982), as per standard methods.

Pollen samples were treated by standard palynological methods, including 10% NaOH to initially disperse the sediments, 10% HCl to remove carbonates, a combination of HF and ultrasonic treatment to remove siliceous material, and acetolysis to dissolve cellulose and to darken the palynomorphs for easy recognition (Faegri and Iversen 1989; Moore, Webb, and Collinson 1991).

Results and Discussion

Spatial Variation in Tidal Amplitude and Water Quality

Assessment of the surface water showed extensive but uneven damage to natural resources such as coral reefs, mangroves, sand dunes, and other coastal ecosystems that acted as the first line of defense from the tsunami. Anecdotal evidence and satellite photography before and after the tsunami event seem to corroborate claims that coral reefs, mangrove forests, and other coastal vegetation, as well as peat swamps, provided protection from the impacts of the tsunami. The damage to coral reefs was mostly due to sediment accumulation due to the turbulent churning of the sea. Coastlines became eroded, with much of the sediment deposited on healthy reefs, agricultural land, and creeks, or even creating new islands. Shallow soils were stripped from some low-lying atolls.

The National Institute of Ocean Technology (NIOT), Chennai, deployed acoustic tide gauges (ATG) at selected sites along the Indian coast and in Port Blair. The tide gauge at Port Blair in South Andaman recorded a gradual rise in water level by 0.9 m (2.97 feet) (compared to the normal tide that would have prevailed) from 06:50 to 07:01 on December 26, 2004, which might have been due to land subsidence caused by the earthquake. At 07:25, the tide gauge showed an abnormally high water level of 3.39 m (11.18 feet), an increase of water level by 1 m (3.3 feet) compared to the level observed at 07:01, possibly indicating the height of tsunami waves.

The tsunami caused significant geomorphologic changes along the coastline, such as eroding sand beaches and enlarging water channels. Post-tsunami studies have confirmed extensive changes in the coastal geomorphology of the Andaman Islands. We observed marked changes in the tidal amplitude at Wright Myo (South Andaman) based on our own observations of this site before and after the tsunami.

In North Andaman, changes in tidal amplitude were more significant than in South Andaman. We compared our post-tsunami data with the existing pre-tsunami records, and found large variations as a result of the massive changes in the geomorphology of the island. Some of the possible reasons could be:

- Changes in amplitude or phase of shelf internal tides, altering surface tides: this may occur because of warming at the surface or at depth, increasing or decreasing stratification. Reduced freshwater discharge may also decrease stratification;
- Changes in estuarine processes: decreased bed friction (due to reduced river flow and sediment transport), channelization (reducing friction), and shoreline alteration (which usually reduces area and volume and funnels the tidal wave) may increase tidal amplitudes. Clearly, tectonic changes have altered tides.

Wave Run-up Level in Andaman

The Integrated Coastal and Marine Area Management (ICMAM) of the Ministry of Earth Sciences, Government of India, carried out a major study (2005) on the run-up levels in the Andaman Islands, and its findings are summarized here. In general, the extent of the vertical run-up of seawater during tsunamis depends on earthquake parameters, geographical location, velocity of the tsunami waves and their frequency, near-shore bathymetry, beach profile, and land topography. Due to these parametric variations in the Andaman and Nicobar Islands, the run-up levels and landward penetration characteristics of seawater were location specific, varying within a location and even within an island. In the North and South Andaman group of islands the run-up levels varied from 1.5 to 4.5 m (4.9 to 14.8 feet), and the distance of penetration from the coast ranged from 100 to 250 m (330 to 825 feet). Little Andaman recorded a run-up of 5 m (16.5 feet), with the distance of penetration 1,200 m (3,960 feet). In the two Nicobar Islands, the run-up levels varied from 3 to 7 m (9.9 to 23.1 feet), with distance of penetration ranging from 50 to 1,000 m (165 to 3,300 feet), with higher run-up levels and longer penetration noted in Car Nicobar. Preliminary conclusions drawn by Bilham et al. (2005) on the slip pattern of December 26, 2004, indicate that due to the high rate of slip in the southern 650 km (404 miles) of the 1,300 km (808 miles) north-south rupture zone of the 2004 Andaman-Sumatra Earthquake, the principal tsunami was generated in the Sumatra area. The time lag between earthquake and land subsidence in Port Blair (South Andaman) on December 26, 2004, which was estimated to be 30–38 minutes, was interpreted as meaning that the rate of slip was slow in the Andaman region, resulting in no tsunami generation in this zone. Therefore, the wide variation in the run-up levels between Andaman and Nicobar Islands was primarily due to the remoteness of North, Middle, and South Andaman Islands relative to the Nicobar group and to the tsunami source zone, and also due to the nature of the land topography in the run-up level measurement locations. The wide variation between Andaman and Nicobar Islands might be attributed also to land subsidence caused by the earthquake.

Table 5.2. Maximum run-up levels in Andaman and Nicobar Islands

Location	Run-up level (m)	Inundation inland (m)
South Andaman (Port Blair)		
Aberdeen	2.9	130
Bamboo Flat	3.5	250
New Wandoor	3.7	215
Wandoor	3.9	215
Chidiyatapu	4.5	130
Sippighat Creek	2	2,000
North Andaman		
Diglipur	1.5	100
Rangat	1.5	200
Little Andaman		
Hut Bay	5	1,200
Car Nicobar		
Malacca	7	1,000
Great Nicobar		
Campbell Bay (central)	3	300
Campbell Bay (north)	6	50
Source: Integrated Coastal and Marine Area Management 2005.		

Table 5.3. Differences in physical and chemical parameters pre- and post-tsunami at Wright Myo, South Andaman						
Parameters	**January 2004**		**April 2005**		**Difference (high tide 2005–high tide 2004 & low tide 2005–low tide 2004)**	
	High tide	Low tide	High tide	Low tide	High tide	Low tide
Salinity: April 2005	30	20	34	17	4	– 3
DO (mg/l)	2.4	4.3	4.9	6.4	2.5	2.1
TSM	31.8	19.2	28.4	453	– 3.4	433.8
NH_4 (µM)	4.2	8.7	150	500	145.8	491.3
NO_3 (µM)	120	380	0.4	14	– 119.6	– 366
NO_2 (µM)	5	20	0.1	0.5	– 4.9	– 19.5
pCO_2 (ppm$_v$)			1,868	6,407	NA	
CH_4 conc. (nM)	282	704	198	585	– 84	– 119
N_2O (nM)	6	13.2	2.7	6.9	– 3.3	– 6.3

Similar types of diversified results were observed in tsunami-affected coastal areas in Indonesia and Sri Lanka. Run-up levels varying from 0.3 to 32 m (0.9 to 105 feet) were recorded in Indonesia and from 2.5 to 10 m (8.25 to 33 feet) in Sri Lanka (Yalciner et al. 2005).

The mixed layer depth, which was inferred from temperature profiles, varied from 50 to 100 m (0.9 to 105 feet) between 80°52' E and 87° E, and thereafter it decreased to 70 m (231 feet) toward Andaman in a transect from Chennai. A temperature maximum was observed at 84°24' E at ~80 m (264 feet). Along the west-east section, the near-surface salinity varied from 32.8 to 33.9, with low-salinity water (31.7) identified near the Andaman Islands. A conspicuous feature identified in the vertical profiles is the occurrence of high-salinity core (35.2) at 100 m between 83° E and 84° E; in the same region the temperature maximum (~29°C) was also encountered. In general, surface freshening occurred near the Andaman region.

Geochemical Investigations of Tsunamigenic Sediments

Geochemical indicators such as major element enrichment (Na, Cl, S, Br, etc.) are used to indicate a marine source for the deposit. When sediment is deposited by a tsunami and preserved, a geological record of that tsunami is created. Analysis of major and trace element variations unrelated to human activity in the sediment column indicates that except for near-surface perturbations (0–10 cm), major compositional breaks are limited to lithological transitions. Reinhart (1991) argues that in protected tidal channels, storms are unlikely to suspend the volume of sediment necessary to produce the deposits observed. When layers are present, their number and thickness are sometimes used to differentiate between a tsunami and a storm deposit (Williams and Hutchinson 2000). Our results suggest that several features in major element chemistry indicate a role for deposition of tsunamigenic sediments. Ca and Si gradients show surface enrichment and a much lower amount of K.

All the major elements, in particular Si, show an anomalous increase at depths between 6 and 8 cm in the mangrove cores and in the adjacent agricultural area, which indicates that sediment was deposited as a result of the tsunami. Another important element, P, shows a distinct depletion, while S shows enrichment at the same depth (6–8 cm [2.4–3.2 inches]) in both the mangrove and agricultural sites.

Similar enrichment of major elements was observed in the mangroves of Wright Myo and the coral reef site of Redskin Island. The mangroves of Wright Myo Creek were not affected by the December 26 tsunami, while the coral reef of Redskin Island experienced large-scale degradation (Ramesh et al. 2006).

The mangroves at Wright Myo protected the shoreline from the giant waves and the only destruction of the surrounding areas was the result of the subsequent aftershocks. On Redskin Island, however, corals were tossed and turned upside down, uprooting them. Even months after the tsunami, the surface water on Redskin Island overlying the coral reef area remained turbid, with a heavy suspended sediment load. Results from the sediment profile reveals this disturbance, showing a surface enrichment of all major elements, such as Fe and Mn, etc., in addition to others.

Chemical Index of Alteration (CIA)

The mobility of the elements calcium, sodium, potassium, and aluminum was investigated in detail using the mobility index (chemical index of alteration). CIA is the molar $Al_2O_3/(Al_2O_3 + CaO + Na_2O + K_2O)$, where CaO refers to Ca that is not contained in carbonate and phosphate (Nesbitt and Young 1982; McLennan 1993). CIA has proven useful in evaluating the degree of weathering experienced by igneous rocks. The weathering of silicates, in particular feldspar, is accompanied by leaching of the more soluble elements (e.g., Na, K, and Ca) and retention of elements that reside in clay minerals (e.g., Al). The CIA of unweathered igneous rocks is generally low (<50) and it increases with the degree of weathering (Nesbitt and Young 1982); shales have a CIA between

60 and 80 (Teng et al. 2004). When evaluating chemical changes associated with weathering, a number of workers normalize absolute concentrations of "mobile" elements, such as lithium, to that of a presumed immobile element (e.g., Al, Ti, Zr, and Nb), in order to evaluate the relative depletion or enrichment of the mobile element.

In general, the CIA shows an overall increase with depth for the study sites, although it is expected that the weathering is predominant in the surface sediments. However, it may be observed that the CIA is greatest at 6 to 8 cm depth in all the study sites, which further strengthens the assumption that the sediments above this layer are the newly deposited ones. Sediment samples below 12 cm depth in all the study sites are highly weathered (CIA = 81–87), with the exception of the Redskin coral reef site (64–78). This suggests that all the sediments (up to a depth of 48 cm) have been newly deposited by the tsunami.

Seawater in the tsunami brought salt to the soil surface, but most land was inundated by the tsunami for a relatively short period, and most of the salt will be, or has already been, washed away by abundant rainfall. The recent FAO survey has found that residual high content of salt is in the layers of clay and silt left behind by the tsunami waves. The clay/silt layer may be identified easily by cracks that spread across the surface of the soil. In many areas, trenching or digging down to a depth of just 20 cm (8 inches) reveals a fine gray layer.

The geochemical heterogeneities found in sediments collected from sections containing a conspicuous tsunamigenic layer match the observed lithological and textural variations. As observed by us in this study, tsunami sands have higher SiO_2, CaO, and Sr concentrations, which are indications of an increasing siliceous-sand component together with variable limestone and marine shell admixtures (Teng et al. 2004). The SiO_2, CaO, and Sr enrichment is related to minor fine sand and carbonate bioclast enrichment within a thin horizon that is correlative with the tsunamigenic sand deposit in adjacent areas. On top of

Table 5.4. Average chemical index of alteration (CIA) for the surface and bottom sediments in tsunami-affected sites of South Andaman

Location	CIA	
	Surface	Bottom
Sippighat: agricultural soil	81	78
Sippighat: mangrove sediment	81	83
Wright Myo: mangrove sediment	84	86
Redskin: coral reef	68	73

this level, sedimentation resumed to silt and clay and displays a significant positive anomaly for MgO and Cl, suggesting deposition on a seawater-dominated environment (Teng et al. 2004).

Trace Metal and Organic Carbon Distribution

The geochemical heterogeneities found in sediments collected from locations of South Andaman containing a conspicuous tsunamigenic layer match the observed variations. Indeed, the estuarine mud displays similar and relatively lower SiO_2/Al_2O_3 and CaO/Al_2O_3 ratios, being enriched in several minor and trace elements (Cu, Cr, Ni, Zn) that are easily incorporated by the clay fraction.

Sharp differences in pH have been observed, particularly at Sippighat (photos 5.1 and 5.2) between the agricultural and mangrove sites. The sediments cored in the Wright Myo mangrove and in the Redskin coral reef sites are quite monotonous with reference to pH. There is surface disturbance in organic matter content, with the exception of Wright Myo, where there is a consistent enrichment with depth. At Redskin Island, surface enrichment of organic carbon is obvious, possibly due to resuspension bringing the organically rich sediment to the surface.

Photo 5.1. Mangrove area in Sippighat, South Andaman, destroyed by inundation of seawater due to subduction of land. (Photo by Ramesh Ramchandran.)

Photo 5.2. Seawater intrusion in agricultural fields adjacent to mangrove area in Sippighat, South Andaman, due to subduction of land. (Photo by Ramesh Ramchandran.)

The results of our preliminary geochemical interpretation of sediment samples from South Andaman suggest that this region and the adjacent land area have been highly impacted by the December 26, 2004, Indian Ocean Tsunami. Salinity levels were considerably higher in the creeks and backwaters than average marine conditions.

Conclusions

Tidal studies carried out at Wright Myo, South Andman, indicated that there is a rise in local mean sea level of an order of 1 m (3.3 feet) due to subsidence. This was ascertained from field surveys and GPS readings during the field survey. Comparison of pre- and post-tsunami water quality from South and North Andaman clearly shows increases in ammonium concentration, probably due to constant inundation and submergence. Although variation in surface salinity and temperature was not significant in the middle Andaman, coral and associated fauna were severely damaged in the Wandoor and Jolly Bouy regions. This could be due to sedimentation and deposition of the debris over the coral reef beds by the large force exerted by the tsunami waves. In the near-shore

Photo 5.3. Mangrove area in Kalighat Creek, North Andaman, exposed during spring tides due to emergence of land. (Photo by Ramesh Ramchandran.)

waters of Viper Island and Minnie Bay, where the intensity of tsunami waves was high, a comparatively high concentration of nutrients, concomitant with high dissolved oxygen, promoted phytoplankton production. The areas with dense mangrove vegetation were least affected, and in such areas beach erosion was greatly reduced. Sediment chemistry indicated enhanced occurrence of major and trace elements both in the mangrove and coral reef areas and in the adjacent agricultural landscape. Our geochemical data suggest that there is deposition and reworking of sediments at least in the top 15 cm (6 inches) in the Sippighat (agricultural and mangrove areas) and >30 cm (12 inches) in the Redskin Island coral reef area. However, the geochemical record is very even in the Wright Myo mangrove creek, suggesting no strong sedimentological impact of the tsunami wave.

Note

The authors wish to thank the BMBF, Germany, and the Department of Science and Technology, Government of India, for the financial support to conduct this work. The authors are grateful to Mr. K. Ravichandran, IFS, Mr. R.C. Jayaraj, IFS, and other

Photo 5.4. Coral reefs ecosystem of the North Reef, North Andaman, exposed during spring tides due to emergence of land. (Photo by Ramesh Ramchandran.)

officials and staff of the Forest Department, Ministry of Environment and Forests, van Sadan, Haddo, Port Blair, for their immense support. Thanks are also due to the project staff of the investigating institutions (IOM, Anna University, and the University of Lüneburg, Suderburg, Germany) for their immense support in field and laboratory. The authors are grateful to ICMAM Project Directorate, Chennai, for providing the run-up level data for this study.

References

Bilham, R., E. R. Engdhal, N. Feldl, and S. P. Satyabala. 2005. Partial and complete rupture of the Indo-Andaman plate boundary, 1847–2004. *Seismological Research Letters*, March 4. http://cires.colorado.edu/~bilham/IndonesiAndaman2004_files/AndamanSRL4Mar.htm.

Faegri, K., and J. Iversen. 1989. *Textbook of pollen analysis*. 4th ed. Ed. K. Faegri, P. E. Kaland, and K. Krzywinski. Chichester, UK: John Wiley and Sons.

Gupta, H. K. 2003. Nature of earthquakes. In *Natural and human induced hazards, encyclopedia of life support systems* (EOLSS). Developed under the auspices of UNESCO. Oxford: EOLSS.

Integrated Coastal and Marine Area Management. 2005. *Preliminary assessment of impact of tsunami in selected coastal areas of India.* Report compiled by ICMAM.

McLennan, S. M. 1993. Weathering and global denudation. *Journal of Geology* 101 (2): 295–303.

Moore, P. D., J. A. Webb, and M. Collinson. 1991. *Pollen analysis.* London: Blackwell.

Nesbitt, H. W., and G. M. Young. 1982. Early Proterozoic climates and plate motions inferred from major element chemistry of lutites. *Nature* 299:715–17.

Page, A. L., R. H. Miller, and D. R. Keeney, eds. 1982. *Method of soil analysis, part 2: Chemical and microbiological properties.* 2nd ed. Madison, WI: American Society of Agronomy, and Soil Science Society of America.

Ramesh, R., R. Arun Kumar, A. B. Inamdar, P. M. Mohan, M. Prithviraj, and S. Ramachandran. 2006. *Tsunami characterization and mapping in Andaman and Nicobar Islands.* New Delhi: New Academic.

Reinhart, M. A. 1991. Sedimentological analysis of postulated tsunami-generated deposits from Cascadia great-subduction earthquakes along southern coastal Washington. Department of Geological Sciences, University of Washington.

Teng, F.-Z., W. F. McDonough, R. L. Rudnick, C. Dalpe, P. B. Tomascak, B. W. Chappell, and S. Gao. 2004. Lithium isotopic composition and concentration of the upper continental crust. *Geochimica et Cosmochimica Acta* 64 (20): 4167–78.

Williams, H., and I. Hutchinson. 2000. Stratigraphic and microfossil evidence for late Holocene tsunamis at Swantown Marsh, Whidbey Island, Washington. *Quaternary Research* 54:218–27.

Yalciner, A. C., D. Perincex, S. Ersoy, S. Presateya, R. Hidayat, and B. McAdoo. 2005. *Report on December 26, 2004, Indian Ocean Tsunami, field survey on Jan 21–31 at north of Sumatra by ITST of UNESCO IOC.* Jakarta: UNESCO.

6

Environmental Damage in the Maldives from the Indian Ocean Tsunami

Koji Fujima

The Sumatra Earthquake occurred at 05:58 on December 26, 2004 (local time in the Maldives). The Indian Ocean Tsunami generated by the Sumatra Earthquake propagated across the entire Indian Ocean and caused serious damage across a wide area.

The Maldives lies 2,000 km (1,200 miles) from the epicenter. The tide gages were present at Hanimaadhoo in the north, Hulhule in the center (Male International Airport, in the neighborhood of Male), and Gan in the south. The Sea Level Center, University of Hawaii (2004), presents the observation results on its homepage, showing that the tsunami arrived at the Maldives at 09:20, approximately three hours after the earthquake, and that several waves followed the leading crest wave. The first wave was the greatest, with a period of 30–45 minutes; the maximum water level anomalies were 1.7 m (5.61 feet) in Hanimaadhoo, 1.5 m (4.95 feet) in Hulhule, and 1 m (3.3 feet) in Gan. Thus, the tsunami amplitude was not high in comparison with that observed in Indonesia and Thailand.

However, the Maldives consists of many low-lying islands, whose maximum ground elevation is approximately 2 m (6.6 feet) above sea level. Thus, the Indian Ocean Tsunami had great effect on people living in the Maldives. The death toll reached eighty-two, with twenty-six people still missing (data from April 1, 2005). Most casualties had been living on nonresort islands in Meemu Atoll, Dhaalu Atoll, Thaa Atoll, and Laamu Atoll. On December 26, 2004, 30,000 people were evacuated out of a total population of 290,000. On January 10, 2005, almost all the residents of thirteen islands had evacuated to

127

other islands. There were approximately 4,000 damaged buildings, and more than 12,000 people lost their homes. The main industries of the Maldives are tourism and fishing; in 2004, tourism directly contributed 33% to the gross domestic product (GDP) and provided employment for 7,500 people; fishing contributed 9.3% to the GDP and provided 14,000 jobs. However, nineteen of the eighty-three resorts sustained damage, leading to four deaths. In addition, over 120 fishing vessels were seriously damaged. Assuming that the mean number of crew members was ten, approximately 1,200 fishermen lost their income-earning opportunity. In addition, the electricity supply failed on 26 islands, communications were temporarily disabled on 188 islands, and Male International Airport was out of operation for ten hours. The total asset loss was estimated at 62% of the Maldives' GDP (National Disaster Management Center 2004; Ministry of Planning and National Development 2005).

Our survey team visited the Maldives from January 31 to February 4, 2005, to investigate the damage and characteristics of the tsunami impact on the Maldives (Fujima et al. 2005, 2006). In this chapter, the environmental damage caused by the tsunami is introduced, and the protective nature of coral reefs is discussed.

Environmental Damage in the Maldives

The Maldives consists of many atolls, which consist of many coral islands gathered closely in a ring (fig. 6.1). The atolls lie in a north-south direction, with a combined length of 860 km (516 miles). The water depth is approximately 30–70 m (99–231 feet) inside the atolls and 300–1,000 m (990–3,300 feet) in the channels between atolls. However, the bottom slope is very steep outside the atolls; the water depth 10 km (6 miles) offshore is about 2,000–3,000 m (6,600–9,900 feet).

The most serious environmental effect of the tsunami for inhabitants was the polluting of groundwater. The tsunami caused many islands to be covered in seawater, as the maximum ground elevation of the Maldives is approximately 2 m (6.6 feet) above sea level. Thus, groundwater became unsuitable for drinking due to its salinity. In addition, the tsunami moved waste that affected the environment, e.g., municipal waste from dump sites, animal carcasses, human excreta, generator fuel, asbestos, batteries, and other hazardous materials. There is a possibility that this waste caused deterioration in the quality of groundwater. Moreover, tanks used for the storage of rainwater were washed away. Thus, the availability of drinking water became a serious problem on some islands (photo 6.1).

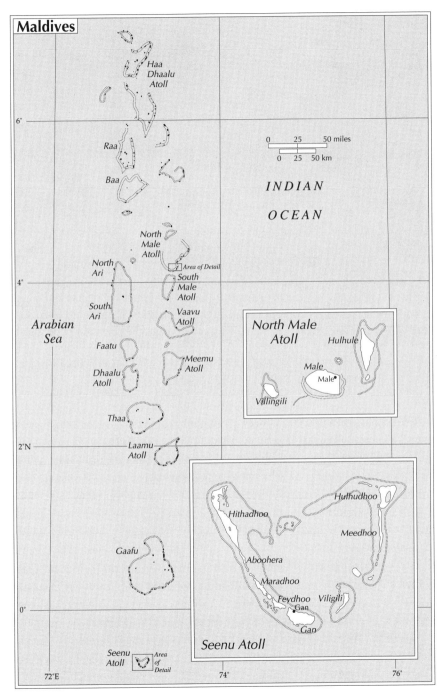

Fig. 6.1. Location of atolls in the Maldives.

Photo 6.1. Contaminated well and damaged water storage tank. (Photo taken by a resident of Muli and provided by the local governor of Muli, Meemu Atoll.)

The tsunami resulted in seawater intrusion into a freshwater lens, as previously described. This occurred on many islands and influenced agricultural land and backyard farming. The National Disaster Management Center (2004) of the Maldives estimated that 73% of agriculture was affected by the tsunami, and, although agriculture is not the main industry of the Maldives, the damage may have had a great influence on Maldivian society. It is possible that saltwater intrusion into wetlands had some influence on flora and fauna; however, this has not been substantiated.

The tsunami destroyed most buildings on several islands and generated substantial waste from materials such as household goods, building materials, and vegetation. These islands lacked the ability to dispose of this waste, and thus waste disposal also became a serious problem for the Maldives.

The direct impact of the tsunami on coral reefs was not serious in the Maldives; however, restricted damage was apparent on the reef. The following list charts the damage to the natural environment observed by resort-island staff and scuba-diving instructors in South Male Atoll:

- A heavy coral rock weighing several hundred kilograms was moved;
- Extensive quantities of silt and sand were moved to deeper zones, where the water depth was 15 m (49.5 feet) or more;
- Turbidity in the channel and atolls due to silt from coral increased and persisted for two weeks after the tsunami hit;
- The seawater around the islands took on a milky appearance;
- Small branching corals were damaged in some places along Vaadhoo Channel;
- Some branching and Poritidae corals rolled from shallow areas into deep areas;
- Some midsized branching corals were also damaged, though no large branching corals over 1 m (3.3 feet) in diameter were damaged;
- Many corals in reefs from the surface to 15 m (49.5 feet) depth were covered by sand, particularly inside the atoll;
- Many varieties of fish disappeared in and around the atoll immediately after the tsunami hit, though all soon returned.

The possibility of indirect damage caused by the tsunami through covering corals at greater depths with sand cannot be denied.

The massive transport of sand by the tsunami was verified by photographs. Male International Airport is shown in photo 6.2; it is clear that the tsunami stirred sand. Similarly, beach erosion such as that shown in photo 6.3 was widely observed in the Maldives.

Photo 6.2. Male International Airport inundated by the tsunami. (Photo by Todd Rempel.)

Photo 6.3. Beach erosion in Muli. The arrow shows the tsunami direction. (Photo by Koji Fujima.)

Coral Reef Dissipation of Tsunami Energy

In Seenu Atoll, the tsunami-trace height was relatively low (1–1.3 m [3.3–4.2 feet]) on the north side, where there was a wide reef (1.5 km [0.9 mile]), and relatively high (1.6–2 m [5.28–6.6 feet]) on the south side, where there was a narrow reef (80–500 m [264–1,650 feet]). This is easily understood by coastal engineers, because coral reefs act as a natural breakwater for high waves. It is thought that the tsunami energy was dissipated on the coral reef in Seenu Atoll. However, may we expect that developed reefs will keep us safe?

In Kulhudhuffushi, located on the east edge of Haa Dhaalu Atoll, the reef is not well developed (less than 100 m [330 feet]), and a high (approximately 2 m [6.6 feet]) dune is formed near the coastline. This dune prevented tsunami inundation from the easterly direction. However, the tsunami propagated into the atoll and Kulhudhuffushi was inundated from the west, where there was a developed reef of approximately 1 km (0.6 mile) width. In Laamu Atoll, the damage was small in Gan, which has a high dune (with an undeveloped reef, less than 100 m [330 feet] wide) and serious in Fonadhoo, which is without a dune (with a developed reef, 500–700 m [1,650–2,310 feet] wide). Heavy damage was thus observed in areas with the wider reef, although such areas were expected to be safer.

In Dhaalu Atoll, no significant difference in tsunami-trace height was observed at the eastern edge of the atoll (Gemendhoo) and the inside of the atoll (Ribudhoo), indicating that the tsunami did not lose much energy as it propagated over the Maldives islands. The tsunami front may have become bore shaped on the reef and wave energy may have been dissipated at the bore front; however, this was negligibly small in comparison with the total energy of the tsunami. Moreover, if the gradient of the water surface at the wave front became steep due to the reef, the wave force may have become large.

On many islands, important facilities are constructed on low-lying areas on the atoll (reef) side, because such areas are safe from ordinary high waves. However, the wavelength of a tsunami is much longer than that of an ordinary wave. Thus, dissipation of tsunami energy over the reef should not be counted on in a protection plan. If land is at its natural elevation, such as in the Maldives, the presence of a surrounding reef does not guarantee safety against a tsunami.

Summary

Several types of environmental damage caused by the Indian Ocean Tsunami were found in the Maldives. The most serious impact for local communities was likely the polluting of groundwater, resulting in a lack of drinking water and damage to local agriculture. Waste disposal was also an important problem. In addition, the tsunami transported massive amounts of sand, covering corals in shallow-water areas, although direct damage to coral reefs was not severe in the Maldives. This does not mean that a coral reef is an effective protection against a tsunami. A part of tsunami energy may be dissipated on a reef; however, it should not be relied upon in a protection plan.

References

Fujima, K., Y. Shigihara, T. Tomita, K. Honda, H. Nobuoka, M. Hanzawa, H. Fujii, H. Ohtani, S. Orishimo, M. Tatsumi, and S. Koshimura. 2006. Survey results of the Indian Ocean Tsunami in the Maldives. *Coastal Engineering Journal* 48 (2): 81–97.

Fujima, K., T. Tomita, K. Honda, Y. Shigihara, H. Nobuoka, M. Hanzawa, H. Fujii, H. Ohtani, S. Orishimo, M. Tatsumi, and S. Koshimura. 2005. *Preliminary report on the survey results of 26/12/2004 Indian Ocean Tsunami in the Maldives.* Yokusuka, Japan: National Defense Academy. http://www.nda.ac.jp/cc/users/fujima/maldives-pdf/index.html.

Ministry of Planning and National Development. 2005. *Statistical yearbook of Maldives (2004).* http://www.planning.gov.mv/publications/yearbook2005/yrb05/all.htm.

National Disaster Management Center. 2004. *Maldives—Tsunami impact and recovery.* http://www.tsunamimaldives.mv/.

Sea Level Center, University of Hawaii. 2004. *December 2004 Indian Ocean Tsunami plots and data.* http://ilikai.soest.hawaii.edu/.

7

Tsunami Disasters in Seenigama Village, Sri Lanka, and Taro Town, Japan

Kenji Yamazaki and Tomoko Yamazaki

This chapter describes the Indian Ocean Tsunami disaster that occurred at Seenigama, Sri Lanka, in December 2004, and analyzes the damage done to the village. Then, in order to offer useful suggestions for developing measures to mitigate the damage from tsunamis, the case of Taro Town in Iwate Prefecture, Japan, which has been attacked by tsunamis many times, is introduced and compared with the case of Seenigama. The structure of vulnerability is also discussed as one of the key issues in analyzing a disaster and providing effective measures for mitigation.

A research trip to Seenigama, Sri Lanka, was made in 2006. In this village on December 26, 2004, the tsunami killed residents, destroyed many houses, and overturned a train. During the field research, actual damages were observed, and survivors, villagers, and officials were interviewed. Maps of the damage of this village were made based on the field observation and interviews. Research trips to Taro Town were made between 2001 and 2007. Taro Town experienced devastating tsunamis in 1896 and 1933, and some remnants of the experiences can still be observed. There were only 36 survivors out of approximately 2,000 villagers in 1896, and just 1,828 villagers out of 5,120 survived in 1933. Since 1933, however, there has not been any loss of human life caused by tsunamis due to the effective damage mitigation measures the town adopted. Survivors from the great tsunami of 1933 and officials were interviewed. Historical documents and data from municipal government archives were also collected.

The Tsunami in Sri Lanka

The tsunami waves reached the coasts of Sri Lanka two hours after the earthquake in Sumatra, Indonesia. All the coastal areas of Sri Lanka were affected by the tsunami. The coasts of the southern and eastern provinces were severely damaged. Seenigama village in Galle province, located in the south, was seriously damaged.

During the visit to Seenigama, the following facts were found:

- A train was overturned by the tsunami waves. The train was crowded and very few people survived;
- Tsunami waves attacked this area many times. The waves reached the ceiling of the first floor of the buildings. Small huts and brick houses were destroyed completely, but some two-story buildings reinforced with concrete were not;
- Tsunami waves traveled up to 1.8 km inland. Many houses were flooded, and the walls were damaged by dirty water.

Table 7.1. Number of casualties and damaged houses in Sri Lanka

Province	District	Affected houses	Evacuated houses	Completely destroyed houses	Partially destroyed houses	Dead	Injured	Missing
Northern	Jaffina	14,767	6,676	6,084	1,114	2,640	1,647	540
Northern	Killinochi	2,754	407	246	NA	560	670	0
Northern	Mullaitivu	6,745	6,007	5,033	424	3,000	2,590	421
Eastern	Trincomate	30,547	30,545	4,830	3,835	1,078	1,328	45
Eastern	Batticatoa	64,151	15,113	12,232	5,376	2,975	2,375	340
Eastern	Ampara	59,275	37,899	14,143	10,547	10,436	6,711	161
Southern	Hambantota	14,344	2,808	2,278	1,752	4,500	434	1,334
Southern	Matara	21,140	2,235	2,223	6,075	1,342	6,652	600
Southern	Galle	24,583	24,165	7,032	7,660	4,330	313	564
Western	Kalutara	11,497	8,134	2,683	3,835	279	401	68
Western	Colombo	9,647	6,702	3,388	2,210	79	64	12
Western	Gampaha	6,827	308	278	414	6	3	5
Northwestern	Puttlam	222	23	23	72	4	1	3
Total		266,499	141,022	60,473	43,314	31,229	23,189	4,093

Source: Government of Sri Lanka, July 2005.

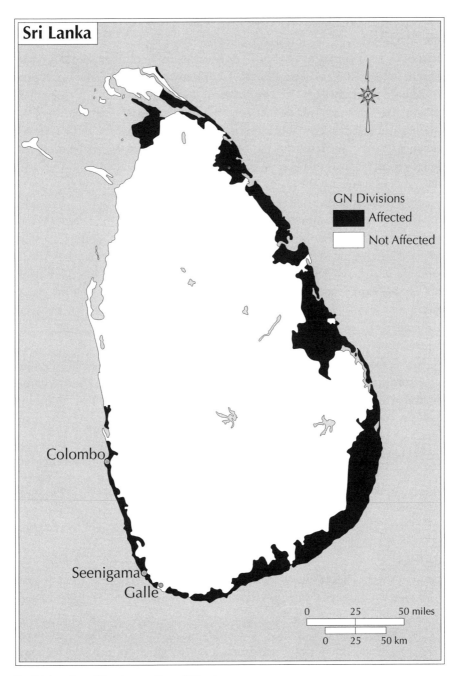

Fig. 7.1. Location of Seenigama village, Sri Lanka.

December 26, 2004, was Poya Day, a full-moon day. As Poya Day is a national holiday, all schools and some government offices are closed. Family members get together to celebrate. Therefore, on December 26, 2004, many people were on their way back to their hometowns by train. The train bound for Matara was crowded. The first tsunami that attacked this area reached the railway. The train stopped near Seenigama station. Many residents, especially women and children and old people living in the area, rushed to the train as a means to escape the danger of the tsunami. The railway officers let these residents get on the train. However, ten minutes later, the second massive wave, like a wall of water, hit the train. The train was overturned and sank under the tsunami wave, together with the people in it.

Another tragedy happened along the seashore. After the first tsunami wave reached the railway, the ebb occurred. Water rolled backward and the sea ground appeared. Thinking that this was a good opportunity to become a landowner, some people staked posts in the sea ground to claim their ownership of the land. In Sri Lanka, most landowners are of the upper caste. Since most fishermen have no land, for them it was a great chance to improve their situation. Moreover, boys and girls rushed to the sea to catch fish flopping on the ground. They had no information or knowledge about tsunamis.

There were 561 houses in the area of Seenigama: of these, 293 (52.2%) were completely destroyed, 26 (4.6%) were partially destroyed but remained inhabited, 130 (23.2%) were partially destroyed and replaced by temporary shelters, 104 (18.5%) were affected with flooding only, and 8 (1.4%) were not damaged because of soil dikes or embankments.

Damage caused by the tsunami varied depending on distance from the coast and height above sea level. In terms of distance from the sea, four categories can be recognized: (A) within 100 m (330 feet) of the coast; (B) 100–200 m (330–660 feet) from the coast; (C) 200–300 m (660–990 feet) from the coast; and (D) farther than 300 m (990 feet) from the coast. In terms of height above sea level, three categories can be recognized: (I) less than 5 m (16.5 feet) above sea level; (II) 5 to 7.5 m (16.5 to 24.75 feet) above sea level; and (III) more than 7.5 m (24.75 feet) above sea level. In total, there are 12 categories. Table 7.2 shows the extent of damage to houses depending on the category of their location.

Nearly 95.3% of the houses in the (A) category were completely destroyed. Less than 68.3% were destroyed in (B). Most of the houses built in a row along the coastline were destroyed. Even in category (D), where houses were built more than 300 m from the coast, 49.4% of the houses were completely destroyed. The division where more than half of the houses suffered from

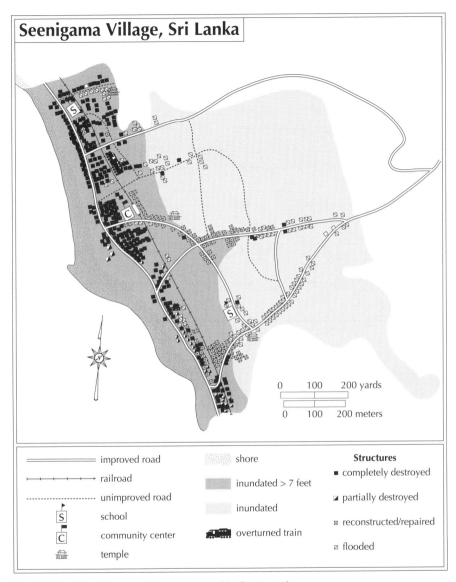

Fig. 7.2. Map of Seenigama and damages caused by the tsunami.

flooding only but were not destroyed was in (C) III. These houses were built more than 200 m (660 feet) from the coast and more than 7.5 m (24.75 feet) above sea level. Furthermore, (D) III shows 80%. This means that houses can still suffer serious damage if they are located less than 300 m (990 feet) from the coast without dikes.

Table 7.2. Location of houses and their damages

Location		I: Under 5 m Number	I: Under 5 m %	II: 5 m – 7.5 m Number	II: 5 m – 7.5 m %	III: Over 7.5 m Number	III: Over 7.5 m %	Total Number	Total %
A 100 m	a	61	95.3	0		0		61	95.3
	b	3	4.7	0		0		3	4.7
	c	0		0		0		0	
	d	0		0		0		0	
	e	0		0		0		0	
	subtotal	64		0		0		64	
B 100 m–200 m	a	156	75.7	23	43.4	0		179	68.3
	b	19	9.2	3	5.7	0		22	8.4
	c	29	14.1	24	45.3	3	100	56	21.4
	d	2	1	0		0		2	0.8
	e	0		3	5.7	0		3	1.1
	subtotal	206		53		3		262	
C 200 m–300 m	a	9	40.9	36	60	0		45	49.5
	b	1	4.5	0		0		1	1.1
	c	11	50	21	35	4	44.4	36	39.6
	d	1	4.5	3	5	5	55.6	9	9.9
	e	0		0		0		0	
	subtotal	22		60		9		91	
D Over 300 m	a	0		1	2.9	7	6.4	8	5.6
	b	0		0		0		0	
	c	0		29	85.3	9	8.2	38	26.4
	d	0		4	11.8	89	80.9	93	64.6
	e	0		0		5	4.5	5	3.5
	subtotal	0		34		110		144	
Total	a	226	77.4	60	40.8	7	5.7	293	52.2
	b	23	7.9	3	2	0		26	4.6
	c	40	13.7	74	50.3	16	13.1	130	23.2
	d	3	1	7	4.8	94	77	104	18.5
	e	0		3	2	5	4.1	8	1.4
	total	292		147		122		561	

Notes: a: completely destroyed houses; b: partially destroyed houses; c: inhabited partially destroyed houses/temporary refuge shelters; d: flooded houses; e: undamaged houses with piled soil.

In August of 2006, two and a half years after the tsunami disaster, thirteen households were living in partially destroyed houses or in temporary shelters. The government prohibits the building of houses (or temporary shelters) within 100 m of the coast. However, these houses are still located in (B) I, (B) II, (C) I, and (C) II and are still in the dangerous zones in terms of tsunami disaster.

It is prohibitively expensive to build high and strong dikes along the coastlines. Therefore, a more feasible and secure measure to prevent disaster damage is to impose controls on housing locations. Analysis of the damage caused by the tsunami of December 2004 indicates that locating houses more than 300 m from the coast is effective in protecting them from tsunamis of the same scale.

Interviews with the Survivors

An interview with a monk: The first wave that attacked the community was as high as the ceiling of the first floor of the house. This monk cried, "Hurry to a temple in a higher place, as soon as possible!" All residents followed this monk's instruction. As a result, there was no tsunami victim in this community (photo 7.1).

An interview with a widow: The lady in photo 7.2 lost all her family in the

Photo 7.1. The temple as community center. (Photo by Kenji Yamazaki.)

Photo 7.2. Waterline showing the height the tsunami waves reached in Seenigama. (Photo by Kenji Yamazaki.)

tsunami. She and her husband, a businessman, had lived in a house reinforced with concrete. Traces of the tsunami waves were observed on the wall of their house. The photo shows that the waves were higher than the widow's height. Massive waves attacked this house, killing her husband, sons, and mother, who were outside or on the first floor of the house. She was the sole survivor because she stayed upstairs at the time of the tsunami.

An interview with a principal: Photo 7.3 shows the inside of a high school principal's house, located 300 m from the coast. When he saw the first tsunami wave, he ordered his family to climb to the top of a small hill behind their home. As a result, all his family members survived the tsunami.

A Traditional-Style House

Photo 7.4 shows a traditional-style house. Such houses, made of wood, straw, and mud walls, are unable to withstand the force of a tsunami. Some houses were broken even by a 1-foot-deep tsunami wave. The force of a tsunami wave is stronger than an ordinary wave. A line marked on the wall by the tsunami wave tells us how high the wave reached. The point where there was finally no trace of waves was near the creek, 1.8 km (1.08 mile) from the seashore.

Photo 7.3. Principal's house in Seenigama. (Photo by Kenji Yamazaki.)

Photo 7.4. Traditional-style house. (Photo by Kenji Yamazaki.)

Photo 7.5. Reconstruction area with government controls in Seenigama. (Photo by Kenji Yamazaki.)

The Government's Control on Reconstruction of Houses

The Sri Lankan government has prohibited people from building houses within 100 m (330 feet) of the seashore. Tsunami survivors have had to move to inland areas to build houses. However, fishermen do not want to move from the seaside areas, and some small huts have been built by the seashore. One of the residents said that the hut was not for living in but for selling things. A temporary bank is also seen on the right side of photo 7.5.

How to Cope with a Tsunami

Interviews in Seenigama illustrate how the survivors coped successfully with the tsunami. Seventeen families were interviewed, and data on how they responded to the tsunami were collected from eighty-eight family members (table 7.2). Their responses were categorized into six types: (1) people who couldn't move from their home; (2) people who went to a temple and climbed a tree or a stupa there; (3) people who climbed a hill; (4) people who climbed a nearby tree or a telegraph post; (5) people who were caught in big waves; and (6) people who stayed out of the village.

Table 7.3. Villagers' responses to the tsunami		Couldn't move from home	Escaped to temple and climbed tree or stupa	Escaped to hill	Climbed tree or telegraph post	Caught in big waves	Stayed out of village	Total
Total		19	23	26	4	23	8	103
Death toll		17	0	0	0	15	1	33
	Male	4	0	0	0	5	0	9
	Female	7	0	0	0	2	1	10
	Children	1	0	0	0	2	0	3
	Over 60	5	0	0	0	6	0	11
Injured		1	1	0	0	4	0	6
Survivors		1	22	26	4	4	7	64
	Male	0	9	8	3	3	3	26
	Female	1	8	10	1	0	4	24
	Children	0	4	5	0	1	0	10
	Over 60	0	1	3	0	0	0	4
Source: Interview investigation by the author, August 20, 2006.								

Among the nineteen people in the first category, seventeen lost their lives. More than half in the fifth category were killed. Fifteen out of thirty-three victims were "vulnerable people": seniors over sixty, children under ten, and one lady in her forties who was ill in bed. Those who escaped to a temple located on higher ground or a hill had to run for more than 500 m. Of the forty-five people who did this, only four were over sixty. At the temple, people climbed a tree or a stupa, helping each other. Four physically strong people were able to climb a tree or a telegraph post.

Reconstruction of Houses

The statistical data in terms of damage to houses in Hikkaduwa, the district in which Seenigama is located, are as follows: 2,333 houses were destroyed and 4,798 were partially destroyed. Within 100 m (330 feet) of the seashore, the destroyed houses numbered 1,076; partially destroyed houses, 2,454. The total number of houses in Hikkaduwa was 27,548.

When inhabitants started to reconstruct houses, the government prohibited them from building houses within 100 m (330 feet) of the seashore. The houses that remained in this zone had to be moved. Instead, the government built new houses in the suburbs with foreign aid. As of August 15, 2006, 971 new houses had been built. According to the seventeen families interviewed whose houses were affected by the tsunami and who lost their family members and furniture, they couldn't start reconstructing their houses right after the tsunami, but were able to later, with the help of foreign aid. There are five types of houses for tsunami victims: (1) repaired houses; (2) reconstructed houses in the same place; (3) new houses for survivors built in the community; (4) new houses in a new village for survivors built in the suburbs by the government; and (5) temporary houses.

Repaired houses and reconstructed houses (types 1 and 2). People who live more than 100 m from the seashore received financial support from the government: 250,000 rupees was given to people whose houses were destroyed, and 10,000 rupees to those whose houses were partially destroyed. However, it costs more than 250,000 rupees to build a house. Long-term housing loans were provided to those whose salary was stable to reconstruct their houses. Some people rebuilt their houses with the help of foreign donor organizations. In such cases, the houses are similar to those built for tsunami victim refugees. Among the seventeen households investigated in this research, two had their houses repaired, and four rebuilt.

Houses for refugees built in the community (type 3). This type of house was built in Seenigama. One of the residents organized a group called the Goodness Foundation. It raised funds from foreign countries and companies to build fifty houses for refugees. Regardless of the 100 m (330 feet) regulation, it gave priority to socioeconomically vulnerable people such as widows and those who had lost their houses.

Houses in a new village for survivors built in the suburbs by the government (type 4). The government built houses for survivors in the suburbs, several kilometers away from the seashore. This project had some problems: First, it has not been able to provide all survivors with houses yet. Although 3,530 houses within 100 m of the seashore were completely or partially destroyed, the government has provided only 971. Second, inexpensive public transportation is necessary for people living in the suburbs to reach the seashore to work or to study. In fact, some students dropped out of school because bus fares were too costly for them. Third, new kitchens require kerosene for fuel, but survivors cannot afford it. Some of them have built a shed with a cooking stove that uses firewood for fuel. Fourth, many building materials contain asbestos, which will cause other problems in the future.

Temporary houses (type 5). Some survivors built temporary houses within

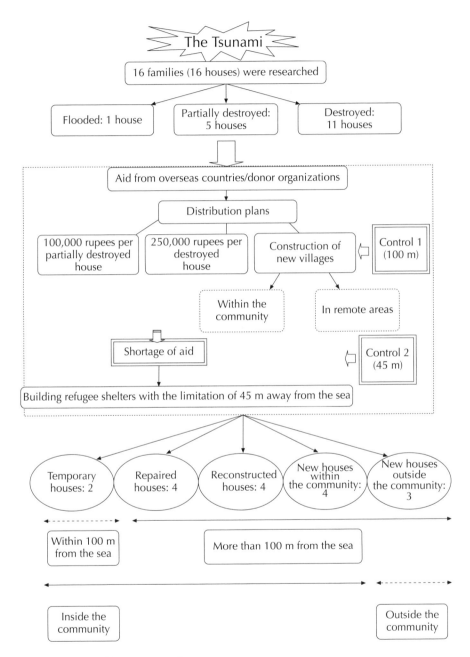

Fig. 7.3. Five types of house construction.

100 m (330 feet) of the coastline, expecting more financial support and alleviation of restrictions on housing zones. In fact, these restrictions are becoming increasingly lax; recently the government has even allowed houses to be built as close as 45 m (148.5 feet) from the coastline. People remain in temporary houses near the coastline, finding it quite difficult to move to a new village in the suburbs built by the government because of unmanageable problems of commuting to work. They are hoping their permanent houses will be reconstructed where they used to live, as building restrictions continue to ease.

Taro Town and Its Tsunami History

Taro Town is located along the Rias coastline of Sanriku, Japan. Sanriku is the ancient name of Iwate Prefecture. Taro Town has a U-carved bay, an ideal fishermen's port. This town has suffered serious damages caused by tsunamis throughout its history. The oldest tsunami recorded occurred in the year 869 (Taro Town 2005).

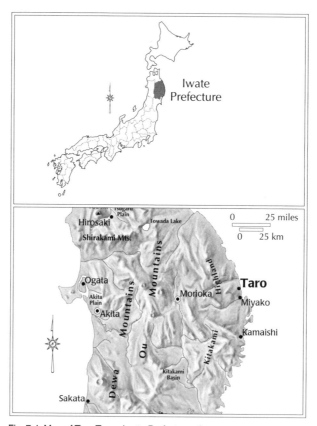

Fig. 7.4. Map of Taro Town, Iwate Prefecture, Japan.

Table 7.4. Tsunami chronology at Taro

Year	Earthquake name	Magnitude	Dead	Notes
869		8.3	1,300 ?	
1611		8.1	3,000 ?	Annihilation
1677		7.1		Destroyed Taro port
1696	Genroku 9			Came from Ishinomak
1751				Came from Chile
1896	Meiji Sanriku Great	7.5	1,859	Destroyed 285 houses
1933	Showa Sanriku Great	8.5	911	Destroyed 506 houses
1952	Tokachi Offshore	8.2	0	5 m high run-ups
1960	Chile	9.5	0	20 ships were lost
1968	Tokachi Offshore	7.9	0	1 ship was lost
2003	Miyagi-ken Offshore	7.1	0	

Table 7.5. The Sanriku Great Tsunamis

Name	Meiji	Showa
Date	June 15, 1896	March 3, 1933
Magnitude	7.5	8.5
Height of run-up (m)	15	10
Destroyed houses	336	506
Dead or missing	1,859	911
Annihilated families	130	66
Survivors	36	1,820
Lost ships	540	990

However, Taro Town is famous for its efforts to mitigate the impacts of tsunami disasters. Taro has created a structural disaster prevention system and has cultivated a tsunami prevention subculture. The researchers compared the damages of two tsunamis, one in 1896 and the other in 1933. In the case of the 1896 tsunami, there were only thirty-six survivors. The chronological table (7.4) shows that Taro has been attacked by tsunamis many times. The damage caused by the one in 1933 was devastating. However, since 1933, even at the time of Chili Tsunami and Tokachioki Tsunami, there has been no loss of human life caused by a tsunami. This is because Taro has found ways to mitigate tsunami disasters.

Photo 7.6. Marks of the run-ups of the great tsunamis in Taro Town. (Photo by Todd Stradford.)

The Size of the Tsunamis

The Taro municipal government marked the height of the massive tsunami waves on the cliff along the seaside road. Every citizen can see the tsunami wave traces. The height of the 1896 tsunami was 15 m (49 feet) and that of the 1933 tsunami 10 m (33 feet) above sea level (photo 7.6).

Photo 7.7 shows Taro Town before March 3, 1933. The houses were arranged closely along the narrow main street. There was little evacuation space in the town. Photo 7.8 was taken after the tsunami. It illustrates clearly that the tsunami washed away the whole village: Taro Town was completely destroyed. The U-curved bay, seen in the photo, accelerated the power of the tsunami.

What Made People Successful in Surviving?

The history book (Taro Town 2005) about tsunami disasters published by the Taro municipal government contains information on destruction by tsunamis. Survivors have repeatedly talked about the Meiji Great Tsunami and what the experience taught them about escaping a tsunami.

Photo 7.7. Taro Town before the March 3, 1933, tsunami. (Photo by Taro Municipal Government.)

Photo 7.8. Taro Town after the 1933 tsunami. (Photo by Taro Municipal Government.)

Table 7.6. Relation between number of deaths in the family caused by the Meiji Sanriku Great Tsunami of 1896 and people's willingness to talk about the tsunami

		Talking about the Meiji Sanriku Great Tsunami	
Dead in a family	Number of family members	Often talked	Rarely talked
0	10	5	4
1	4	1	3
2–3	1	0	1
4–6	2	0	2
More than 7	1	0	1
Only 1 survivor	2	0	2
Total	20	6	13

It was the early morning of March 3, 1933. While almost everyone in Taro was asleep, a sudden, powerful earthquake occurred. People woke up, worried about a tsunami. What did they do at that time? People's responses can be categorized into two groups. One group, remembering the lessons of the tsunami of 1896, instituted escape plans, rushing to the hill or preparing for evacuation. The other group, lacking active or useful information about tsunamis, wasted time, only watching outside or checking the well. As it was a cold day, many people went back to bed.

Suddenly someone shouted, "Tsunami!" People rushed to the hill, but it was dark and the roads were too slippery and too narrow for many people to go at one time. Before they could reach the hill, the massive wave swallowed them. People living in the Sanriku area are familiar with the phrase *Ten-den-ko*. This means that you should disperse and escape, without caring about others, and that everyone should help themselves.

After the Showa Great Tsunami in 1933, the prefectural government proposed to the residents of Taro that they should emigrate to Manchuria. The residents rejected this proposal, and they started to build dikes to protect their town from tsunamis. At first, the prefectural government and the central government did not financially support this project. However, the town received financial aid from foreign donor organizations to build the dikes. The following year, the prefectural government contributed to supporting the project. Even after World War II, the residents continued to construct the dikes. Finally, in 1978, the construction was completed. The total length of the dikes is 2,400 m (7,874 feet), and they are called Taro Great Walls (Taro Town Board of Education 2005).

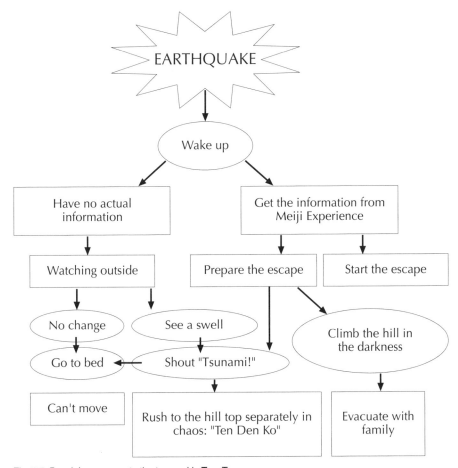

Fig. 7.5. People's response to the tsunami in Taro Town.

Photo 7.9. Dikes of Taro Town.
(Photo by Todd Stradford.)

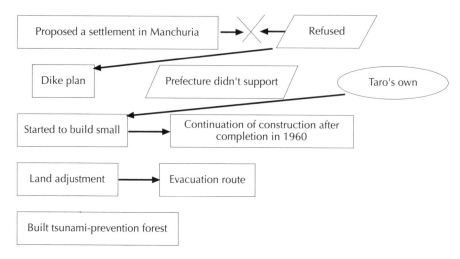

Fig. 7.6. Taro reconstruction plan.

How to Reduce the Damages of a Tsunami Disaster

It is very important to connect the structural adjustment and the nonstructural adjustment in order to reduce the damages of a tsunami disaster. One of the nonstructural adjustments is to pass down tsunami history. For instance, Mrs. Tabata, a survivor of the 1933 tsunami, created a picture story and has been a volunteer who plays the show at many schools for more than thirty years (Yamazaki 2008). (Picture stories are a popular form of entertainment for children in Japan. Pictures are drawn on large cards and a storyteller tells a story, showing picture cards one by one in a dramatic fashion, acting the scene.) At first, she played the show for her grandchildren, who had just moved to Sanriku, because she thought they should have vivid information about tsunamis to prepare them for another if need be. Mrs. Tabata believes that her picture story show can serve as a warning and as a guide to dealing with a tsunami when it strikes. In the picture story, children learn how to escape from a tsunami.

After the 1933 tsunami, the survivors built a cenotaph for its victims. Every year on March 3, the elementary schoolchildren sang two songs in front of the cenotaph: one to mourn the victims and the other cheering for the survivors who reconstructed the town. But this ceremony was stopped at the time of the Pacific War.

It has been said that Sri Lanka has no history concerning tsunamis. But the author saw a picture of a tsunami painted on the wall of the Kelaniya Temple. This temple, one of the most famous in Sri Lanka, is located 7.2 km (4.5 miles)

Photo 7.10. Mrs. Tabata presenting her picture story of her tsunami experience. (Photo by Todd Stradford.)

Photo 7.11. Monument commemorating the victims of the 1933 tsunami. (Photo by Kenji Yamazaki.)

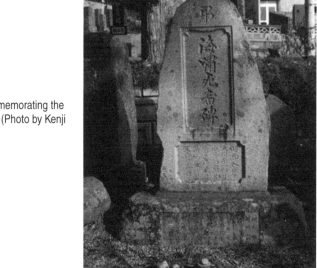

east of Colombo. The wall painting of this temple tells the story of how Buddhism was introduced into Sri Lanka when a group of Buddhists advocated the religion to the king. A group of Buddhists were staying at the king's royal palace, in what is currently Colombo. One monk wrote a love letter to the queen but lost it. Unfortunately, the king found the letter and, thinking that the writer must be the leader of the monks, ordered his men to kill the leader

Photo 7.12. Wall painting of Kelaniya Temple. (Photo by Kenji Yamazaki.)

with boiling oil. Then, big waves attacked the country. The king offered one of his daughters as a sacrifice to the sea. She floated in a small boat, which drifted until it reached a beach near Matara. The king of Matara married this princess, and established the kingdom. The big waves described in this story may be a tsunami. Physical evidence exists to support this, as a deposit of sand carried by tsunamis has been found near Matara.

As the wall paintings of the temple show, the tsunami of 2004 was not Sri Lanka's first. However, the people of Sri Lanka did not pass on their sad experiences of a tsunami to their descendants—or perhaps it could be said that their efforts to pass on their experiences by means of wall paintings were not successfully understood. Thus, many people could not escape from a tsunami with waves and ebbs because they did not have adequate knowledge of tsunamis.

Creating a Disaster Subculture

One's raw experiences of a tsunami can be verified scientifically, and they can be developed or transformed into active and valid experiences. These experiences can be used to create evacuation plans. Not only will "active and valid experiences" be able to create various kinds of soft adjustments, such as telling

Photo 7.13. Another view of the wall painting. (Photo by Kenji Yamazaki.)

an experience to a younger generation, but also they will be effective in making a structural adjustment to tsunamis.

Teaching materials, cenotaphs, local history, and evacuation drills are constantly examined so they will become valid as "active experiences." These processes create a disaster subculture that can protect the community (Iwate University and Iwate Prefectural Government 2006).

The Structure of Vulnerability

From the interviews, it was apparent that people living in Seenigama had neither knowledge nor information about tsunamis before December 2004. On the other hand, the citizens and the government of Taro Town are well prepared for a tsunami: After the devastating tsunami in 1933, they have created both hard and soft adjustment systems to tsunamis through their hardship (Ito 2005).

It can be said that socially and economically vulnerable people tend to be affected by natural hazards more seriously. Issues of vulnerability are crucial and inevitable for hazard researchers. Vulnerability has several aspects. Depending on the situation or the environment people live in, the damage they suffer varies. If they live in a wealthy environment, they suffer slighter damages. If

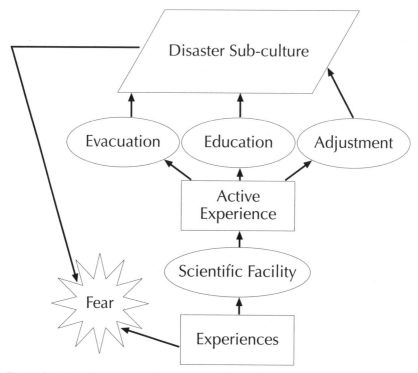

Fig. 7.7. Structure of how raw experiences are transformed into active experiences.

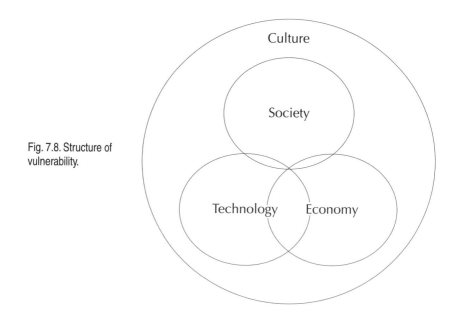

Fig. 7.8. Structure of vulnerability.

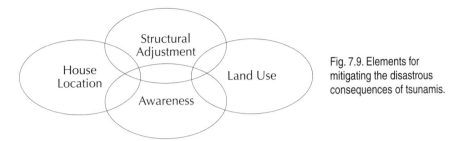

Fig. 7.9. Elements for mitigating the disastrous consequences of tsunamis.

they live in a poor environment, they suffer more serious or sometimes devastating damages.

Concluding Remarks

We would like to point out three factors concerning tsunami disaster reduction. The first is location of housing. If a house is built in a high place, it is less likely to be damaged by a tsunami. The second is hard adjustment, such as building dikes and shelters and establishing a warning system. The third is soft adjustment, such as cultivating a tsunami subculture. With the help of improvements in these three factors, residents along the seashore would be armed with the knowledge and ability to enable them to succeed in escaping tsunamis.

References

Ito, Kazuaki. 2005. *Tsunami Bosai wo Kangaeru* [Consider the tsunami disaster prevention]. Tokyo: Iwanami.

Iwate University and Iwate Prefectural Government. 2006. *Tsunami Bosai Kyozai* [Teaching materials for tsunami disaster prevention]. CD-ROM. Iwate: Iwate University.

Taro Town. 2005. *Chiiki Gaido* [Regional guide]. 7th ed. Iwate: Taro Town.

Taro Town Board of Education. 2005. *Taro Choshi Tsunami Hen* [The history of Taro Town: Tsunami]. Iwate: Taro Town.

Yamazaki, Tomoko. 2008. *Kodomotachi ni Kataritsugu Tsunami Taiken—Kamishibai Tsunami* [Passing on a tsunami experience to children—A picture story show by Yoshi Tabata]. Iwate: Gorokudo Insatsu.

Part 2

Socioeconomic Dimensions of Recovery, Reconstruction, and Response

Post-tsunami Recovery in South Thailand, with Special Reference to the Tourism Industry

David Zurick

The Indian Ocean Tsunami tragedy was unprecedented. It prompted worldwide humanitarian relief efforts on a historic scale and mobilized governments to address public and private sector challenges in natural hazard preparedness, public health, infrastructure, and economic recovery. Several years later, many affected communities across the region remain devastated by the disaster. In Thailand, however, where the tsunami was the greatest natural disaster in the country's history, the recovery has been remarkable.

The tsunami hit southwest Thailand along a 400 km (240 mile) stretch of coastline and offshore islands. The affected provinces include Phang Nga, Ranong, Satun, Trang, Krabi, and Phuket—the core of southern Thailand's tourism industry. The concentration of tourist services and activities near the beaches made them especially vulnerable to the devastation of the tsunami. The fast-growing Khao Lak resort in Phang Nga province, for example, with its string of low-lying beachside bungalows, suffered almost complete destruction. Similarly, on Phi Phi Don, a small island at the mouth of Phuket Bay in Krabi province, where most of the tourism facilities are packed onto a narrow isthmus averaging less than 2 m (6.6 feet) in elevation, the devastation was enormous. The tsunami surged across the isthmus, killing 1,700 persons and destroying 70% of the structures in the tourist center of Ton Sai village.

The immediate post-tsunami recovery efforts in Thailand were motivated by basic humanitarian needs felt across the affected region. They focused not only on tourists and tourism resorts, but also on the coastal indigenous fishing villages and low-lying agricultural zones, where many people lost their lives or the means of making a living. The tsunami caused major damage to fishing boats (4,300 boats were destroyed in Phang Nga, Krabi, and Phuket provinces), as well as to aquaculture ponds. The waves washed across farmland, destroying crops, uprooting trees, carrying away livestock, and inundating soil with salt-water. The urgent need during the days and weeks following the tsunami was to help the survivors cope with their losses and to account for the victims. The longer-term recovery efforts were designed to rebuild livelihoods and restore crucial infrastructure. In the tourism areas, which contribute substantial revenue not only to the local communities but also to the national economy, the most pressing need was to get the tourism industry back on track as fast as possible (Scott and Laws 2007).

The tsunami-affected areas of southern Thailand are located along the Andaman Sea, a region known best for its exquisite natural landscapes and marine resources. Phuket, Phang Nga, and Krabi provinces have international reputations as tourism destinations. Together, they account for 20% of the total annual tourism revenues in Thailand. Khao Lak in Phang Nga province, the newest of the areas developed for tourism, was hardest hit by the tsunami, with a death toll of over 4,000 (half of whom were foreign tourists) and property damage in excess of U.S.$350 million. The other tourism destinations in southern Thailand suffered varying degrees of damage. The beach resorts on Phuket Island are well established, dating to the early 1980s, and support the highest level of commercial mass tourism in the southern provinces. The smaller Phi Phi Islands in Krabi province constitute a spectacular cluster of islands accessible only by boat from Phuket or the Krabi mainland. These islands are popular among budget-conscious travelers and backpacking tourists for their crystal-clear snorkeling waters, imposing cliffs, sandy beaches (including the beautiful Maya beach made famous in the Hollywood film *The Beach*), and budget accommodations. To the east of the Phi Phi Islands, on the mainland of Krabi province, the Rai Ley beaches are popular among young travelers who come to climb the towering limestone cliffs that overhang the ocean or to kayak on the inland waterways.

The post-tsunami rebound in tourism in all these areas was speedy, given the scale of the disaster (Rittichainuwat 2006). Their international reputation and the revenue generated from foreign tourists partially explain why the coastal communities here recovered so quickly after the tsunami when the coastlines of many other affected countries remain bleak and depopulated. The success of the post-tsunami recovery in Thailand, however, is attributable to a constellation of factors, not simply to the motivations of the tourism economy. In fact, many of the affected communities were located away from the tourism resorts, inhabited by indigenous traditional communities, and in need of assistance quite different from the tourism centers (United Nations Development Project 2006).

On the one hand, the short-term humanitarian responses were immediate and multifold. The Royal Government of Thailand provided comprehensive emergency response in the region by mobilizing the entire civil and military agencies of the government. The urgent needs of the survivors were met by an integrated crisis coordination center combining the efforts of the Thai military and international search and rescue missions. The identification of victims was facilitated by forensic science technologies and an information-sharing Web site set up by the Ministry of Information and Communication. Relief operations were centralized under the Ministry of Public Health. The Ministry of the Interior mitigated the plight of victims by providing direct compensation to families for the loss or disablement of members, while the Ministry of Labour provided onetime payments to individuals who had lost their livelihoods.

These short-term measures were designed to mitigate the most immediate and severe impacts of the tsunami. The long-term consequences of the devastation, meanwhile, were addressed in a mix of livelihood recovery efforts, social programs, early warning systems, and environmental conservation strategies. These programs include fisheries and agriculture initiatives, broadly defined community and social development strategies; and, in the coastal towns and resorts, investments to rebuild tourism. Much of this chapter examines the tourism component of the post-tsunami recovery landscape in southern Thailand, focusing on the major tourist areas of Phuket, the Phi Phi Islands, and the coastline of Krabi province. Arguably, and notwithstanding the more generalized human tragedy of the tsunami, it is precisely because tourism in the southern provinces is important for the country as a whole that the recovery efforts there were so speedy and comprehensive. Moreover, the fact that almost half of the tsunami casualties in Thailand were foreign tourists, and much of the property damage was sustained by internationally owned resort properties, meant that the country's recovery needs became an immediate worldwide concern.

There is surprisingly little research on the impacts of natural hazards on tourism, despite the fact that many of the world's most popular tourist destinations are subject to catastrophic natural events or societal crises (Laws and Prideaux 2006). Alpine tourism, for example, must contend with the ever-present threats of avalanches, floods, and, in many mountain systems,

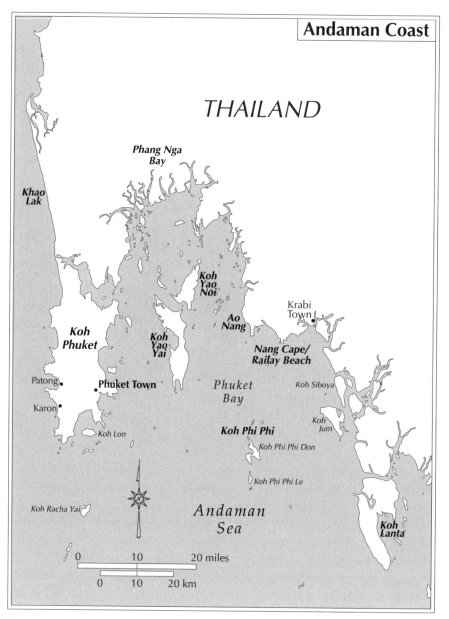

Fig. 8.1. Map of tsunami-affected areas of south Thailand.

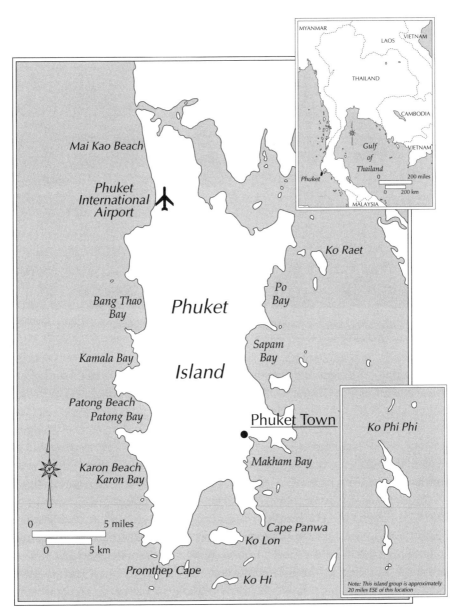

Fig. 8.2. Map of Phuket Island tourist resorts.

Photo 8.1. Entry point to Krabi province, August 2008. (Photo by David Zurick.)

earthquakes (Nothiger and Elsasser 2004). Oceanic volcanic islands, such as those in the Caribbean and South Pacific as well as in Southeast Asia, pose the potential problems of explosive eruptions and toxic gases being spewed into the air (Meheux and Parker 2006). The impacts of the Indian Ocean Tsunami on tourism in Thailand were of an especially large scale, and they extended beyond the infrastructural damage suffered by the industry to the psychology of tourists and the international reputation of the destinations (Ichinosawa 2006).

In some cases, tourists may actually be drawn to places of tragedy out of curiosity—a phenomenon called "thanatourism" (Lennon and Foley 2000; Seaton 1996). In a minor way, this attraction to places of tragedy is suggested to have been a motivating factor among some of the tourists who first visited southern Thailand in the immediate wake of the tsunami (Rittichainuwat 2007). More commonly, however, the tsunami destruction in Thailand kept tourists away, and the industry's concern, once the infrastructure damage was repaired, was to rehabilitate the reputation of the region as a safe place to visit.

Regional Background

The attraction of southern Thailand for both domestic and international travelers lies in its diverse geographical attributes. Phuket is the largest island in the country, measuring approximately 570 km^2 (228 sq. miles), and it contains interior hills covered in rubber plantations and rainforest, wetlands and estuaries on the east coast, and a succession of beaches on the west side of the island, facing the Andaman Sea. The west coast beaches host the majority of tourism spots. The economy of Phuket is largely dependent upon tourism, which, in addition to the commercial resorts, is based upon a variety of natural landscapes on the island—forests, mangrove estuaries, a succession of sandy beaches and ocean reefs, and a vibrant cultural life. A small patch of interior rainforest (20 km^2 [8 sq. miles]) is protected by the Khao Phra Thaeo reserve, and the Sirinat National Park on the northwest coast protects a 90 km^2 (36 sq. mile) area of marine environment that is important for nesting sea turtles. These natural areas host flourishing ecotourism activities such as hiking, wildlife viewing, and kayaking. The commercially developed beach resorts on Phuket Island include Karon beach, Kata beach, and Kata Noi beach—all relatively quiet places that are popular with families and expatriates. The most intensively developed beach on Phuket is Patong. Here, the hotels and bungalows, restaurants, shopping centers, and bars compete for space in a dense business strip situated alongside the ocean. The word *Patong* literally means "forest filled with banana leaves." This label still would have made sense as a description of the place twenty-five years ago, when the resort was in an early stage of tourism development, but now the town is a hyperconcentration of tourist services and activities, void of natural areas, and best known for its bars and nightlife.

Two hours by ferryboat east of Phuket are the Phi Phi Islands—considered by many to be among the most beautiful islands in the world. The Phi Phi cluster of islands is dominated by two relatively large ones—Phi Phi Don and Phi Phi Leh. Phi Phi Don is the only permanently settled island in the group and is where the tourism services are located. Daily boat excursions to Phi Phi Leh are offered to travelers staying on Phi Phi Don, with the main attractions being Maya beach and numerous smaller bays and snorkeling reefs. Most of these places are located within the Koh Phi Phi National Park. Phi Phi Don was first settled in the 1940s by Muslim fishermen. In the early 1980s, a single row of bungalows supported the few tourists who arrived there by long-tail fishing boats. By the mid-1990s, the island was a flourishing center for budget travel. Shortly after the Hollywood movie *The Beach* appeared in 2000, tourists flocked to the island in huge numbers, surpassing the tourism-carrying capacity of the island and turning it into an overcrowded and overwhelmingly busy place.

The majority of Phi Phi Don's inhabitants work in the tourism industry, and, along with the tourists, inhabit Ton Sai—a tiny village situated on a shelf

Photo 8.2. *Bangkok Post* front-page photo showing the destruction on Phi Phi Don, December 27, 2005.

Photo 8.3. The isthmus of Phi Phi Don, showing a recovered landscape, August 2008. (Photo by David Zurick.)

of low-lying land set between towering limestone rock cliffs. The 2004 tsunami completely inundated Ton Sai when it rolled across the island isthmus. The main reason for the concentration of people and buildings in this vulnerable spot is because it is the only significant piece of flat land on the island. Elsewhere, the topography is more varied, and the tourism resorts are scattered in a few small cove beaches or atop small ridges in terraces of bungalows and restaurants overlooking the rocky shoreline. Many of these isolated resorts are spectacularly situated and well appointed, supporting high-end enclave tourism, but outside of Ton Sai the geography of Phi Phi Don simply does not allow intensive tourism development on a large scale. Ironically, the outlying resorts on Phi Phi Don were largely spared much damage from the tsunami because of their higher-elevation locations.

The province of Krabi is one of Thailand's most spectacular places. The Phi Phi Islands described above are the offshore components of Krabi. The mainland portion of the province is filled with steep limestone mountains, solitary cliffs, caves, and rainforests. Many of the caves show signs of Thailand's oldest settlements, some dating to 35,000 BCE, and their interior walls are covered in elaborate paintings. The rainforests harbor rich biodiversity as well as ancient monasteries and meditation centers. Small islands, mangrove estuaries, and cove beaches dot the shoreline. These natural and cultural features support a range of tourism activities, including jungle safaris, scuba diving, cultural tours, rock climbing, kayaking, and beach resorts. For the most part, Krabi is less intensively developed than Phi Phi Don or Phuket, and its tourists tend to prefer solitude and nature-based activities. The atmospheric quality of Krabi is a good complement to these quieter tourism pursuits.

Scale of Tsunami Impacts

In all, the tsunami killed 5,291 persons and injured an estimated 8,500 in southern Thailand. Sixty thousand additional persons were otherwise directly affected by the tsunami, including those forced to evacuate or resettle elsewhere in the country. The household property damage included more than 3,000 destroyed homes and in total exceeded U.S.$25 million. Among the most vulnerable communities were the fishing villages and the sea gypsy households (75% of the latters' homes were damaged or destroyed by the waves). The sea gypsies are indigenous nomads who sail the mangrove coastlines to fish and to collect shells. Their origins are unknown, but they speak their own language, follow local beliefs, and are extremely poor. Their small settlements were the hardest hit of all the indigenous communities on the southern coast of the Andaman Sea, and an immediate concern arose that a total cultural loss might occur in the longer wake of the tsunami if these people permanently relocated to inland areas.

An early issue of post-tsunami recovery in Thailand was the impact of the waves on the coastal environment. Ironically, as it turns out, the biggest environmental problems stemmed from societal debris washed by the tsunami waves out from the tourism resorts, swept along the coastline, and deposited in pristine habitats that are spatially removed from the centers of human activity, rather than from any direct impact of the waves on the coastal habitats. The debris that despoiled many of the tourist beaches prompted immediate and successful cleanup campaigns. Of greater concern was the damage of debris to coral reefs, which are world famous for their scuba-diving prospects.

Altogether, an estimated 13% of the reef area in the southern provinces was affected. The greatest concentration of debris occurred among the reefs located off the western coast of Phuket, where the reef destruction exceeded 80%. The debris wash also inundated mangrove estuaries and sea grass beds, some of which are important sea turtle conservation areas. It is difficult to quantify the amount of debris, but on Phi Phi Don it was estimated at 35,000 tons. The marine environments are critical tourism resources, and, consequently, they garnered worldwide attention for cleanup, including the efforts of volunteer divers from around the world who came to clean the coral reefs (United Nations Country Team 2006).

The tsunami destroyed infrastructures across the region, but the overall damage was localized and relatively minor. Sixty-nine electrical subsystems were damaged at an estimated cost of U.S.$6 million. Nineteen water supply systems required replacement or repair. Roads and bridges were destroyed or damaged to varying degrees. The total impact on transport and communication, including asset damage and loss of revenue, was estimated at U.S.$20 million. Public infrastructure damage was offset by special budget assignations set up within the government sectors, making possible fairly speedy repairs and replacements. The private sector, on the other hand, which is where most of the structural impacts were felt, required time-consuming insurance assessments and capital investments that many individuals found difficult to manage.

Approximately 2,000 ha (5,000 acres) of farmland were affected by the tsunami, including rice fields and oil palm plantations. The agricultural sector suffered direct crop damages in excess of U.S.$10 million. Most of the coastal aquaculture ponds were destroyed, with total damage estimated at U.S.$30 million, and the coastal fishing fleet suffered U.S.$43 million in damaged assets (boats and gear). The total economic impact on livelihoods in agriculture, fisheries, and related industries was estimated to be over U.S.$350 million (asset loss and loss of productivity).

As large as they may seem, the numbers cited above are dwarfed by the economic losses suffered by the tourism industry, which exceeded an estimated U.S.$2 billion. The impact of the tsunami on tourism included extensive damage to hotels, restaurants, and other services, as well as the loss of tourism income and productivity. The ripple effects of tourism losses were felt across the region and throughout the communities of the Andaman Sea coast, while their magnitude was exacerbated in the cases of Phuket, the Phi Phi Islands, and coastal Krabi province, all of which are heavily invested in tourism.

Tourism Effects

The tsunami-affected provinces in southern Thailand generate an estimated one-fifth of total tourism revenues for the country. While the immediate impact of the waves on both local and national economies was great—the damage to tourism assets such as hotels, restaurants, and related service infrastructures was estimated to be about U.S.$400 million, the loss of future revenue from international tourism was an even greater concern for local communities and the national economy. Many of the tsunami victims were local people employed in the tourism industry, as well as migrant workers from elsewhere in Thailand or neighboring countries. Included among the casualties were an estimated 2,392 foreign tourists, comprised of thirty-seven nationalities, dominated by Swedes (543 deaths), Germans (468 deaths), Finns (158 deaths), Swiss (79 deaths), Norwegians (79 deaths), Britons (79 deaths), and Austrians (69 deaths). The death of the Westerners heightened the level of attention paid by the international media to the tourism areas, and, together with the actual damage sustained by tourism infrastructures, predicted a precipitous drop in tourist arrivals. This indeed happened. Hotel bookings in Phuket, for example, dropped 90% in the month after the tsunami, and, overall, tourist arrivals in Thailand dropped 35% from the previous year. An estimated 100,000 persons lost their jobs in the tourism sector. The overall loss of tourism revenues attributed directly to the tsunami exceeded U.S.$1.4 billion (United Nations Development Project 2006).

The tsunami impacts were not felt equally among all the Andaman Sea destinations. Phang Nga province reported 4,225 persons killed, with foreign tourists accounting for almost half the death toll. In Phuket, the tsunami killed 279 persons, of whom about 40% were foreigners. The number of foreigners killed in Krabi province was 204, approximately 30% of the total deaths. These numbers fail to account for the missing persons (about 2,817 in total) who

Photo 8.4. Tsunami destruction in Patong Beach, December 27, 2005. (Photo by Thorfinn Stainforth.)

were swept out to sea. The varying death tolls relate not only to the size of the waves, but also to the topography of the coastlines, the density of settlements, and the types of tourist accommodations found at a destination. On Phuket, for example, where the death toll was relatively low despite the large size of the coastal settlements, the land rises quickly a short distance from the beach, and many of the hotels are multistoried and located on higher ground, effectively placing people out of reach of the wave inundations. In contrast, the high death toll in the Khao Lak resort in Phang Nga province stems from the fact that the tourist bungalows were one-storied affairs and located directly on the beach.

The tsunami destroyed or damaged 25% of total room capacity in the provinces of Phuket, Phang Nga, and Krabi. The damage was not spatially even. It was greatest in Phang Nga province (45% of total lodgings), notably because of the extensive destruction of high-end tourist bungalows in Khao Lak (Calgaro and Lloyd 2008). The loss in Phuket amounted to 28% of the total room capacity. The other Andaman Sea destinations suffered varying degrees of destruction (with Phi Phi Don recording almost total loss in Ton Sai). The damage to infrastructures and houses apart from the tourism facilities, as well

Photo 8.5. Patong Beach fully recovered, August 2008. (Photo by David Zurick.)

as to agricultural holdings and fishing fleets, show a similar spatial cluster-ing. In all cases, Phang Nga province was hardest hit. Despite the geographi-cal patterns showing Phang Nga to be the most devastated place in southern Thailand, the international attention to the tragedy has centered largely on Phuket. This is mainly because the island is the best known of all the tourism places on the Andaman Sea and is extremely popular among foreign tourists from throughout the world.

Despite the widespread destruction, though, within two weeks many of the affected resort areas had reopened, and the tourism industry embarked on an international campaign to lure foreign tourists back to southern Thailand.

Recovery Efforts

The immediate responses following the tsunami were search and rescue efforts for stranded survivors, emergency aid to casualties, and identification of vic-tims. The neighboring communities were first to respond, followed by govern-ment action and international assistance. The relief efforts initially focused on Phuket (Patong and Kamala beaches), Phang Nga (Khao Lak resort), Phi Phi

Don, and the coastal beach resorts of Krabi province (especially Ao Nang). Thailand's navy and police were put into service for the search and rescue operations. Rescue teams from throughout Asia, Europe, and North America assisted these efforts. Relief supplies delivered to Phuket were distributed by the army. Local communities were made responsible for cleaning up the debris and coordinating aid delivery. Forensic teams identified bodies (however, over 1,000 bodies remain unidentified; their DNA samples were collected and stored for future identification). Evacuation centers were set up to house tens of thousands of persons left homeless by the tsunami. These were run mainly by Thai volunteers and local community organizations. In the case of Phi Phi Don, the entire island was evacuated and closed for several months while cleanup crews combed the island and officials drew up new zoning plans for future development.

Foreign victims of the tsunami required special attention. The Thai government coordinated the evacuation of survivors, paying for their lodging and food and flights back home. Within ten days, the Immigration Bureau had assisted 5,000 foreign tourists to return home. The Ministry of Tourism also covered the expenses of foreigners who flew to Thailand in search of relatives, as well as the funeral expenses of victims. Students from throughout Thailand were mobilized to provide assistance to foreigners in the way of logistics and communications, including language translation, food, and transportation. In the immediate aftermath of the tsunami, foreign tourists commented often in the media about the high quality of assistance they received from both the Thai government and volunteer organizations, and praised the efficacy and compassion shown by relief personnel toward both them and the Thai tsunami casualties.

The effectiveness of the short-term emergency response in Thailand is attributed to several factors. The scale of destruction in Thailand was smaller than in some other countries, notably Indonesia and Sri Lanka, and institutional mechanisms were already in place in Thailand to handle disaster mitigation. The Thai community (both local and national) responded with the immediate provision of volunteer assistance and relief supplies. The various agencies of relief operations—civil, military, NGOs, and charitable organizations—were effectively coordinated by a centralized crisis center. International assistance arrived quickly and was efficiently distributed to the affected communities (Nidhiprabha 2007).

Once the immediate relief assistance was implemented, the recovery focus shifted to longer-term rehabilitation and reconstruction efforts. The damage to infrastructures such as roads and bridges was relatively slight in Thailand compared to other affected countries. Most of the structural damage affected tourism facilities. Hotels near the beaches were hit particularly hard. Phuket lost 25% of its hotels but less than 10% of rooms, since the larger hotels were situated inland and untouched by the tsunami. In Phang Nga province, on the other hand, two-thirds of the hotels were damaged or destroyed, resulting in a room loss of 70% (much of this was concentrated in the Khao Lak beach resort area). The hotels in Krabi were less impacted, with a total room loss of about 10%. Throughout the region, tourism corporations worked with local communities not only to repair the damage sustained by hotels and related structures, but also to address the broader societal needs of the affected communities (Henderson 2007).

With the exceptions of Khao Lak and Ton Sai, where tourism facilities were almost completely obliterated, the overriding concern in the industry centered not so much on infrastructure damage as on the projected shortfall in future tourist arrivals. The international media focus on the destruction led to the overwhelming perception among prospective tourists that southern Thailand was totally destroyed and to be avoided. This, in turn, led to a sharp decrease in tourist arrivals for several months after the tsunami. Hotel occupancy rates dropped on average 60% across the affected provinces in the three months following the tsunami. While the tsunami effects were felt most acutely by the tourism industry, the agricultural and fisheries sectors of the provincial economies also experienced economic downturns. The rehabilitation efforts included investments in all livelihood areas, with tourism accounting for the majority of the expenditures.

The Thai government allocated U.S.$1.7 billion for immediate tsunami relief and reconstruction. Twenty percent of this amount went toward emergency measures, including survivor rehabilitation and infrastructure reconstruction. The largest budget allocations went to tourism entrepreneurs in the form of low-interest loans to rebuild tourism facilities. This was a top priority because so many people in the affected provinces were dependent upon tourism for their earnings. The high unemployment rates among tourism workers immediately after the tsunami proved to be relatively short term, and many of the workers found employment at tourism destinations elsewhere in Thailand (including the resorts on the Gulf of Thailand side of the Malay peninsula, which were unaffected by the tsunami and actually experienced a spike in tourist arrivals as foreign visitors rerouted their itineraries). Within two years, however, tourism in the Andaman Sea provinces had rebounded to the pre-tsunami levels, workers had moved back into the region, and the economy was again booming.

In addition to recovery aid in the affected areas, Thailand invested in a tsunami warning system for the entire country. This system includes new technologies, for example, a system of sensors and buoys placed in the Andaman Sea and tied into the new National Disaster Warning Center, as well as more effective communication links to coastal communities. The latter incorporates an "alert system" of tsunami warning towers (fifty-five in total for Phuket, Phang Nga, and Krabi provinces) and a set of marked evacuation routes for the coastal communities. Handbooks were prepared for distribution to schools, fishermen, and tourism workers, and regular evacuation drills are now part of daily life for persons living in the coastal communities. The disaster management efforts also included substantial investment in geospatial information, including remote sensing analysis and geographic information systems, intended to assist mitigation experts in the affected provinces to plan for future natural disasters (United Nations Development Project 2005).

Of special concern for long-term recovery were the fishing villages and sea gypsy communities damaged by the tsunami. Many of these persons had no legal claim to land, a problem exacerbated in recent years as tourism and other commercial development spread along the coast and into the indigenous areas. The fishermen had lost boats and gear in the tsunami and, without land rights, faced the dilemmas of both where and how to live. Soon after the tsunami, the Royal Thai Government announced a policy of providing free housing in designated areas located several kilometers inland to the tsunami victims who had no land ownership papers. Most of the affected people, however, chose simply to return to their coastline homes and rebuild rather than relocate away from the sea. The land rights problem continues to plague many of these communities. Protests and conflicts are common, and most villages destroyed by the tsunami are still embroiled in court battles over land tenure, even as they battle with large-scale tourism developers for prime coastline.

Because the Indian Ocean Tsunami had affected world-famous tourism destinations in Thailand, the country was inundated with international offers of assistance. They came from foreign governments, multilateral donor agencies, corporations, and individual philanthropists. The offers of financial assistance from foreign governments were turned down by the Thai government with the rationale that other, less prosperous countries needed help more than Thailand. Foreign technical assistance, however, was accepted, mainly for search and rescue missions. Economic assistance in the tourism sector included large investments and donations by multinational corporations doing business in the region. These included hotel chains, restaurants, spa facilities, and entertainment venues. Within a year following the tsunami, over U.S. $62 million of international donor assistance had been distributed in the affected provinces, with Phuket and Phang Nga accounting for half the allocations (United Nations Country Team 2006).

The long-term concern of the tourism industry was the impact of the tsunami on tourist psychology and related travel behavior. The grim picture of the tsunami painted by the international media was considered to be an important factor in deterring tourists from visiting the affected communities in the future. Surveys conducted by the industry, however, have shown the negative impressions to be relatively fleeting. After the first quarter of 2005, when tourism was at a low point, international tourists began trickling back into the region, and the pace of arrivals quickened throughout the post-tsunami year, so that within about fourteen months the tourist arrivals had matched pre-tsunami levels. To a large extent, this quick recovery was linked to a media blitz by the tourism industry showcasing the speedy rate of infrastructure rebuilding and effectively portraying the region as being safe and essentially "back to normal." Indeed, much of the post-tsunami rebuilding was very fast and led to superior tourism facilities and expanded services and activities. Moreover, the tourism promotions suggested that, by visiting Thailand, tourists could actually aid in the recovery process (Pacific Asia Travel Association 2005).

Nowadays, across the region, there are few reminders in the landscape of the scale of the disaster that struck the coastline in December 2004. Within a year, 80% of the hotels on Phuket were back operating normally (Kurlantzick 2005). A large number of new hotels have been built or are currently under construction. Indeed, the frenzy of construction in the affected provinces is perhaps the clearest sign of both the disaster and the intensity of recovery. The tourism industry also is diversifying its product, moving away from an exclusive reliance on beach resorts and toward alternative sustainable options, including cultural and ecotourism developed among the inland communities previously underserved by the tourism industry. A broadly conceived regional recovery plan seeks to situate the new tourism developments within a more comprehensive planning strategy that diversifies the local economies and gives greater control over the design of tourism projects to the local communities (Asian Development Bank 2008). This is considered to be especially important in light of the threat that in the wake of the tsunami, large business interests might take over indigenous land claims and outcompete the small-scale entrepreneurs.

Field studies conducted by the author in summer 2008 in Phuket, Phi Phi Don, and Krabi revealed almost total recovery in the tourism sectors. The numbers of visitors were at all-time highs, the economies were generally booming, and the coastal infrastructure had been rebuilt. Little evidence of the tsunami exists now in the landscape. Ao Nang beach in Krabi province has a

Photo 8.6. Tsunami destruction in Ton Sai, Phi Phi Don, December 28, 2005.

Photo 8.7. Hotel construction in Ton Sai, Phi Phi Don, August 2008. (Photo by David Zurick.)

small memorial to tsunami victims, as does Patong Beach on Phuket. Phi Phi Don contains signage to show evacuation routes for pedestrians. Otherwise, the main indicator of the tsunami destruction is the rapid pace of construction that has occurred in its wake.

Much of the new construction fails to adhere to building codes proposed to make the structures safe in the event of a future tsunami. The tourism center of Ton Sai on Phi Phi Don, for example, is being rebuilt from the ground up, but much of the construction is substandard, with minor regard for the new safety provisions. Furthermore, despite zoning provisions that require the replacement construction on Phi Phi Don to be at a lower density than the pre-tsunami settlement, the tourist center at Ton Sai is being rebuilt even more intensively than before, with new bungalows, restaurants, and other tourist services jammed tightly within the core area. In all the affected tourist provinces, the planners had proposed that new developments be scaled back and placed further inland on high ground. A survey of the rehabilitated tourist spots in Phuket, Krabi, and Phang Nga, however, shows that this advice has been only partially heeded.

Despite the specific problems with some of the new constructions, the general response of tourism in southern Thailand to the tragedy of the Indian Ocean Tsunami provides a lesson in good governance. The Thai government is widely considered to have managed a successful response to the disaster, reacting swiftly and with full capacity. Beyond the immediate need of emergency assistance (search and rescue missions and relief aid to victims), there was no need for large-scale food assistance, and only localized and short-term disruptions occurred in basic infrastructures and services. Southern Thailand did not suffer the problems that plagued other tsunami-affected countries in the Indian Ocean region (e.g., civil unrest, military conflict, extreme poverty, and lack of basic infrastructure), thus providing greater stability and resources to the recovery efforts (Robinson and Jarvie 2008).

The Andaman Sea provinces rely heavily upon tourism revenue, so the efficacy of their post-tsunami recovery has an important ripple affect across the entire economy. In many places around the world, tourism does not fare well after crises, be they of natural or societal origin (Laws and Prideaux 2006). The resilient nature of tourism in southern Thailand, however, which results from a combination of diverse tourism products and effective industry management, provided a stable platform for the recovery of the region as a whole. Within little more than a year, the tourism industry was back to "business as usual," revenues were up to pre-tsunami levels, the evacuated workers and residents had moved back into the region, and the beach resorts were busy and prosperous once again. Moreover, the tourism programs initiated after the tsunami have shifted focus slightly away from the highly commercialized models of "mega-resorts" and toward the new designs of "green tourism" and community-centered development. In this regard, post-tsunami tourism in southern Thailand follows more closely the precepts of sustainable development, where environmental conservation and economic equity are important considerations.

References

Asian Development Bank. 2008. www.adb.org/tsunami.

Calgaro, E., and K. Lloyd. 2008. Sun, sea, sand, and tsunami: Examining disaster vulnerability in the tourism community of Khao lak, Thailand. *Singapore Journal of Tropical Geography* 29 (3): 288–306.

Henderson, J. C. 2007. Corporate social responsibility and tourism: Hotel companies in Phuket, Thailand, after the Indian Ocean Tsunami. *International Journal of Hospitality Management* 26 (1): 228–39.

Ichinosawa, J. 2006. Reputation disaster in Phuket: The secondary impact of the tsunami on inbound tourism. *Disaster Prevention and Management* 15 (1): 111–23.

Kurlantzick, J. 2005. Return to paradise. *New Republic* 233 (12): 42.

Laws, E., and B. Prideaux. 2006. *Tourism crises*. New York: Routledge.

Lennon, J., and M. Foley. 2000. *Dark tourism: The attractions of death and disaster*. Cornwall, UK: Thomson.

Meheux, K., and E. Parker. 2006. Tourist sector perceptions of natural hazards in Vanuatu and the implications for a small island developing state. *Tourism Management* 27 (1): 69–85.

Nidhiprabha, B. 2007. *Adjustment and recovery in Thailand two years after the tsunami*. Discussion paper 72.Tokyo: Asian Development Bank Institute.

Nothiger, C., and H. Elsasser. 2004. Natural hazards and tourism: New findings on the European Alps. *Mountain Research and Development* 24 (1): 24–27.

Pacific Asia Travel Association. 2005. *Tsunami recovery travel facts*. pata.org/~pata/newsletter/news05/Impact17jan05/htm.

Rittichainuwat, N. B. 2006. Tsunami recovery: A case study of Thailand's tourism. *Cornell Hotel and Restaurant Quarterly* 47 (4): 390–404.

———. 2007. Responding to disaster: Thai and Scandinavian tourists' motivation to visit Phuket, Thailand. *Journal of Travel Research* 46 (2): 422–32.

Robinson, L., and J. K. Jarvie. 2008. Post-disaster community tourism recovery: The tsunami and Arugam Bay, Sri Lanka. *Disasters* 32 (4): 631–45.

Scott, N., and E. Laws. 2007. Tourism crises and marketing recovery strategies. *Journal of Travel and Tourism Marketing* 23 (2–4): 1–13.

Seaton, A.V. 1996. Guided by the dark: From thanatopsis to thanatourism. *International Journal of Heritage Studies* 2 (4): 234–44.

United Nations Country Team. 2006. *Tsunami Thailand: National response and contribution of international partners*. Bangkok. www.un.or.th.

United Nations Development Project. 2005. *End-to-end warning system and preparedness for tsunamis and other natural hazards in southern Thailand*. Bangkok: UNDP and Government of Thailand, Department of Disaster Preparedness and Mitigation.

———. 2006. *Building back better in Thailand tsunami affected areas*. Bangkok: United Nations Development Program, Inter-Agency Support Unit.

9
—

The Role of NGOs in Tsunami Relief and Reconstruction in Cuddalore District, South India

Muthusami Kumaran and Tricia Torris

The intent of this chapter is to illustrate the role of nongovernmental organizations (NGOs) in the recovery, relief, rehabilitation, and reconstruction of coastal communities affected by the 2004 Indian Ocean Tsunami. It is a case study of NGOs involved in tsunami relief in Cuddalore district, one of the worst-affected coastal areas in Tamil Nadu, South India. Section 1 of the chapter provides an overview of NGOs in India and their role in tsunami relief in general and in Cuddalore district in particular. Section 2 presents the first-person report of coauthor Tricia Torris, a trained and experienced professional, who spent two months (May and June 2005) in Cuddalore working on tsunami aid with a network of NGOs. It highlights the situation on the ground, providing a human face to the issue of disaster relief and rehabilitation. In each section, major lessons learned in the aftermath of the tsunami disaster are outlined and a few recommendations to improve the disaster management capabilities of NGOs are presented.

The Role of NGOs in Tsunami Relief: The Case of Cuddalore District

NGOs in India

In the twenty-first century, NGOs appear to have become an integral part of Indian society. Indian NGOs are organized at local, regional, national, and international levels and are usually task oriented and managed by people with common interests; they perform a variety of services and humanitarian functions and bring citizen concerns to the government. The wide array of initiatives, interventions, services, advocacy, and knowledge that Indian NGOs provide to society makes it difficult to formally define them and provide a set of their characteristics. The World Bank (1995, 13) defines NGOs as "private organizations that pursue activities to relieve suffering, promote the interests of the poor, protect the environment, provide basic social services, or undertake community development." This World Bank document, titled *Working with NGOs,* further explains: "In wider usage, the term NGO can be applied to any non-profit organization which is independent from government. NGOs are typically value-based organizations which depend, in whole or in part, on charitable donations and voluntary service. Although the NGO sector has become increasingly professionalized over the last two decades, principles of altruism and voluntarism remain key defining characteristics" (13–14).

The NGOs in India reflect a wide spectrum of organizations, playing the role of an independent force outside the realm of government and private businesses. They include religio-political institutions, social movements, voluntary organizations, community-based or grassroots organizations, welfare associations of religious organizations, associations for the promotion of art, science, and culture, research groups, and organizations that provide services to the needy and the poor. Like the NGOs in many developing countries, Indian NGOs have emerged in recent decades as a dominant force in providing an impressive range of direly needed social services, community development, and grassroots activism. Unlike in the United States of America, where the nonprofit sector has been well established through a facilitative taxation system, excellent volunteerism, and substantial government contracts, the NGO sector in India is still in its infancy both in terms of resources and volunteerism.

According to IndianNGOs.com, a Web portal dedicated to providing information and knowledge exchange for Indian NGOs, there are about 1.5 million NGOs functioning in India. NGOs are registered as "Societies" or "Trusts" or "Section 25 Companies" (under section 25 of the Indian Companies Act), and estimates of their number ranged from 50,000 to 100,000 in 1993. However, since then, there has obviously been an explosion in the number and variety of these organizations. During the past two decades, the Indian government has recognized the contributions and importance of NGOs in the country's socioeconomic development through services that governments are unable to provide. Beginning with the Indian government's seventh Five-Year Plan (fiscal years 1985–1989), the funding for NGOs has been steadily increasing, further contributing to the rise of the sector. The NGO sector has also thrived on foreign donations and funding sources, which in 1999–2000 contributed more than U.S.$ 1 billion (Sooryamoorthy and Gangrade 2001).

While Indian NGOs had made tremendous strides in socioeconomic developments and reforms such as the women's movement, environmental conservation, rural development, poverty alleviation, and HIV/AIDS prevention, it was the massive disaster relief they launched in the wake of the December 2004 tsunami that brought visibility to their effectiveness, efficiency, collectivism, issues, and concerns like never before. It was also the first time in India that NGOs of various kinds rallied around a single cause.

The Indian Ocean Tsunami of 2004

On the Indian subcontinent, the Andaman and Nicobar islands were the first to experience the tsunami's wrath, followed by the coastal districts of Andhra Pradesh, Kerala, Tamil Nadu, and the Union Territory of Pondicherry. The tsunami affected a total of 2,260 km of India's coastline besides the entire group of Nicobar Islands, and the death toll was listed as 12,405: 8,009 in Tamil Nadu, 3,513 in Andaman and Nicobar islands, 599 in Pondicherry, 177 in Kerala, and 107 in Andhra Pradesh (United Nations 2005). In terms of mortality, injuries, and damage in Tamil Nadu, Nagapattinam and Cuddalore districts were reported to be the hardest hit.

The scope and magnitude of this natural disaster sparked an extraordinary mobilization of resources for humanitarian relief. Hedman (2005) reported that governments, NGOs, individuals, and corporations responded to the needs of the affected people in an unprecedented manner. A complicated and collaborative network of people and organizations delivering assistance and relief was activated and deployed. The scale of relief needed, especially in inaccessible areas, required the services of national and/or foreign military forces.

NGOs operating in the sectors of health, psychosocial counseling, shelter, sanitation, food and water, education, livelihood, and environment actively involved themselves in relief and rehabilitation activities. Participating organizations included international agencies such as World Vision, CARE, Catholic Relief Services, Project Concern International, ECHO, Oxfam, Dhan Foundation, League for Education and Development, and local agencies like Social Need Education and Human Awareness, Tamil Nadu Voluntary Health Association, and Bhumika (Kumaran 2008). The stages of the tsunami relief, recovery, rehabilitation, and rebuilding are illustrated in table 9.1.

The Role of NGOs in Tsunami Relief, Rehabilitation, and Reconstruction

NGOs from across India and around the world mobilized communities, private individuals, donor agencies, international, national, and local organizations,

Table 9.1. Major relief, recovery, rehabilitation, and rebuilding activities provided by NGOs after the tsunami

Immediate relief (first 60 hours)	Post-disaster relief (1 week–2 months)	Recovery and rehabilitation (3 months–9 months)	Rebuilding (9 months–)
Rescuing victims trapped under debris; first aid for injured; moving the seriously wounded to medical facilities; retrieving, burying, or cremating the dead; transporting victims to relief camps; making arrangements for food, water, sanitation facilities, clothing, and shelter for all victims; grief counseling, etc.	Providing food, clothing, and transitional housing; providing psychosocial care and child trauma assistance; removing debris, etc.	Providing psychosocial support; upgrading quality and facilities of temporary housing; social reintegration to address trafficking, health, and nutrition; disease prevention and care; education, etc.	Rebuilding livelihoods; providing compensation packages; developing shelters and habitats; safeguarding water supply, sanitation, and hygiene; providing security, etc.
Source: Kumaran 2008.			

and the corporate sector to respond to the needs of the tsunami-affected areas. As a first step, NGOs brought in substantial amounts of resources and expertise to help provide immediate relief to the affected people. The early and rapid response helped create space and time for both the government and communities to seek more effective ways of responding to the multiple impacts of the disaster. The collaboration between a large number of NGOs and international nongovernmental organizations (INGOs) enhanced the overall effectiveness of the relief and rehabilitation efforts. NGOs' advocacy was critical in highlighting concerns of those on the margins of society and the less visible victims of the tsunami (Tata Institute of Social Sciences 2005).

The wide spectrum of NGOs participating in relief operations also meant an equally diverse number of approaches to the issues of relief, rehabilitation, reconstruction, and development. Humanitarian aid agencies and international development agencies such as the United Nations, the World Bank, and INGOs had the ability to mobilize resources on a large scale. These resources were channeled through their partners, mostly local NGOs. For the most part, while international development organizations advocated the rights-based, sustainable development perspective to relief and rehabilitation planning and implementation, charitable foundations, religious orders, and corporate bodies tended to work on the welfare and charity aspect of tsunami relief and rehabilitation. Local NGOs approached the rehabilitation and reconstruction process as an opportunity for laying the basis for short-term and long-term changes in local social, economic, and political structures. Interest groups and associations with a membership base in the affected communities (e.g., fisherfolks' organizations) focused largely on protecting the interests of their own constituency.

Another category of NGOs included advocacy groups, research organizations, technical institutions, watchdog organizations, and citizen collectives. Most of these organizations were not directly engaged in relief or rehabilitation work themselves, but focused on independent and often well-informed analysis of policy and practice. Using the media, the courts, and/or mobilization of affected people and communities, these entities highlighted key issues of concern. Given their noninvolvement in the actual administration of relief and rehabilitation, they often acted as watchdogs trying to examine the situation from the wider perspectives of transparency, accountability, and fair distribution of relief aid.

Fritz Institute, a San Francisco–based nonprofit organization that specializes in global research on the challenges of delivering humanitarian relief to vulnerable people, conducted a study of NGOs and tsunami-affected families in India in 2005. This study, with the purpose of understanding the dynamics of the relief operation and gathering data to inform future relief efforts, was conducted nine months after the tsunami and involved interviews with 226 NGOs and surveyed about 1,000 families from 100 villages affected by the tsunami. According to the study report, 64% of the affected families surveyed said that they had received overall help from NGOs in the first forty-eight hours following the tsunami (Fritz Institute 2005). Table 9.2 shows the types and percentages of assistance received by the surveyed families from the government and NGOs.

The data from table 9.2 reveal that NGOs provided the bulk of the immediate tsunami relief and rescue, except for assistance in burying the dead and providing medical care—both of which were beyond their scope. Table 9.3

Table 9.2. Assistance provision during the first 48 hours after the tsunami

Assistance providers	Rescue (%)	Burial of dead (%)	Food (%)	Water (%)	Clothes (%)	Shelter (%)	Medical care (%)	Counseling (%)
Government	23	40	24	40	8	32	57	26
NGOs	59	34	65	48	71	53	31	51
Corporate sector	0	1	9	10	5	3	1	3
Unknown	18	25	2	2	16	12	11	20
Source: Fritz Institute 2005.								

Table 9.3. Satisfaction level in assistance received		
Type of assistance	Government	NGOs
Psychosocial counseling	3.4	3.8
Livelihood restoration	3.2	3.1
Shelter service	3.2	3.2
Source: Fritz Institute 2005. Note: Mean scores on a scale of 1–5, 5 being the highest level of satisfaction.		

shows the satisfaction level of surveyed families in the assistance provided by the government and the NGOs in the Fritz Institute survey.

The Fritz Institute study report (2005) also shows that 70% of the NGOs interviewed collaborated well with each other. Most collaboration involved national or international NGOs working with local community-based organizations.

The Tsunami's Devastation in Cuddalore District

Cuddalore district is a northeastern coastal district of Tamil Nadu (fig. 9.1). Cuddalore ("Ocean Town" in Tamil) city's industries employ a large portion of the district's population. Cuddalore district was heavily damaged by the tsunami waves, with several fishing hamlets disappearing altogether. About 700 people lost their lives and several others were reported missing. About 100,000 people belonging to fifty-one fishing hamlets were affected severely by the tsunami disaster. A total number of 11,804 families were affected, and 61,054 people were evacuated and provided shelter in temporary camps as a part of rescue and relief operations (Cuddalore Collectorate 2005).

Roads were either washed away or covered with debris, cutting off many villages. According to the Cuddalore Collectorate (2005), problems included the bursting of water pipelines, seawater incursion and subsequent salination of agricultural land, destruction of horticulture activities, and loss of livelihood for fishermen. The entire village of MGR Thittu, a small island 600 m off the coast, was reduced to rubble. More than 125 people died in this village alone. Every hamlet along the Cuddalore district's coastline was affected in varying degrees, depending upon factors like the distance of the residential area from the coast, land elevation, tree cover, and type of house.

NGOs and Tsunami Relief in Cuddalore District

Although local NGOs in Cuddalore district swung into action to begin the recovery and rescue phase almost immediately after the onslaught of the tsu-

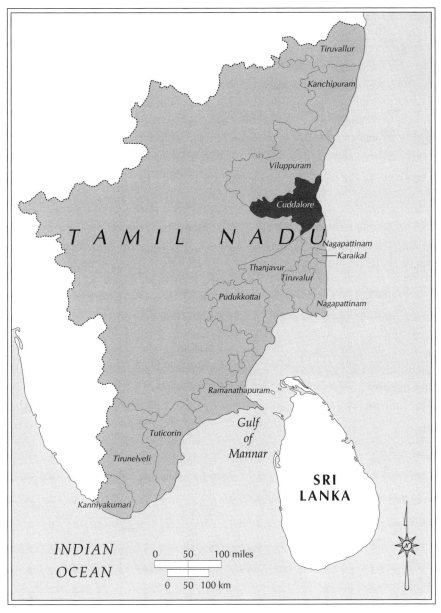

Fig. 9.1. South India location of Cuddalore district. (Source: http://cuddalore.nic.in/images/maps/1.jpg.)

nami waves, the local NGOs experienced significant and rapid shifts in their organizational functions. For the first two weeks, in spite of a rapid, early response to the disaster, the organizations' employees and volunteers, just like the affected people, were all in shock, working long hours, unsure of what to do, but continuing to strategize, move forward, and help people. Many of them had come together for the first time to form collaborative teams, setting aside their differences in the wake of the emergency. Once the first rush of recovery and relief was over, many of them were unsure of how to organize themselves and whether they would continue onto the rehabilitation phase. It was during this time that the NGO Coordination Center at the district collectorate in Cuddalore was established to serve as the "hub" for all NGO operations in tsunami aid (Cuddalore Collectorate 2005), and, through this center, several INGOs worked along with local, regional, and national NGOs. Overall, most of the NGOs approached disaster relief work through four distinct phases—rescue, relief, rehabilitation, and reconstruction.

The Rescue Phase

In the immediate aftermath of the deluge and destruction, local NGOs such as Dalit Munnurimai Koottamaippu and religious groups were among the first responders. Hundreds of volunteers helped the trapped, rushed the injured to hospital, and fed thousands of survivors in the villages until the government and the army stepped in.

The district administration set up thirty-eight temporary shelters that accommodated some 62,000 affected people (Cuddalore Collectorate 2005). NGOs provided food and water to the people in these temporary shelters and also set up temporary community kitchens with the assistance of district administration. NGOs also took part in the grim task of removing the debris and locating and burying the dead.

The Relief Phase

The relief phase focused on providing immediate aid and succor to the victims of the tsunami. Interventions included the provision of temporary shelters, food, emergency medicines, clothes, means of communication, and counseling. When evacuation of people from their villages was called for, the district administration sought the help of NGOs to identify and provide the most suitable form of alternative accommodation. Of the total number of 2,502 temporary shelters provided for the tsunami victims in Cuddalore district, only 925 were provided by the government; 1,577 shelters were built by NGOs (Cuddalore Collectorate 2005).

Table 9.4. NGOs' involvement in temporary housing in fisherfolk hamlets in Cuddalore district		
Hamlet	NGO involved	Number of houses constructed
Sonankuppam	World Vision	324
Devanampattinam	Khalsa Aid & Project Hope	723
Akkaraigori	World Vision	50
Periyakuppam	VR. Sa. Dhan	7
Pettodai	Isha Foundation	6
Reddiyarpettai	TDHCT	12
Madavapallam	Sumanahalli	11
Kumarapettai	BLESS & Oxfam	9
Velangirayanpettai	BLESS & Oxfam	10
Pudhukuppam	BLESS & Oxfam	96
Pudhupettai	Sadhu Vasvani Mission	81
Chinoor (north)	BLESS & Oxfam	10
Chinoor (south)	BLESS & Oxfam	55
Indira Nagar	Sadhu Vasvani Mission	13
Annankoil	Sumanahalli	27
Chinnavaikal	CREED	62
Pilumedu	CREED	81
Total		1,577
Source: Cuddalore Collectorate 2005.		

Another major need during the relief phase in the affected coastal communities was psychosocial counseling. Affected people in coastal communities, particularly women and children, who were gripped with fear and panic on seeing giant waves, developed trauma and psychological blocks causing disruption to their normal life. For the first time in their living memory, the fishing community developed a "fear of the sea" (Helping Hand 2008). The psychological effects were especially severe for children from villages where the death tolls were quite high. The NGO Family Care Foundation and its partners (2005) reported that many of these children didn't want to see the sea again. Many had nightmares and yet others repeatedly asked their surviving parents and relatives to move away from the ocean to interior towns. Adults also suffered severe psychological trauma. For the first time in their lives, many adult fishermen who had always depended on fishing for their livelihoods refused to go into the sea. Many women and fishermen who lost their family members and boats could not find the energy to rebuild their broken lives and dreams.

Acknowledging the importance of counseling at these critical times, Tamil Nadu state government's Social Welfare Board set up several post-disaster trauma counseling centers. Responding to the government's appeal for experienced counselors to operate these centers and provide effective delivery of services to the affected people, the NGOs promptly sent in social workers. Several trained students and faculty from universities across the state of Tamil Nadu and other parts of India assisted NGOs in dealing with the demand for psychosocial counseling. Family Care Foundation, Helping Hand, Save the Children, and Family Services India were among the first NGOs to provide direly needed psychosocial counseling to the affected people, serving thousands of traumatized victims and also providing emotional healing programs for young children.

The Rehabilitation Phase

People who were already struggling to cope with the loss of their family members and personal belongings also faced the problem of destruction of their landholdings, fishing boats, gear, and other means of livelihood. Since the tsunami had wiped out many communities' means of livelihood, the rehabilitation phase by NGOs focused on both short- and long-term goals, concentrating on programs to resurrect affected industries such as fishing and river trade. Focus on livelihood support reflected the adaptation of a popular proverb: "Give a man a fish and you feed him for a day. Give a village a fishing boat and you feed them for life" (Family Care Foundation 2005).

As many communities affected by the tsunami were marginalized even before the disaster, NGOs also concentrated on programs that would bring education and other benefits to them. The fisherfolk, farmers, and laborers of the coastal communities in Tamil Nadu were perhaps some of the poorest in the country even before the tsunami, with the average person in the three most affected districts (Nagapattinam, Cuddalore, and Kanyakumari), living on less than $1 per day (Oxfam 2005). To address this problem, NGOs adopted an innovative approach by converting the erstwhile boat laborers into boat owners. Those fishermen who had worked as laborers in pre-tsunami days were identified by the NGOs for assistance and supplied with fishing units comprised of boats with engines, nets, and gear. The beneficiaries were assembled into groups of four or five persons, and agreements with necessary terms and conditions were entered upon between them and the NGOs regarding the collective ownership (Oxfam 2005). The initiative resulted in two dynamic shifts

Table 9.5. Number of fishing units provided by NGOs in Cuddalore district				
Boats	**Nets**	**Catamarans***	**Engines**	**Thonies***
1,182	1,932	193	865	169
Source: Cuddalore Collectorate 2005. *Catamarans and thonies are small wooden boats with paddles traditionally used by South Indian fishermen.				

in the fishermen community—the social status of a wage earner was uplifted to that of a boat owner, and a sense of collective well-being and cooperation spread among the fishermen (Kumaran 2008).

NGOs also provided necessary training to farmers to improve their tsunami-affected saline agricultural land. Self-help groups that formed among the farmers were assisted by NGOs in obtaining quick relief assistance from the government for damaged crops. Many women's rights NGOs provided alternative employment options to the women of affected communities through skills training in small cottage industry products. Those who underwent training were also given microloans to start their own small businesses.

The Reconstruction Phase

The reconstruction phase focused on helping families and communities rebuild infrastructure like homes, roads, public buildings, hospitals, and bridges destroyed by the disaster. According to the Cuddalore Collectorate (2005), all the permanent houses for the tsunami-affected people in Cuddalore district were constructed only by NGOs through contracts from the government and contributions from international donations. Prescribed procedure was followed, with letters of intent from various NGOs received in advance before the actual number of houses to be constructed was determined. The district administration allotted permanent housing construction in villages based on the records submitted by NGOs as prescribed by the government and based on their previous operations and contacts with the affected community. To ensure fairness, these allocations were made in consultation with a committee representing various NGOs, and attempts were also made to involve the beneficiaries during the planning and designing process for permanent housing.

Lessons Learned

The 2004 Indian Ocean Tsunami left in its wake unprecedented destruction of life and resources in coastal South India and posed a huge challenge to the government and NGOs, both of which played positive and decisive roles in relief, recovery, and reconstruction efforts. The tsunami and the crisis that it created brought out the underlying humanitarianism among the NGOs, general public, and all sections of the society. Such a spontaneous outpouring of generosity for the victims of the disaster was a welcome feature despite the tsunami's extensive damage to life and property. It is clear that a synergy of NGOs' strengths has been an important factor in ensuring some level of comfort for the people affected by the devastation.

Despite the many positive actions and outcomes of the NGOs in the wake of the tsunami, there were many vital lessons learned in its aftermath that can help Indian NGOs be better prepared for disaster management in the future:

- There should be greater coordination among relief agencies and better sharing of information about disaster impacts and victims' needs. Coordination, dialogue, and information sharing between NGOs are crucial to avoid problems stemming from duplication, wastage of resources, competition, and differences in approach. Networking between organizations working toward a common goal will serve not only to optimize and maximize individual efforts, but also to ensure accountable and transparent disaster response interventions. Given the involvement of a wide range of actors (about 400 NGOs and INGOs, government and UN agencies) responding to the relief, rehabilitation, and reconstruction of tsunami-affected communities, coordination needs to be strengthened to ensure adequate attention to all areas (sectoral as well as geographical) and to avoid duplication of efforts.
- There is a need for knowledge networking and partnership building to support policy making and recovery planning. Access to knowledge resources and updated information is crucial for long-term planning and implementation. While the lack of prior experience in managing a disaster of such magnitude must be taken into account while assessing the progress made in the relief measures, the question remains as to what prevented the state and the NGOs from consulting their experienced counterparts in other parts of the world about their positive and negative experiences and also involving the directly affected people in assessing their actual needs.
- Relief provided to disaster victims should be need driven, not supply driven. Examples of unsuitable and therefore wasteful spending after the tsunami included the supply of temporary shelters made out of metal sheets, which were suffocating and dangerous in the stifling temperatures, and donations of thousands of items of Western winter clothing given to

people living in hot, humid climates. These and other similar abominations are inexcusable, and an insult to the beneficiaries.

- A vibrant interface and partnership between the state and NGOs needs to be in place to minimize corruption and to ensure that people's concerns are addressed by both policy and practice. The government played a vital role in promoting the state-NGO synergy, as demonstrated in several districts. Equally important is the necessity for NGOs to engage constructively not only with the government but also with each other.
- NGOs working among local communities must educate them about their rights and motivate them to make demands on the government. Citizens must be encouraged to become self-reliant rather than depending on NGOs for everything.
- An early warning system must be put in place in every village, and local NGOs must be trained and provided with information and a clear protocol of action in disaster situations.
- While individual NGOs that assisted in tsunami relief and recovery have reviewed their own operations, released reports, and shared their lessons, a sectorwide review of all NGOs involved is needed. Such a review could uncover important ways in which future relief efforts can be improved and coordinated.

Although the NGOs and Cuddalore district administration proclaimed by the end of 2005 that "several long pending requests of the people of the affected area have been suitably addressed now and it is expected that the face of coastal villages of Cuddalore district will have changed beyond recognition in a matter of one year or so" (Cuddalore Collectorate 2005, 64), not all changes envisioned have materialized and the reconstruction is far from over.

Many NGOs that actively participated in the tsunami relief and recovery by dramatically addressing the immediate needs of hunger and health care should have realized that with time, they needed to focus away from addressing the symptoms toward addressing community building and rehabilitation projects that would have a longer-term impact for the affected communities and their residents. An NGO that provided food to tsunami victims for several months after the devastation, for example, could put pressure on the government and INGOs to provide resources for economic development in the area.

Closer coordination among NGOs to avoid overlap and redundancy is imperative and needs to be supported by government agencies and donors including INGOs in the disaster management field. It is important for all NGOs to speak with a single voice on a number of issues relating to disasters.

All NGOs, big and small, are susceptible to internal and external pressures. As NGOs are asked to do more, and the incidence of complex disasters involving natural and man-made factors increases, all NGOs should collectively develop basic standards to govern the way they work in disaster assistance. Such standards will greatly improve rapid response and facilitate better coordination and pooling of resources, resulting in efficient and effective disaster relief. And as the number of active NGOs in the field has considerably increased in India, the focus should now shift from disaster relief to a more long-term disaster management approach. Such long-term commitment is clearly the way to turn relief into sustainable development that can make devastated communities flourish once again.

Reflections on My Tsunami Recovery Experience in Cuddalore

Background

I spent two months (May and June 2005) in Cuddalore district, India, with Action Aid India (AAI), an INGO providing aid to tsunami-affected coastal communities. The work was part of my master's degree practicum requirement, and I volunteered for the project because of my interest and training in emergency management and disaster relief. Through volunteering with the American Red Cross (ARC) and the Federal Emergency Management Agency (FEMA) in the United States and attending several training sessions and multiagency simulations, I had acquired training in emergency management and humanitarian assistance. My hands-on experience included deployment as an ARC mass care technician to Caguas, Puerto Rico, after Hurricane Georges, and a Level 4 disaster relief effort in Dededo, Guam, after Typhoon Chataann. I had also continued to serve ARC as the lead person for the Oahu Shelter Team, an operator for the ARC hotline, and as a co-captain for the Disaster Action Team, which responds to fires, floods, and other disasters on the island of Oahu, Hawaii.

It was as part of the practicum requirements for the master's degree in public administration that my academic advisor, Professor Muthusami Kumaran, made arrangements with his alma mater, Madras Christian College (MCC), Chennai, Tamil Nadu, to be the host institution for my work with tsunami aid NGOs in South India. The Department of Social Work at MCC facilitated my fieldwork at tsunami-affected coastal communities. In May 2006 I earned the master's in public administration degree and a graduate certificate in disaster management and humanitarian assistance from the University of Hawaii–Manoa. The following section presents reflections on my experience working with Action Aid and its partner NGOs during the months of May and June 2005.

My Experience with NGOs and Tsunami Relief in Cuddalore

I arrived in Tamil Nadu, India, in May 2005, five months after the December 2004 tsunami, to work in the tsunami-affected areas of Cuddalore district. Initially, I worked with Action Aid India (AAI), the Indian branch of the INGO Action Aid International, and several of its partner agencies. During the latter part of my stay, I also visited Oxfam India and the Indian Red Cross, Tamil Nadu branch (IRC–Chennai) offices and observed their operations. AAI addresses disaster-related issues by supporting established local grassroots NGOs. Thus, during my two months of tsunami relief work with AAI, I was also closely associated with the following AAI partners:

- Dalit Munnurimai Koottamaippu (DMK), which literally means the Federation for Dalit's Advancement. I spent the majority of my time with this NGO;
- Human Rights Forum for Dalit Liberation (HRFDL);
- Institute for Social Education and Development (ISED);
- Social Need Education and Human Awareness (SNEHA).

The coastal population served by DMK and AAI were from the Dalit, or the lowest caste, of India's social hierarchy. One group that makes up this caste is called Chembadavan. According to AAI staff, they were among the most backward classes in the Indian caste system, only second to the lowest caste in the hierarchy. To deepen my understanding of the group's socioeconomic conditions and historical placement in the society, I did some background research.

I was told that in Tamil Nadu, the Dalits make up 25% of the population, are the poorest in this state, have the highest incidence of illiteracy, and have been fighting for land rights for generations. My experience indicated that despite the many struggles, the Dalits were resilient to the tragedy spawned by the tsunami and had even begun working on some of their preexisting issues, so that they would be able to achieve greater stability and prosperity than before this tragic event.

While working with AAI, my focus was on understanding how the organization functioned during a disaster of this magnitude. I began by looking at the areas of advocacy, psychosocial counseling, and livelihood. The fisherfolk who were affected by the tsunami, as well as the Dalit people, were being serviced not only by NGOs but also by the Indian government, religious groups, and numerous private individuals and organizations. Although AAI was providing a substantial amount of aid, it was still only a very small part of the services being rendered by a multitude of NGOs—local, regional, national, and international—to meet the needs of the affected people of Cuddalore district. Needless to say, the reconstruction efforts required multiple sources of funding, workers, and advocates in bringing some normalcy to the communities affected by the tsunami's destruction.

AAI and its partner NGOs had two major approaches to their role in tsunami relief:

- A human rights–based approach in disaster management/relief;
- To work toward improving the entitlements, including food, shelter, relief, and human rights, that had long been denied to the marginalized people even before the tsunami.

AAI looked not only at the immediate needs but also at long-term goals for the affected people. For example, they trained people within the villages as counselors to address mental health needs (train the trainer). AAI's intentions were to work with the tsunami-affected people for three to five years after the disaster and provide necessary skills and training for them to take care of themselves. The rationale was that by training members of the community, those affected would come together to address their own needs. AAI and its partners also foresaw the need to train community members as human rights advocates, land rights advocates, counselors, and job skills trainers. Thus, instead of treating the symptoms, they helped to address the underlying issues that had affected these communities for decades.

Shelters

After such a large disaster, I expected to see NGO workers, volunteers, government workers, and social workers providing assistance to the community, carrying out tasks such as monitoring the shelters or answering people's questions. But I never saw any such activities. The reason for this could have been that I had arrived five months after the disaster, or that at this point it was the responsibility of the people to go to the offices of the NGOs and other representatives. But it was apparent that there were still many people in need and some did not have the resources or time to take from their wage-earning labor to go to the NGO or government offices. Barriers to seeking assistance included inadequate transportation, lack of finances, and loss of time from doing their regular, paid work.

In May 2005, the temperature on an average day was between 38°C and 46°C (100–115°F), with extreme humidity. There were still thousands of people displaced by the tsunami who needed assistance, and villagers were still trying to meet their basic needs such as shelter. They did this by finding shade underneath palm trees or among the rubble of their tsunami-devastated homes. When I visited Devanampattinam village, I noticed that not everyone was utilizing the temporary shelters that had been provided by an NGO. The shelters were in one long row structure and had dirt floors, corrugated metal siding, and thatched roofs. The structures were separated about every 3 m to make separate dwellings for the families. Occupants rigged makeshift doors by putting up fabrics or just left the entrance to the unit open with absolutely no privacy for the occupants. The one room, measuring approximately 2.4 by 3 m, was used by a family for sleeping, cooking, eating, and children playing. This was where they had lived since the tsunami, and they would probably continue to do so for a projected year to come. Many people preferred to make do with what they were able to salvage out of their homes and stay in a larger space, where they could have separate areas for cooking, sleeping, and other activities. Staying in the vicinity of their fishing hamlets and homes also allowed them to keep an eye on the boats and other fishing gear that was necessary for their livelihood.

As I walked through the shelters, I was surprised at the quiet and the degree to which people had adjusted to the difficult living conditions. I compared the situation to what I had seen on television of Hurricane Katrina evacuees on the U.S. Gulf Coast and wondered whether the response in the tsunami-affected area had been more organized from the start, thus making the transition from home to a shelter much easier. In the shelters I visited, there were groups of men sitting in circles repairing fishing nets, most women preparing meals, and the children playing or helping their mothers. Of course these people had been living in this situation for a while and had had time to adjust to this type of living, but nonetheless I think that they dealt with the tragedy's aftermath with remarkable grace and dignity.

While visiting those shelters, I was privileged to witness men going back to the ocean to fish for the first time after the tsunami disaster. It was amazing to see a part of the actual steps in the recovery process. Restoring a few individuals' economic situation and their livelihood was a success not only for themselves but also for their families and the community.

Inequality in Services

The extent of the lack of communication and cooperation between organizations that provided services to disaster-affected people was staggering. One community in Marakkanam, Cuddalore, had been given high-quality tents by

Photo 9.1. Several NGOs, such as Missio Austria, focused on child welfare (health, nutrition, and education) in tsunami-affected areas of Cuddalore district. (Photo by Tricia Torris.)

an NGO to live in until the people were able to rebuild. The families that I visited were quite happy with the tents, which were very practical and functional. People were able to take the tents back to where their homes were before the tsunami so that they could work on repairing their homes without traveling back and forth from the shelter to their home. The ability to stay on their land

Photo 9.2. Inappropriate housing for tsunami victims built by the government in Cuddalore district. (Photo by Tricia Torris.)

also supplied them with a sense of security, in that they were able to keep an eye on their properties as well as their livelihood.

Two blocks over, in the same village, families were living in metal-sided, thatched-roofed, multiple-family shelters. Separating these families was the NGO service boundary! That is, one NGO had provided the tents and another the multiple-family shelters. The latter families were not satisfied with their shelters because they offered little if any privacy. Also, these shelters were located far away from their previous homes, and so the occupants could not keep an eye on their fishing boats and other gear. The inhabitants wanted to know when they were going to get tents like their neighbors. But the NGO that was providing services in their community had already spent their sheltering funds on the metal-sided thatched-roof shelters and had no funding available for tents.

A different type of shelter was being offered in a neighboring village. These government-built shelters, made entirely of metal sheets, could never be used because they were too hot to live in. The community had to make do with what little they already had. From the perspective of the affected people in the villages, there was an unequal distribution of shelters provided from block to block and village to village. Much of the disparity could have been corrected, perhaps not during the initial phase of the relief operation, but surely five or six months after.

Preexisting Issues

For many NGOs, the tsunami seemed to work as a catalyst for addressing many of the preexisting issues of the affected population. The organizations that I worked with were addressing not only the needs created by the tsunami but also preexisting needs such as insufficient housing, lack of financial stability, health-related issues, absence of land rights, ineffective political structure of the villages, dismal women's rights, and wide gender gap issues. My perception of the affected population was how pleased people were that there was an organization present, willing to listen to their needs, and then do something about it! It was terrific to witness how proactive the villagers were about their own well-being. Women, who before the tsunami would not have spoken out, were now rallying together to form coalitions for women's rights. Men who were not in leadership positions in the village local governments (Panchayats) were now able to have a voice in village meetings. Although this new activism had repercussions within the community, the majority of the people seemed to be in favor of the changes.

Working with Indians in India after one of the largest natural disasters in history gave me a sense of a culture that is proud, of people who are strong willed, and of a country that is determined to prosper in health, wealth, and knowledge from the grassroots level upward.

The Oxfam Approach

While I was with the Oxford Committee for Famine Relief (Oxfam), India, I was exposed to the organization's education program that was created in six different fisherfolk villages within the areas of Thazhanguda, Akkaraigori, Rasapettai, Sothikuppam, Singharathoppu, and Naicherpettai. The limited outreach of Oxfam was in contrast to the operations of AAI, which was trying to serve almost every community that had been affected by the tsunami in Tamil Nadu. The Oxfam mission was to create community centers within these six villages as well as long-term job opportunities. They worked with two to four women from each of the villages, brought them to the office in Cuddalore for computer training, and then put these women in charge of the newly built computer and information centers in their own villages. Most of these women had no prior experience with a computer or even a typewriter, so the training was extremely intensive and thorough.

The information centers were designed to connect all six villages. More specific tasks included the daily announcement of the average prices of locally grown crops and locally caught fish. This practice ensured that the village farmers and fishermen knew that they were receiving a fair price for their produce and hard work. The information center was also a place where people of all ages could be trained in basic computer skills that they could then use when given the opportunity. The information centers also provided the village folks access to the Internet and computer games for schoolchildren.

Oxfam had funding for these centers for one year, within which time it planned to make the centers self-sufficient by seeking funding from other sources. This would ensure that the time invested would not be wasted. My fear was that the projects would thrive as long as Oxfam representatives were involved and perhaps for about a year afterward, and then interest would die out and so would the funds. However, I believe that the project will give the trained women the confidence and opportunity to seek and find jobs using computers outside their villages.

The Indian Red Cross Society Approach

I was very impressed with the range of services offered by the Indian Red Cross, Tamil Nadu branch (IRC–Chennai). The IRC operated a day hospital where there was at least one full-time doctor on the floor at all times as well as two part-time doctors who provided medical service to people in need. The hospital had several sections, including a general clinic as well as specialty departments such as cardiology, ophthalmology, gynecology, dermatology, psychiatry, dentistry, and internal medicine. In India, medical insurance is virtually non-existent, and people pay the provider directly for medical services. Providers are mostly individual physicians who have health clinics in the community; emergency surgery or other treatments are provided at a larger hospital. This system makes it difficult for low-income people, such as fisherfolks, to access medical services when needed even under normal conditions. After a disaster of the magnitude of the tsunami, many local residents could not afford any medical expenses. So, the presence of the IRC day hospital was a benefit to the affected people.

The IRC also operated an on-site training center with four different areas: tailoring, drafting, typing, and machinist training—all very practical and useful for obtaining local employment. The main reason for the IRC's success in providing efficient and effective relief after the tsunami was its well-established presence within the communities. While the IRC's response to the tsunami was swift, Oxfam India and many other NGOs' responses were slower and less efficient, especially during the initial rescue and recovery efforts. This was mainly due to their lack of familiarity with the local culture and the needs of the people. They needed time to assess the situation before taking action. Another major difference between the IRC and AAI was that, while the IRC provided free-of-charge services such as medical attention at its hospital, a blood bank, physical therapy, and artificial limbs directly to the affected people and communities, AAI provided indirect services by funding other organizations that, in turn, provided direct services.

Unsuitable Assistance with Good Intentions

Often I was told by local people that government and "outside" or unfamiliar organizations offered/provided services or products that weren't suitable for them. Good examples of such unsuitable relief measures were the shelters built by the Indian government and several NGOs. The shelters were rows of metal temporary structures built far away from the shore and in the sand. These were never used because they were too hot to live in—at times reaching 120°F. Other inappropriate products given included the thousands of items of winter clothing donated by people from Western countries that were totally unsuitable for the hot and humid conditions of coastal South India. The resources wasted in bringing these and other such useless items could have been well spent on most needed and simple items such as locally made cotton clothing and material. Not only would these items have been more suitable for the affected population, but purchasing locally made items like clothing and supplies would have provided a much-needed financial boost to the local economy.

In many affected fisherfolk villages, I saw water containers that had been provided by an NGO thrown away as garbage—they were of poor quality and became damaged quickly. They just added to the piles of rubbish already littering the beaches. A primary goal of NGOs should have been providing multipurpose, reusable items. The last thing an NGO should do is to contribute to the already large problem of trash.

Relocation of Affected People

There was a perception that the Tamil Nadu state government was using the current situation of the displacement of the local fishing villages as a way to transition from fishing coastal communities to tourist coastal communities. I also heard that the existing coastal communities, specifically the communities that were affected by the tsunami, were being pushed back away from the ocean, and the government was selling the coastal property to resorts and hotels. I was told that while the government was providing financial incentives to assist people to rebuild, there were different rankings of financial assistance based on location: if people rebuilt where they had originally lived on the beaches, they would receive no money. If they rebuilt 200 m back from shore, they would receive 100,000 Indian rupees, or U.S.$ 2,300. If they rebuilt 500 m back, they would receive 150,000 rupees, or U.S.$3,450.

While there was no hard evidence of the government's motivation for this process, I noticed that many local NGOs were planning protests and seeking assistance from larger NGOs and civil society organizations to persuade the government against such measures. I was impressed by the active role taken by many NGOs to prevent any such attempts by the government.

Uniting the Fisherfolk Villages

To create more self-sufficient and prepared communities within the fisherfolk villages along the shores of coastal Tamil Nadu, NGOs need to emphasize the common aspects of the villagers' lives and their interdependence. Many of the villages have lived at odds with each other for generations because they compete with one another in their livelihood of fishing. With each family's livelihood depending on the sea or neighboring lands for its survival, people have become protective of their land and waterways, which has led to long-standing conflicts between the villages. During times of disasters the rift between neighboring communities makes it difficult for NGOs or local officials to provide services to those who are in need. For example, an NGO may get misinformation from one village about the needs or status of neighboring villages for the simple reason that villagers do not have close enough relations to be able to accurately inform the organization's representative.

Another aspect of this issue for NGOs is that they strive to remain neutral within the villages. If an NGO is servicing a "rival" village, the neighboring village may not trust that it is receiving the same treatment/services as the other. In times of need it is important that the different agencies receive accurate information to reassure all interested parties that every affected community is given an equal level of services.

Need for Networking and a Coordinating Entity

An additional issue that needs to be addressed to help create a better response system within disaster-affected areas is the necessity of a coordinating agency to ensure that all the needs of the affected communities are being met. At the beginning of the tsunami relief effort there was an active NGO coordination center that was created for NGOs to network, to make contact with each other and assess the disaster situation. This was an ideal situation in place at the beginning of the relief process, but eventually this space disappeared, and the NGOs no longer had a central location for discussion and the exchange of information.

A common thread between Hurricane Katrina, the tsunami of 2004, and many more recent disasters is inequity in service provision: there were communities that didn't receive services, while others were "over" serviced. In some areas supplies were wasted because no one knew where to distribute them. Different kinds of agencies, such as NGOs, private organizations, and local, state, and federal governments, provide services in the aftermath of any disaster. With each of these agencies working on a specific issue, such as food supply, shelter, or health care, gaps can easily be created and provision of services overlooked. This problem is heightened by the fact that multiple agencies often provide the same service without communicating efficiently with one another. The repetition of the problem across the world underlines the need for an outside organization to act as a coordinating or monitoring agency and information source throughout the relief process. This agency should be tasked to keep track of the types and quantity of services required and provided, the recipients, and also what service is still needed. A common problem that I have noticed in many disaster situations is that each agency (for example, the Red Cross, FEMA, Civil Defense) goes out and collects information, makes assessments of whom to serve, the kinds of services needed, and what can be provided, and then takes the action it deems necessary. The result of this individualistic approach is that the survivors of the disaster are approached by multiple people from multiple agencies multiple times and then often receive nothing or only a portion of the services they need, due to the jurisdictional or service-specific nature of NGOs providing relief services. This can be frustrating and demoralizing to the individuals in need.

Typically, NGOs specialize in a particular service and do not work in coordination with one another. Thus, without coordination, affected communities may end up receiving less than adequate services though there are multiple sources ostensibly providing them. An example of this occurred during Typhoon Chataann in Guam. While the American Red Cross provided short-term relief, including shelter and food, FEMA provided long-term relief such as funding to rebuild homes and replace large appliances. There were other organizations that supplied medical relief and referral information. As a result of the lack of coordination in relief services, individuals were receiving inadequate services from four or more different agencies. If individuals weren't at the right place at the right time, they may have missed the information or services offered by one of these agencies. I saw similar hardships faced by people in almost all the villages I visited in India.

A well-organized coordinating agency would see the big picture and then coordinate efforts to make sure that everyone who needed services received them. The first major task of this coordinating agency would be to conduct a quick and practical assessment of needs before the bulk of the service delivery by various NGOs began. Such a coordinating agency would need to work with NGOs without hampering their independence. The agency could work regionally to focus on monitoring the relief process and ensuring that the demands/needs of the affected people were being met by adequate supplies. It would also serve as an information hub in the affected area for any agency, whether an NGO or a private or public agency. The agency would also provide information on the current challenges in the affected area to NGOs unfamiliar with the situation on the ground, such as what areas are unreachable or how the current weather has affected the roads. Such coordination would not only make the work of all NGOs more effective; there also would be much less chaos and frustration.

"Do not make the survivors of a disaster beggars for services," in the words of my friend Archana, an employee of AAI. The sentiment sums up the requirement that relief and development systems must be organized enough so that individuals or whole communities don't fall through the cracks of receiving aid. Survivors of disasters shouldn't have to beg for their basic needs of food, shelter, and medical attention. The adage is applicable universally to all disasters, natural or man-made, and it forms the basis for considering disaster relief aid as a human rights issue rather than one of giving away handouts!

Language Problems Faced by INGO Representatives and International Volunteers

Numerous representatives of INGOs and volunteers from across the world participated in tsunami relief efforts. One major problem faced by these "foreign" volunteers and relief workers was the language issue. As learning even the basics of a new language, especially the complex Tamil language, in a short period of time is very difficult, the next best alternative for international volunteers is to have access to volunteers of local NGOs who can also function as translators or interpreters. Although I was fortunate to work with a few social work students and AAI staff who spoke excellent English, I faced difficulties when helping people in the field. I did not always know whether I was hearing a translation laced with personal interpretation or if I was receiving a literal word-for-word translation of what people were telling me. Often I was unsure of the accuracy of the information I was getting from the translators. While a word-for-word translation can be confusing, the embellishment of what has originally been said with varying personal interpretations could make things worse.

While it is not fair to expect local NGOs to provide comprehensive translation or interpretation services, local NGO networks can develop a referral system through which groups of foreign volunteers can get language assistance from a pool of volunteers. Better yet, one NGO can specialize in this language "service" and seek funding for it from INGOs.

The Changing Role of Women in Fishing Communities

As a woman born and raised in the United States, I found myself in uncharted waters when it came to understanding the role of women in fishing communities of Cuddalore district. Most young women in these communities are educated only to the age of fourteen. Then they marry and begin their lives as housewives, mothers, and supporters of their fishermen husbands. In many of these fishing villages, women don't work outside of their households, and they are not allowed to leave the village unescorted.

In these more traditional communities, the women don't have a "paid income." They make their homes, raise children, cook for the family, and also help with different aspects of the fishing process such as drying the fish, transporting them from the boats to the trucks, and icing them. But they are not paid for their work. If a woman has lost her husband she has no income, and if a man has lost his wife he has no one to run his household or take care of his children. During the tsunami many men and women lost their spouses. The structure of the family unit makes survival difficult without both parents. So, very quickly after the tsunami, people began to remarry, but many who did not do so became beggars. In order to prevent this tragedy, many NGOs were successfully offering assistance to widows for alternative means of income. Due to lack of facilities, NGOs were training women in their village temples. Skill training included small-scale food processing, tailoring, and micro cottage industry products.

Thus, once again, the tsunami acted as a catalyst for change within the affected fishing communities. NGOs created new women's movements in these communities. These movements have allowed more and more women to take jobs outside of their homes, initially only to survive but later motivated by a desire to be a part of the workforce. I saw not only women who had lost their husbands at these training sessions but also young women and girls who were eager to learn a trade. It would be interesting to study whether these women continued to use their training to make a living on their own or went back to their more traditional role of wives once the men were able to resume their role as the breadwinners.

Photo 9.3. Appropriate temporary shelters built by NGOs. (Photo by Tricia Torris.)

Working with or around the Leaders of a Community

A recurring issue within many fisherfolk villages in Cuddalore was the fallout resulting from NGOs following the traditional method of distributing supplies or aid money. In this traditional method, the leaders of the villages (Panchayats) distribute aid to the affected people within their village. Many complaints came back to NGOs from villagers stating that they had received very few or none of the items they should have received from the Panchayat leaders and were afraid of asking them about it. NGOs have a responsibility to all of the people in the villages who were affected by the tsunami. That means the NGOs may have to take a less traditional approach when distributing supplies. NGOs also have a duty to be aware and respectful of the practices of the people they are trying to service. This requires delicate and mature handling of the situation.

My experience leads me to believe that an NGO may have to work side by side with the village leaders and monitor the distribution instead of allowing the Panchayats to take sole charge of it. It would be very difficult for an NGO to initiate such a procedure, as it would be working against a long-standing custom, which is related to the caste system. At the same time, NGOs would have to stay true to the mission of their organization. Had the standard of distributing supplies directly to each person or family been set from the beginning instead of initially allowing the Panchayat leaders to handle the distribution, the relief effort would have been easier for everyone to commit to; instead, matters were complicated through trying to change the practice in midstream.

Conclusion

The two months of fieldwork and assistance I contributed to the affected coastal villages of Cuddalore was my way of honoring the lives that were lost and the lives that were forever changed by the tsunami. I have acquired extensive formal training and experience in disaster management and humanitarian assistance and am always willing to contribute my expertise by volunteering for disaster relief. But every time I go to a disaster-affected community, I am amazed and humbled by the way human dignity prevails even in the face of catastrophes and tragedies. Most of the time, it is indeed the glorious presence of NGOs and volunteers that helps the survivors of disasters overcome their grief and gives them hope to rebuild their lives.

Since the devastating Indian Ocean Tsunami, there have been a multitude of changes to the affected communities, and the potential for future changes and advancement is endless. My hope for the affected areas is that the NGOs that came to be a part of the disaster recovery and reconstruction process continue to successfully transform them until they flourish. In order to help them do that, these NGOs should keep their focus on addressing not only the needs that were created by the tsunami but also the preexisting needs of these communities and their long-denied human rights.

In spite of several uncertainties, the NGOs that came to help were the lifelines in this massive disaster relief operation—without their support, so many people would have been left behind. My experience has taught me that efficient and effective disaster management and humanitarian assistance require communication, and that communication is vital not only within an NGO, but between all the players. All entities involved—the NGOs, INGOs, the civil society, governments, individuals, communities, and the corporate sector—need to take a holistic approach when providing assistance to communities in distress.

References

Cuddalore Collectorate. 2005. *Tsunami and one year after: Report by the Relief and Rehabilitation Department.* Cuddalore: Cuddalore Collectorate.

Family Care Foundation. 2005. *India tsunami: Insights from humanitarian aid and relief teams.* http://www.familycare.org/network/i06.htm.

Fritz Institute. 2005. *Recipient perceptions of aid effectiveness: Rescue, relief and rehabilitation in tsunami affected India and Sri Lanka.* http://www.fritzinstitute.org/PDFs/findings/NineMonthReport.pdf.

Hedman, E. 2005. The politics of the tsunami response. Special issue, *Forced Migration Review.* http://www.fmreview.org/FMRpdfs/Tsunami/full.pdf.

Helping Hand. 2008. *Tsunami update from the Tamil Nadu, India.* http://www.helpinghandonline.org/Tsunami_india_c_report.html.

Kumaran, M. 2008. The civil society in India. In *Comparative perspectives on civil society,* ed. R. Dibie. Lanham, MD: Lexington Books.

Oxfam. 2005. *Targeting poor people: Rebuilding lives after the tsunami.* http://www.oxfam.org.uk/resources/policy/conflict_disasters/downloads/bn_tsunami_6months.pdf.

Sooryamoorthy, R., and K. D. Gangrade. 2001. *NGOs in India: A cross-sectional study.* Westport, CT: Greenwood.

Tata Institute of Social Sciences. 2005. *The state and civil society in disaster response: An analysis of the Tamil Nadu tsunami experience.* Bombay: Tata Institute of Social Sciences.

United Nations. 2005. Tsunami—One year after: A joint UN report—India.

World Bank. 1995. Working with NGOs: A practical guide to operational collaboration between the World Bank and non-governmental organizations. Operations Policy Department, World Bank.

10

Sociocultural Frame, Religious Networks, Miracles

Experiences from Tsunami Disaster Management in South India

Seiko Sugimoto, Antonysamy Sagayaraj, and Yoshio Sugimoto

Natural hazards and disasters happen all over the world, and they bring great losses to human beings and their assets. The physical sciences, especially geophysics, geology, seismology, and meteorology, have been vying with each other to develop a model to predict these sudden events correctly in terms of time, place, and magnitude and to contribute to more effective disaster management. As greater concern has arisen among administrators and policy makers to find an acceptable way to attend to the needs of affected people, scholars of area studies, policy studies, and city planning have also participated in policy making for restoration after disasters. In contrast, the social sciences, especially anthropology, sociology, and human geography, have not been very active in the field of disaster management. However, our field research in the tsunami-affected areas of South India has shown various problems in the recovery process caused by the lack of knowledge of the culture and socioeconomic relations of local communities. We examine the experiences of the recent tsunami disaster in South India and argue that the social sciences play an essential role in effective disaster management, illustrating the importance of understanding sociocultural factors.

In the first section of this chapter, "The Importance of Sociocultural Perspectives," we will discuss the issue of the significance of sociocultural information on local communities in four phases of disaster management—rescue, relief, rehabilitation, and disaster prevention—pointing out examples of troubles caused by irrelevant relief measures undertaken based on stereotyped images of tsunami victims and by inappropriate aid policies for rehabilitation that disregard local demands. In the second section, "The Role of Religious Institutions in Relief," we will examine the existing sociocultural networks in local societies, focusing especially on religious networks that could attend to the needs of disaster relief immediately. In the third section, "Socioreligious Power Relations and the Post-tsunami Spread of Miracle Stories," we will discuss the new dimensions of socioreligious power relations that appeared in the tsunami-affected areas of South India.

The Importance of Sociocultural Perspectives

Scholars from the natural and political sciences gathered data and tried to estimate the physical and material damages of the tsunami disaster at the national, regional, and district levels from a macro perspective. NGOs that rushed to disaster-stricken towns and villages for relief activities got information of damages at village and household levels, from a microscopic perspective. However, it seems that the advisories based on such research and activities were not enough to get an overall picture of the damage inflicted on local society, and therefore fell short for planning appropriate restoration policies. In addition to the macroscopic and microscopic perspectives, there may be another perspective in the middle range wherein the principles of anthropology, sociology, and human geography may have relevance, as they recognize regional socioeconomic relations in examining the damages in detail. Also, we should not ignore the influence and impact of local sociocultural factors and power relations in assessing the damages caused by natural processes like tsunamis. Sometimes the natural disaster itself must be understood as in part the result of man-made conditions. For example, to understand the extensive damage inflicted on Muslim fishermen, who had lived on a riverbank near Nagapattinam town, by the backflow of water from the tsunami waves, we should not overlook the sociocultural conditions of the victims—they had to select domiciles in such a risky area because of their occupation as river fishermen and their low social status, which guaranteed no land rights. In another case, the destruction of the environment caused by the development of shrimp farms, which necessitated cutting palm trees along the seashore, might have increased the damages of natural disasters. The difference in how much knowledge people had of natural hazards was also a crucial factor in determining whether potential victims would suffer heavily or be equipped to ward off calamity. We should also note man-made disasters such as unequal distribution of relief measures and delay in the reach of help with reference to different social groups; moreover, in terms of the accessibility of relief measures, the degree of solidarity of local communities matters much.

Disaster management consists of four phases: rescue, relief, rehabilitation, and disaster prevention. One of the most important points to note through all these phases is that the disaster-stricken area is a sociopolitical space. In the beginning, in the rescue and relief stages just after a natural hazard has happened, it is important to collect information immediately on the status of each village and on the local demand for relief, which differs depending on the sociocultural characteristics of the affected community; at the same time, it is vital to circulate among victims information on the distribution of food and other relief items by government and NGO agencies. It goes without saying that without knowledge of the socioeconomic constructs of people and of their multilayered local networks, such as those of kinship, caste, fishermen's cooperative societies, political parties, and religion, we cannot start effective rescue and relief activities, and instead we may face unnecessary hurdles in relief operations.

The area south of the lighthouse area at Marina beach in Chennai along the coast to the Adayar river mouth is dotted with fishing hamlets occupied by multistory apartments constructed by the Slum Clearance Board of Tamil Nadu. Nochikuppam, at the northern end of this stretch, is one of the well-known fishing hamlets in the city. In the south, abutting the river Adayar, is Srinivasapuram, located in the Foreshore Estate area of the city. Srinivasapuram reported great damages to property and people during the 2004 tsunami. Although it is called a fishing village, it has a large number of nonfishing households, comprised of people coming from outside to live there. Human loss during the tsunami was greater among those nonfishing households. It is said that when aid was given immediately after the tsunami, friends and relatives of members of these nonfishing households arrived in this fishing village to claim a share of the donations, although they were not residents of the hamlet. The fishing households and the leaders of the fishing community of this hamlet objected to this, insisting that aid agencies distribute relief through them only. Thus some conflicts among the households came to the surface. Aid agencies distributed more boats than were required in this hamlet with its number of nonfishing households. They distributed catamarans, too, which are not much used for fishing these days. In another rehabilitation village near Chennai, occupied by uprooted fisherfolks, a solar-powered fish drier donated by an NGO was completely useless, as the people there catch fish only for local markets.

Our field research in the tsunami-affected areas on the Nagapattinam coast has indicated various problems in the recovery process, which seem to surface mainly from the gap between the simple stereotyped images held by aid agencies about the affected regions and the demands of the affected people, which vary from community to community. After the tsunami, various international and local organizations participated in the relief and rehabilitation of the victims in South India. Our research indicated that Christian and communist organizations started the initial efforts quickly and effectively provided relief and rehabilitation. These organizations already had a close relationship with the local people through their daily activities and also had wide national and international networks through which they could smoothly gather the human power and materials to conduct relief measures. On the other hand, sometimes the relief provided by international NGOs, based as it was on stereotypical notions of victims of natural hazards, actually hampered effective relief and rehabilitation work. The general image that fishermen are poor encouraged the aid agencies to provide boats and to distribute used clothes, but fishermen were not ready to accept used clothes. The construction of temporary shelters with tin roofs and without floors in an area of hot climate and monsoon rains was not an effective remedy.

The fishing industry at Nagapattinam area is characterized by an economically stratified society. Most of the fishermen who own big boats and fiber boats with an outboard motor are Kallars or Chettiyars. (Kallar is the name of a caste group found largely in the Thanjavur district of Tamil Nadu. Chettiyars are a trading and farming community in South India.) Those shipowners hire their relatives and Dalit (low-caste) laborers, realizing a reasonable profit with coastal fishery for one day and deep-sea fishery for three days. Their total catch is classified into several categories: prawns are sold to export companies; big, high-priced fish go to fish traders, who transport them to big towns in other states like Kerala; and the rest is for local markets, where many of the peddlers of the fish are women from the fishing community. From May to July, fisherfolks who have an outboard motorboat sail out almost 120 km (72 miles) away from Nagapattinam, for example, to Jagatapatinam and Malipattu in the north in Tanjavur district, and to Tondu and Kattumavary in the south in Pattukottai area. Some fishermen escaped the damages of the tsunami as they had left their boats with partners in those remote areas. Dalits, who live in quarters near the seashore, are laborers in fishing or fishing-related activities onshore. The fishing industry in Nagapattinam supports many from nonfishing households, too, such as laborers, traders, and peddlers. However, the tsunami relief fund was distributed mainly to fishermen in the form of compensation for fishing boats because of the stereotypical idea that the tsunami waves hit the fisher-

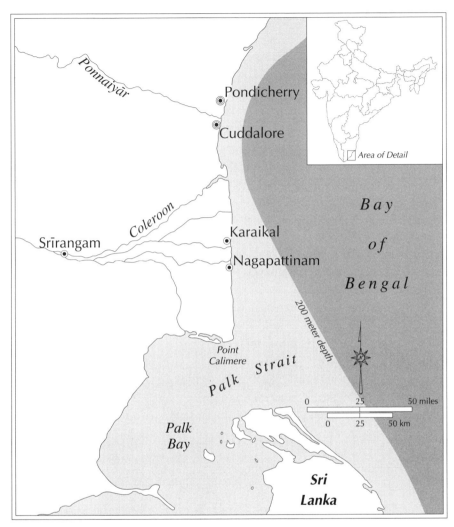

Fig. 10.1. Map of the Nagapattinam coast.

men only, and, in fact, because fishermen's cooperative societies in the area enjoy very strong political patronage. As a result, the disparity between rich fisherfolks and poor laborers has grown since the tsunami.

The economy of the Nagapattinam area consists mainly of four characteristic aspects: a large-scale fishing and fishing-related business; a large tourism industry of holy places; agriculture in suburban areas; and the aquaculture of shrimp farming. The affected communities were not composed only of fishermen—nor only of people directly related to the fishing industry—but also of other constituents who engaged in the other three industries, especially farmers, to whom the aid for relief and rehabilitation was delayed and sometimes neglected. In Nagapattinam, farmers consist of various castes: Iyars, Chettiyars, Kallars, or Dalits. Most of the Dalit farmers are agricultural laborers or small-scale landowners. They cultivate mainly rice, though a few of them grow cash crops like tobacco, jasmine flowers, cashew nuts, or mangoes. They suffered from scanty harvests caused by dry weather in 2002 and 2003, and, in 2004, their crops were badly damaged by saltwater intrusions thanks to the tsunami. However, they did not receive enough from the distribution of the relief fund. Many farmers have been forced to sell some portion of their land to the owners of shrimp-farming aquacultures, most of whom are rich businessmen from outside the Nagapattinam region. Aquaculture has already worsened the situation since seawater from aquaculture ponds has seeped to nearby farmlands. Thus farmers, besides damages from the tsunami, face man-made environmental damages, too. Yet, the relief provided to them was comparatively very small.

In Velanganni, a holy town situated 10 km (6.2 miles) south of Nagapattinam town, many pilgrims, both from inside and outside of the district, and workers engaged in tourism lost their lives to the tsunami. Most of the merchants and traders were Chettiyars, Christians, or Kallars, and migrant workers were from various areas like Kelala, Madurai, Tirunelveli, Pondicherry, and Mumbai. Though the tsunami was a severe blow to tourism, the damages to this industry were not eligible for compensation. In addition, victims who were not permanent inhabitants of the Nagapattinam region could not receive compensation money.

From the above experiences in the recent tsunami in South India, we realized that the difficulty of affected people was caused both by natural disaster and man-made social differences. That is why anthropological, sociological, and human geographic research should contribute to disaster management: in the relief phase, for assessment of damage and for collecting detailed data of the real demand of each local community; in the rehabilitation phase, for restoring businesses and confirming rights to lost assets and for proposing the rehabilitation policy suitable to each local community to prevent further difficulty caused by man-made conditions. These social sciences should also take part in the disaster prevention phase. In Japan, after the Kobe-Awaji earthquake in 1995, anthropologists and human geographers began to join in various activities for disaster prevention. For example, in Kushimoto-cho in Wakayama Prefecture, in cooperation with teachers of local secondary schools, anthropologists have encouraged and supported schoolchildren in collecting memories of past big earthquakes and tsunami waves as an educational endeavor and have assisted inhabitants in disseminating local knowledge of natural disasters. In the Ogura area in Kyoto Prefecture, as a part of precautions against earthquakes and floods, geographers and anthropologists have done research on both written histori-cal materials and oral accounts of large natural disasters that have hit this area in the past. And geographers have prepared maps of disaster-stricken areas to promote awareness of disaster prevention so as to strengthen the prepared-ness of the citizens. Anthropologists have participated in constructing effective local networks for emergencies through local online networking systems. If we were to pool these experiences gained in Japan and put them to good use in disaster prevention in tsunami-stricken areas in South India, we would be better equipped to establish a disaster management system in India.

The Role of Religious Institutions in Relief

The deadly tsunami of December 26, 2004, brought extensive damage to people, infrastructure, and utilities. Hours before the official (government) agencies or NGOs arrived, it was religious organizations that rose to the occasion by collecting the corpses, providing medical treatment to the injured, digging through devastated structures to extricate those who were trapped, handing out food, comforting and counseling the traumatized, and sheltering the dis-placed. The second author of this chapter participated in relief works in the Kanyakumari area during January 2005 and carried out fieldwork in the same area from February 20 to March 5, 2005, on the questions of the role of reli-gious institutions in relief and rehabilitation works.

In this section of the chapter, the group communication enacted by religious networks in managing the tsunami disaster is examined. First, concepts, defi-nitions, and types of communication are underlined, and the role of religious networks immediately after the tsunami is analyzed. The study looks into the communal disharmony (in the case of Nagapattinam) or harmony (in the case of Kanyakumari) that was noted during the relief and rehabilitation activi-ties, apart from the caste equations within Christian circles in Kanyakumari. Organizations belonging to three major religions—Hinduism, Christianity, and Islam—are included in the present observations.

Signs and symbols must have been the initial devices for human beings' communication, and then speech and language gave us a great facility to express and to conceptualize thoughts in a more systematic way. Language became an important vehicle for interpersonal and group communication. The next stage within this process of development was the slow and steady discovery of writing. Writing seems to have developed from drawing simple pictures and

paintings of animals, later moving on to expressing ideas with pictures or styl-
ized drawings, and from there using simple letters to convey specific sounds.
The invention of the printing press is considered one of the most important
developments of modern civilization. The third and current stage of progress
is the "communication revolution," variously known as the age of mass media,
information technology, the information superhighway, and so on. Communication is now very much associated with mass media, including print media,
radio and television, and the Internet. An act of communication includes an
initiator, a recipient, a mode of conveyance, a message, and an effect. For this
study, it is important to understand the concept of the receiver of the message—in other words, the audience. These are the listeners, viewers, and readers
of all the information and messages. Communicators shape their messages to
fit the perceived needs of their audience; they modulate according to the level
of receptiveness, the degree of readiness to accept, and the mode of delivery;
sometimes there is an extra factor in the communicator-audience situation.
The audience situation is central to a process that is essentially interactive and
subject to a wide range of social, cultural, economic, political, religious, and
environmental influences. There are two types of audience, *audience-as-public*
and *audience-as-market*. The audience-as-public relates to people as receivers
of messages of information, knowledge, education, and enlightenment as well
as entertainment. The difference between audience-as-public and audience-
as-market is simple but at the same time quite profound: audience-as-public
defines its function as being to *serve*, whereas audience-as-market thinks only
of how to *sell*.

Types of Communication

There are four basic levels or types of communication: intrapersonal communication, interpersonal communication, group communication, and mass
media communication. Mass communication gets maximum emphasis and
priority and is very popular too. By definition, it is a communication that is
aimed at the masses, and this requires a greater need for technology. Whereas
in interpersonal communication, the sender and the receiver are either present
to each other or can hear one another (as in long-distance telephone conver-
sation), making communication a two-way reality, the same cannot be said
of mass communication. Mass media communication takes its messages to
all the members of a larger audience simultaneously. The current technology
of the Internet is also a part of mass media. In the event of a disaster, which
may disable communication technology, group communication seems to be
more dependable. In my fieldwork, I observed that group communication was

adopted by various local religious networks that were familiar with the local population and enjoyed its regard and respect.

In this chapter, a plea is made to state and central governments to recognize the role of religious institutions and organizations—which have a vast local, national, and international network—in the four phases of disaster management: rescue, relief, rehabilitation, and disaster prevention. Governments can profitably utilize religious organizations' services by collaborating with them at all levels of disaster management.

The 2004 Tsunami

Mutual intolerance often is a source of tension among different religious communities in India. After the tsunami, however, religious organizations rose above prejudices and united for the service of humanity. The churches, mosques, and temples worked together to help the people.

Velanganni, located 10 km (6.2 miles) from Nagapattinam, houses the magnificent seventeenth-century shrine the basilica of Our Lady of Health. Known as the Lourdes of the East, Velanganni attracts not only Catholic pilgrims but also people of other religions from different parts of India and abroad. On December 26, the numerous lodging houses in the town were overflowing with pilgrims who had gathered for the special Christmas Mass. The killer waves hit while the Mass was being held in Malayalam. (The shrine holds mass in Tamil, Telugu, Malayalam, and English on specified days.) Hundreds of pilgrims, including many children, were taking a dip in the "holy" sea, and scores of children from the local communities were playing close to the sea. Shops lining the shore were crowded with pilgrims looking for mementos. Most of these people had no chance against the giant waves.

A 100-member team of volunteers from a Hindu *muth* (organization) of Kundrakudi in Sivaganga district, about 150 km (93.2 miles) away, led by Ponnambala Adigal, the head of the muth, and a 15-member team of Muslim youth from Nagore, 20 km (12.4 miles) away, also a tsunami-affected village, worked with local people and volunteers from many districts to bury the dead. They also helped clear the debris to open up the roads for vehicles. Ponnambala Adigal, following his predecessors, rushed to help the needy people, recollecting the service of his muth during the Mandaikkadu communal riots in Kanyakumari district in the late 1970s, when Hindus boycotted Christian fishermen. Then the senior Adigal helped fishermen resume the sale of fish by himself taking out a fish and launching the sale. "The killer waves did not discriminate between men, and many closed ranks to face the challenge," said Ponnambala Adigal, who also distributed food and clothes. Rector Fr. Xavier said the church had accommodated victims of all faiths. Its canteen provided food to the affected people, and relief materials were pouring in from different parts of the country and abroad, he said.

The Parankippettai Islamic Ikkya Jamaat (United Islamic Society of Parankippettai village) rushed to the help of people around the little town near Chidambaram, another popular pilgrim center. Within minutes of the information reaching it, the Jamaat Committee launched massive relief operations in places such as Chinnur, Indira Nagar, Puduppettai, Pudukuppam, and Velingarayanpettai. The youth of the community, numbering about 5,000, rescued many people and arranged for the hospitalization of the injured. An ambulance given as a gift to the Jamaat by a Singapore-based devotee came in handy for the purpose. The volunteers saved about 400 people. "Our boys joined the efforts of the district administration in rescuing people and recovering bodies," said O. A. W. Bawajan, secretary of the Jamaat. The organization also took up relief operations, sheltering and feeding about 15,000 persons in four camps. The Jamaat provided shelter to non-Muslims, too, in mosques. Mr. Bawajan commented, "For us, human lives are more important than the sanctity of places of worship."

In Nagore also, where hundreds of people died and a large number of families were displaced, the Saint Hazrath Saiyed Shahul Hameed Qadir Oli Dargah, which attracts pilgrims from all communities, did remarkable service. The *dargah* (mosque or shrine) provided shelter to about 4,000 people, and its volunteers played a key role in retrieving bodies, arranging for burial or cremation, and providing assistance to the survivors. Relief materials were received from hundreds of regular visitors to the dargah from all over the country and distributed to the victims. About 250 bodies of fishermen and others, including 18 Hindus killed by the tsunami, were buried in the dargah compound, relaxing the usual religious rules, said a spokesperson of the dargah.

Temples in several places were also serving as camps for victims. At Thirumalai Rayan Pattinam in Karaikal, the affected fishermen from Pattinacherry were accommodated in a Siva temple. A camp office of the Pondicherry government functioned from there. One of the trustees was seen distributing kerosene stoves to the families sheltered in the temple.

The Catholic Relief Services in India and Caritas India jointly responded with twenty-three local partners in Tamil Nadu, Andhra Pradesh, Kerala, and the Andaman and Nicobar islands to alleviate the suffering of 430,000 displaced victims in 299 relief camps. St. John's Medical College Hospital of Catholic Bishops' Conference of India (CBCI) was asked by the World Health Organization to set up a disease surveillance cell for the Nicobar Islands. Indo-Global Social Service Society (IGSSS) and Action for Food Production (AFPRO) are other church-related NGOs involved in the relief and rehabilitation work on the southern coast of India.

Thus the different religious groups were at the frontlines of the disaster response and continued to bring relief and long-term aid to the hardest-hit states of South India. The tsunami program of the religious organizations in India represents perhaps the best illustration of their work with partners and their investment in disaster preparedness and mitigation. Religious institutions and their networks on the ground responded literally within hours of the tsunami, providing food, water, shelter, and clothing. They provided emergency tents, temporary shelters, and permanent homes. In addition to rebuilding homes, they also repaired or built major infrastructure such as hospitals, roads, bridges, schools, and other community buildings. Emergency assistance, restoration of livelihood education, and child protection were other areas in which religious institutions helped maintain the continuity of life in coastal communities. Special efforts were made to ensure children were attending school and to keep the learning environment intact. Religious groups provided teacher training, school equipment, and uniforms and other materials. The interventions were intended not only to ensure the continued education of children but also to protect them from exploitation or dropping out of school. Religious organizations thus spent millions of rupees to provide food supplies, basic household items, and other emergency needs in the wake of the disaster and through the course of the year. Measures to provide safe water and sanitation, vital needs for a healthy environment, were taken. They helped in reconstructing the health delivery system, training health care workers, and providing trauma counseling and community health education.

Socioreligious Power Relations and the Post-tsunami Spread of Miracle Stories

On December 12, 2004, repairs to one of the well-known churches of South India, Santhome Cathedral, located at Chennai, Tamil Nadu State, in South India, were completed. It was expected that thousands of visitors would assemble at the church, which attracts many tourists because of its tomb venerating St. Thomas, one of the apostles of Jesus. Velanganni, located south of Chennai in Nagapattinam district, is a pilgrimage center for Indian Christians as the holy place of the shrine basilica of Our Lady of Health, and it is well connected by road and rail. With improved facilities, new rail station, and broad-gauge link, this holy place will receive further crowds of visitors. Both Chennai (Santhome) and Nagapatinam (Velanganni) are the places where mainly Portuguese settled and as such became the two bases for Portuguese Catholics.

In the 2004 tsunami, the shrines at Santhome and Velanganni did not suffer any loss, though the surrounding fishing community did suffer. The fact that the shrines and the pilgrims assembled therein were safe during the tsunami led to the spread of modern "miracle stories" among Christian followers (e.g., "Two Catholic Churches in India Were Miraculously Saved from Terrifying Tsunamis," http://www.tdm.org/News/TwoChurchesInIndiaSavedFromTsunamis .htm). For instance, the article titled "Santhome Miracle" in the *New Indian Express* was circulated among Christians through Web sites and other media. On the other hand, there were criticisms by anti-Christian religious adherents questioning why St. Thomas and Mary had not saved all believers. In times of disaster, religion plays a great role, both materially, as we have seen above, and spiritually, as a savior. At the same time, it brings hidden conflicts and disputes to the forefront.

Santhome Cathedral

The history of Christianity in South India starts with St. Thomas, one of the twelve apostles of Jesus; "the St. Thomas legend" is widely believed in both India and Sri Lanka. Christianity in South India can be traced quite far back: by AD 200, the Orthodox tradition had been established in the region. It is known that a bishop was sent from Jerusalem to India in AD 345, and Cosmas Indicopleustes, a Greek writer of the sixth century AD, reported the presence of Christian communities in the southwest and in Sri Lanka.

There are various theories as to whether St. Thomas came to India or Sri Lanka, and no conclusion has yet been reached on this point. But from the point of view of anthropological studies, it is certainly true that such kinds of legends have been actively narrated, and people do believe in them. With reference to the legends of the life of St. Thomas, the following pilgrimage spots in Chennai are some of the revered ones for Christians:

- Little Mount (Chinnamalai) cave, where St. Thomas was believed to have hidden himself. The church was built in 1559;
- St. Thomas Mount, from which place, it is said, he was taken away and attained martyrdom. It was built on the hill in 1523 by the Portuguese (see photo 10.1);
- Santhome Cathedral, the great shrine where St. Thomas's relics are kept. It was established in 1606 (photo 10.2).

(above) Photo 10.1. St. Thomas Mount.
(Photo by P. P. Karan.)

(right) Photo 10.2. Santhome
Cathedral, Mylapore, Chennai.
(Photo by P. P. Karan.)

St. Thomas is known as Sao Thome (San Thome) in Portuguese, and the area around the church is called Santhome. Santhome Cathedral is located within the city of Chennai in the Mylapore area, which is close to the seashore. In the neighborhood are the Kapaleeshwarar temple and the famous Marina and Eliot beaches, which attract tourists in large numbers. According to believers, St. Thomas was originally enshrined in this place, but it was not until 1522 that the Portuguese constructed the present church, to which the tomb and relics were shifted. In 1606 the church became a cathedral. It was destroyed in 1893, and in 1896 the present beautiful Gothic-style structure was completed. The relics of St. Thomas are enshrined in the underground area in front of the altar in the cathedral.

It seems that since ancient times miracle stories centering around St. Thomas have been recorded and widely propagated in the European world. It is needless to say that the miracle is an indispensable factor in the divinity claims of saints, holy men, and even Jesus Christ. Since the beginning of Christianity, almost all miracle stories pertain to the cure of diseases or the prevention of disasters. There are the miracles St. Thomas is said to have performed, all carefully catalogued by the Portuguese: 19 people raised from the dead, 260 exorcised of their demons, 330 cured of leprosy, 250 of blindness, 120 of paralysis, and 20 of dumbness. And there is a famous curse of Cochin, that its inhabitants might suffer from elephantiasis, which is now called St. Thomas Foot (D'Souza 2009).

Medieval European travelers also reported miracle stories pertaining to St. Thomas. For instance, the Italian missionary Monte Corvino stated that "if the soil from the holy tomb of the saints is applied on the patient, the injury will be cured immediately, and the vacuum created by the removal of soil will automatically be filled the next day as original" (Yule 1866). Moreover, Marco Polo also believed in such miracle stories (Latham 1958, 15). He noted that the Christians who went there on pilgrimage collected soil to carry home from the place where St. Thomas was killed. A potion made from this red soil, it was believed, cured a sick person immediately. Marco found it true with four sick persons, and he himself brought some of this soil to Venice and cured many people with it. Even today the shop at Santhome Cathedral sells St. Thomas cards along with a tiny packet of this red soil.

Many other wondrous miracles are believed to happen in this place daily, especially the healing of Christians who are crippled or deformed. On the one hand, such miracle stories increase the religious value of a holy place. On the other hand, they can bring social and political conflicts to the forefront. In India these conflicts take the form of communal riots. In the succeeding paragraphs, miracle politics in the case of Velanganni Basilica shrine, a pilgrimage place for Christians, are looked into in a larger context.

St. Thomas's Miraculous Pole

On December 26, 2004, the Indian Ocean Tsunami devastated the coast of Tamil Nadu. Though it is impossible to know exactly how many deaths occurred, per the official records there were about 8,000 deaths in Tamil Nadu, of which Nagapattinam district alone reported 6,065 persons dead (2,406 women, 1,883 men, and 1,776 children). As it was a Sunday morning, the child victims were mainly those who usually go out to the shore to collect small fish and sell them for pocket money. Of the adults who died, most victims were older people, those who would have passed on traditions to the next generation; it is a great blow to the fishing community.

In Chennai, there were large numbers of victims from the northern part of the city, known as Kasimedu, where the small-scale fisherfolk lived, and from the citizens' relaxation spot of Marina beach and its southern Santhome beach. Kasimedu hamlet of fishermen stretches for about 2 km along the shore north of Chennai port, near Ennore fishing harbor. It is occupied by the tiny huts of fishermen.

Most of the victims of this area are poor fisherfolk, and, moreover, most of them have built their huts illegally within 500 m (1,640 feet) of the shore, against coastal zone regulation laws. Although the state government built rehabilitation structures beyond 500 m from the coast, many people did not move to the new dwellings because their workplace is the seashore. The state government decided to render partial assistance to those who lived in the area 200–500 m (656–1,640 feet) from shore and not to give any assistance to those who lived within 200 m. However, in reality there has been no strict enforcement of coastal zone regulation laws.

Santhome beach, located in the stretch from the lighthouse to the Adayar river mouth, witnessed large-scale destruction due to the tsunami waves. Here Santhome Cathedral is one of the central landmarks of the area. This area is inhabited largely by Christians, and many of the fishermen in the coastal area are also Christians. The area near the Adayar mouth was the most affected. To the south, there lies a large expanse of the Theosophical Society and an elite residential area where damage was minimal.

Santhome Cathedral is a little away from the seashore. When the tsunami waves hit the area of Mylapore, they reached the backshore area, but the shrine was not at all affected. This is considered by Christian devotees another Santhome miracle. Father Lawrence Raj, the parish priest of the Santhome Cathedral basilica, has been asked numerous questions about the story of St. Thomas's miraculous pole, supposed to have kept the sea away on December 26. The 450-year-old church, located a few meters away from the water, remained unaffected by the tsunami, even though buildings in line with it got wet by tsunami waves. The belief, says Father Lawrence, is that when St. Thomas planted the pole at the top of the steps leading to the cathedral, he said the sea would not pass that point. "But that is the legend," stresses the father. "Nobody knows whether it is true." The priest sounds wary of declaring it a miracle. He offers logical explanations, like perhaps the church was spared because it is built on a higher level. "But, then," he reasons, "the lighthouse is on roughly the same plain, and the water reached it."

This pole is just like an ordinary flag-hoisting tower on the side of the building facing the sea, and it was not at all remarked upon before the tsunami, neither by tourists nor by devotees. But today, if you look carefully at its position, it certainly appears to be preventing the flowing in of water from the sea. Further, recently an inscription has been added to the pole on the church side: "ST. THOMAS POLE: IN GRATITUDE TO GOD FOR SAVING SANTHOME FROM TSUNAMI 2004" (photo 10.3 and photo 10.4).

This pillar has an additional story relating to St. Thomas and the floods. The story goes that a village in the Mylapore area was flooded when a huge tree trunk fell across the river. The local king brought a royal pachyderm to lug it away, but the task seemed impossible. Then St. Thomas came along, removed the girdle from around his waist and handed it to a bystander, asking him to yank the log with it. He did so and the log moved easily. There is a mural illustrating the episode in the cathedral museum. The story of the wooden log that St. Thomas miraculously lifted was borrowed from the Jagannath Puri *stala purana* (place history as narrated by religious works) by the Portuguese ("St. Thomas Saved Himself, Abandoned Fishermen," http://hamsa.org/ tsunami,htm). Bishop Raj's miracle stories were introduced through various media, initially in the national newspaper *New Indian Express,* Chennai edition, on January 4, 2005, in an article written by Susan Muthalaly titled "Santhome Miracle." This story was further disseminated on the Internet in "How Tsunami Waves Did Not Touch Santhome Cathedral" (January 4, 2005). In addition, many other Catholic sites quoted this, causing the story to be further known. However, the bishop himself does not say whether the story is true or false.

Velanganni and Miracle

Velanganni shrine is located about 10 km south from Nagapattinam town. The neighborhood of Nagapattinam has been a base for marine trade since the

(right) Photo 10.3. St. Thomas Pole at Santhome Cathedral. (Photo by P. P. Karan.)

(below) Photo 10.4. Marker at the base of St. Thomas Pole, which Christians believe saved the area from the tsunami. (Photo P. P. Karan.)

Greco-Roman period. Tharangambadi (Tranquebar), north of Nagapattinam, was the base of Denmark's religious propagation mission during the colonial trade era and later. The shrine faces the Bay of Bengal, and the original shrine is located about 1 km away to the west of the current main church.

Velanganni is a small town, having a population of 10,000 people, but during the pilgrim season hundreds of thousands of pilgrims make this place as lively as a large city. Particularly during the great festival season from August 29 to September 8, every nook and corner is filled with pilgrims who visit the shrine, arriving on foot from all over Tamil Nadu. The devotees, with a strapped pair of bundles slung over their shoulders, daring the scorching heat, tread a path hundreds of kilometers long to reach the far-off Velanganni basilica. This pilgrimage is as important to Christians as the pilgrimage to Sabarimalai in Kerala is to Hindus.

While Velanganni is a typical pilgrim center, it has also developed into a business area around the basilica. The town is provided with a post office, bank, police station, hospital, primary school, middle school, and other amenities. In addition, there are welfare institutions such as asylums for orphans and the elderly. Among these activities, lodging facilities for the pilgrims and gift shops are in a way "sacred business," and this may draw our attention to the power of the great shrine.

The basilica is built closer to the sea than the earlier one, and the building of the clergy, the museum of offerings (to the shrine), storage areas for basilica goods, and so on are located around the eastern entrance. In addition, on both sides of the road facing the sea there are rows of shops selling various gift items, and beggars are found sitting all along pleading for aid from visitors.

Most of the shops and residential houses in front of the gate to the shrine were washed away. In all probability the beggars lining the road must have also been dragged off to the sea by the tsunami waves, which reached a maximum height of 12 m (39.6 feet). The tsunami further moved up the river running along the side of the shrine and flooded the bus terminal at the backyard of the shrine, causing damage all around. However, the water just reached the stairs in front of the main gate of the shrine itself, and there was no damage at all to the shrine building. It is a fact that the water did not enter the shrine, which is of the same height as the maximum height of the tsunami waves. Therefore, the more than 1,000 people inside the shrine saying Christmas prayers when the tsunami hit were all safe and sound. All these factors formed part of the "miracle." Places far from the shoreline suffered due to floods, but not the shrine, which is close to the shore. This also added to the belief in a miracle, although the topography around the shrine must have played a role in influencing the varied impacts and flood reaches during the tsunami.

In the latter part of the sixteenth century, when Velanganni became a historic place, strained relations between the Portuguese and the Tanjavoor Nayaks at times resulted in religious conflicts. The Jesuit Manuel Barradas, who visited Nagapattinam in about 1615, recorded interesting local tales. The Amman temple at Nagapattinam had a large column of black stone in it, which was believed to have emerged from the sea. The Portuguese decided to steal it. But as they were about to do so, a cow let out a bellow so great it was heard by the Naique (chief of the community) in Tanjaor (Tanjavur), two days' journey away, and he prevented the Portuguese from taking it. Here again conflicts between Hindus and Christians are narrated, and as usual the Hindu symbol of the holy cow, as will be discussed later, appears. In legends of the origin of the Velanganni shrine and the history of Velanganni, the motifs of the holy cow and the Portuguese distinctly appear.

There are three miracle stories relating to Maria (Our Lady of Health) enshrined in Velanganni. The first two stories are the basic sources of myths involving the curing of diseases and the prevention of epidemics, and therefore this shrine has become a favorite among other religious devotees. The motif of the holy cow and milk appears very frequently in the origin of the mythology of Shiva temple. That is why this miracle story is very easily acceptable to Hindu religious devotees. Besides, Maria is worshipped as one among the innumerable goddesses, and therefore the difference in religion does not become an issue at all. It is said that both in daily life and during the great festival from August 29 to September 9, about 80% of the visitors are followers of the Hindu religion. It is the followers of Christianity who make the difference of religion an issue, when during the Mass religious confession and Holy Communion take place. Further, the prayer hall used by Christians for Mass is separate in the church from the main hall where most of the pilgrims assemble.

The third myth is the story of the prevention of marine disasters and calamities. Sometime during the sixteenth century, Our Merciful Mother rescued a few Portuguese merchant sailors from a violent storm that wrecked their ship. When the merchants reached the shore of Velanganni, they were taken by local fishermen to the thatched chapel. To give thanks and pay tribute to Our Lady, they built a small permanent chapel on their return trip. On subsequent visits they improved it. The merchants dedicated the chapel to Our Lady on September 8 to celebrate the feast of her nativity and to mark the date of their safe landing at Velanganni.

In the immediate aftermath of the tsunami, the number of people visiting the shrine dropped, and the tourism business suffered. Hotels and restaurants were closed down. Street vendors lost their business. As a result, nonfishermen, too, were disappointed with the loss of occupation and business. As the BBC put it, Velanganni, previously one of the busiest pilgrimage centers of Tamil Nadu, had become a "ghost town." The Christian population in the neighborhood of Velanganni village may not be large enough to support the shrine; patronage must come from far and wide. This is probably why the three stories of miracles arose, after the arrival of the Portuguese, and they were intentionally woven, taking their cue from the beliefs of the Hindus. This mythological common factor and the interchangeability of the Hindu goddess Maria and the Christian Mary enable the large number of Christian and Hindu pilgrims to assemble for the festivals and feasts. With this construct, religious influence may be seen with the life and routine of the people.

Since the great shrine does not have a foothold in the community of devotees, at times social and political issues come to the fore. Those who believe in the supremacy of Hinduism, especially Rashtriya Swayamsevak Sangh, are highly critical, questioning whether there is forcible conversion to Christianity under the pretext of assistance to sufferers around the shrine. There were cases at times when such criticism developed into violence against the fathers and nuns. As a result those associated with Christianity had to work secretly and conduct their activities in a subdued manner.

Velanganni also became involved in conflicts with Hindu nationalists and had to face the storm of communalism. As narrated in the miracle story, a ship sailing along the Cholamandalam (Coromandel) coast was wrecked offshore and saved by Maria; at that time the sailors offered prayers at the Velanganni Devi Kovil in that area. However, this temple of the goddess, Mada Kovil, was overpowered by the shrine of Velanganni, and at present it remains deserted a little away from the shrine. A recent report indicates that the stone statue of the goddess had been removed.

The Politics of Miracle Stories

The modern miracle stories created in the context of the great earthquake in the open sea and the great tsunami in the Indian Ocean are restricted neither to India nor to Christianity. James Pinker, on his Web page *Tsunami Miracle* dated January 17, 2005, searched via Google and stated that at that time there were 352,000 hits (www.tcsdaily). That number has now exceeded 1 million. Of course, most of them pertain to a somewhat different kind of "miracle"—of returning to normal life after disaster, the saving of life, and so on. However, religious miracle stories are also found in plenty. It is quite interesting to note that about ten stories of this variety centering around Christianity were included on the German Web site *Die Maechtige hand Jesu hat sie vor dem Tsunami Gerettet* (http://www.jmanjackal.net.deu/deups91).

The following is the most widely known story of such a miracle. On December 25, 2004, Christians in the town of Meulaboh in Aceh wanted to celebrate Christmas in a combined service, but the Muslims in that town objected and told them that if they wanted to celebrate Christmas they would have to do it outside the town area because Meulaboh is a Muslim town. The 400 Christians complied with this and went to a hill outside the city perimeter to hold their Christmas program there. As we know, the following morning there was an earthquake and the tsunami that followed destroyed the whole town of Meulaboh and almost everybody in it. The population of Meulaboh was practically wiped out—except for the 400 or so Christians who celebrated Christmas on a hill outside the town.

A few survivors of Meulaboh remarked, "The god of the Christians has punished us." Some of them asked, "Why are there so many of us who died in this disaster, and none of the Christians are destroyed?" If the 400 Christians had insisted on celebrating Christmas in that town according to their original plan, they would have perished, too. They can see this as the direct intervention of God to save his children in Meulaboh. This is the famous story told in "Saved by Humility" (http://www.snopes.com/religion/tsunami.asp).

Unfortunately, there is not enough evidence to support this story. On the other hand, it is well known that the person behind the story's spread is the pastor Willem Heckman. It is said that this pastor heard it from the pastor Arnold Abraham of Ambon, that Pastor Abraham got it from three Chinese pastors in the United States, and the Chinese pastors heard it from Meulaboh devotees.

Thus several modern miracle stories originated and spread. Miracles are the core of religion, and there are plenty of stories with such content, which may accelerate religious conflicts. There is an especially large number of such stories among Christians, who are fond of miracles. In the case of Muslims, photographs of the mosque on the shore that stood solid without any damage during the tsunami were collected and spread through the Net. With Hindus, there are examples given of how the idols of God on seashore shrines remained intact. However, at present miracle stories about Hindu temples are not as prevalent as those regarding Christian church miracles. Regardless, in India, whatever may be the religion, the power of miracle stories is unquestionable.

During great disasters religion, as well as spiritual salvation and miracles, provides substantial relief and rescue. Religion has an important meaning to that extent. In the case of the tsunami disaster, one important "miracle" was the disappearance of religious differences and conflicts. Citizens, unmindful of religious differences, helped all sufferers quite voluntarily. The Hindu temples, Christian churches, and Muslim mosques functioned as shelters. Santhome shrine and Velanganni shrine functioned as refugee shelters, and the famous Nagore mosque also was opened to refugees irrespective of their religion. The area around the dargah is usually known rather as a place of Hindu-Muslim conflict; but at the time of disaster such conflict disappeared.

The mythology and miracle stories of the earthquake and tsunami pertaining to both the St. Thomas shrine and the Velanganni shrine had political relevance. The miracle stories were used as tools in religious conflicts. In the case of India, this was reflected in the relations between Hindu nationalists and Christians, and, in the case of Indonesia, it was reflected in the relations of various sects of the majority of Muslims and the minority of Christians. Aceh in Indonesia, which felt the brunt of the disaster, is the state where originally the conflict between the two religions was critical, and, further, in India, particularly in Tamil Nadu among the fisherfolk affected by the tsunami, Christians were comparatively in the majority. Meanwhile, in Tamil Nadu the conflict between Hindus and Muslims was not as severe as in North India, and, moreover, in the context of the tsunami, the targeted Muslims were just a few. However, since the miracle stories by definition had a strong religious tint, their propagation, whether intentionally or unintentionally, amounts to the external elimination, both openly and covertly, of other religions. In that sense, the miracle stories have strong political meaning.

Especially in India, the activities of the Christian Church, NGOs, and social welfare and charity establishments were thought to be aiming at religious conversion, and as such invited the enmity of the Hindu nationalists. The Christian community has a very strong information network and is thus highly organized. The state government of Tamil Nadu also tried to use the strength of the Christian groups positively.

The Mata Amritanandamayi Mission of the State of Kerala, which has a following in Japan, too, donated 10 million rupees toward the relief and rehabilitation of tsunami victims. There were also other organizations, such as the Rishikesh Swamy Dayananda Educational Trust, which offered a positive helping hand. An NGO of Japan, the Japan Platform, received a request from the government to help, and this aid agency, a Christian one, played a key role in channeling aid. As a matter of fact, the Christian organization was the chief entity involved in aid. Though the consulate general of Japan in Chennai had planned a number of schemes, it could not implement them, as India did not allow the direct involvement of foreign governments. That may be the reason why it is written on the walls of the shelter: "This project is funded by your Japanese friends and the government of Japan through Japan Platform."

A look at the disputes surrounding the miracle of St. Thomas Pole and the Velanganni shrine shows that the tendency to criticize the unscientific attitude of Christianity is growing stronger. It is because the waves of communal conflicts and religious antagonism have been increasing since the 1990s. In the current age of the Internet, these miracle stories are circulated widely and instantaneously. As such, instead of fading, it appears that religious importance is strengthening. And, there is the hidden possibility of the modern religions turning as various blades of the sword in the form of relief and conflicts in every aspect of the age of globalization.

Note

Section 1, "The Importance of Sociocultural Perspectives," was written by Seiko Sugimoto; section 2, "The Role of Religious Institutions in Relief," by Antonysamy Sagayaraj; and section 3, "Socioreligious Power Relations and the Post-tsunami Spread of Miracle Stories," by Yoshio Sugimoto.

The field research was conducted from February 20 to March 5, 2005, by Dr. Seiko Sugimoto, Dr. Yoshio Sugimoto, Dr. Fukao Junichi (Takushoku University), Dr. S. Subbiah (Madras University), and Dr. Antonysamy Sagayaraj. The research was funded as a part of the Grant-in-Aid for Special Purposes by the Ministry of Education, Culture, Sports, Science and Technology, Japanese government, titled "Understanding the Whole Picture of the Sumatra Earthquake Tsunami Disaster in December 2004" (project leader: Professor Yoshiaki Kawata, Disaster Prevention Research Institute, Kyoto University).

References

D'Souza, Herman. 2009. *In the steps of St. Thomas.* Chennai: Disciples of St. Thomas.
Latham, Ronald Edward. 1958. *Marco Polo: The travels.* London: Penguin Classics.
Yule, H. 1866. "Notices of Cathay." *Proceedings of the Royal Geographical Society,* 270–78.

11

Achievements and Weaknesses in Post-tsunami Reconstruction in Sri Lanka

Martin Mulligan and Judith Shaw

Aside from Aceh in Indonesia, Sri Lanka suffered the worst impacts of the December 2004 tsunami. It took almost a year to compile accurate figures on what was lost, but the final tally made by the Sri Lankan government was that 35,322 people died, and a further 516,150 lost their homes; 65,275 homes were totally destroyed, and 38,561 were partially destroyed.[1] In the weeks and months following the tsunami, Sri Lankan civil society did a remarkable job in coming to the aid of the victims. Those who survived the waves, volunteers from Colombo, and international aid workers took quick action to collect the bodies, get everyone into temporary shelter, provide fresh drinking water, repair damaged roads and mangled bridges, and clear the debris. People went house to house in Colombo to collect donations of food, clothes, and medicine, and television studios and the national film school in Colombo became the clearinghouses for such donations. Privately owned trucks were made available, and they left—loaded with donations and volunteers—for the south and the east. Most people assumed that the mangled railway line that had connected Colombo to the south would take years to repair, yet it was made operational again within months.

Volunteers from around the world rushed to Sri Lanka and other countries impacted by the tsunami to help. A leader of the post-tsunami recovery effort in the badly affected town of Hambantota, Azmi Thassim, later reported that such volunteers included a few teams of highly organized and professional people who knew exactly what to do without getting in the way of the locals.[2] However, he stressed that many of the volunteer "experts," however well-meaning they may have been, expected overworked locals to make the necessary arrangements for them to offer their services and, as such, they were more trouble than they were worth. One writer (Rajasingham-Senanayake 2005) even suggested that the airfares and per diems used to support young and inexperienced volunteers who could not speak local languages might have been better used to build temporary houses. More usefully, perhaps, the aid response from Western governments and private individuals, the multilateral aid agencies, and international NGOs was swift and generous. In 2005 the Sri Lankan government received $93 million in grants for tsunami reconstruction projects, in addition to substantial concessional loans and debt relief (Central Bank of Sri Lanka 2006). It soon became apparent, however, that the politicization of aid processes and failures in public sector capacity and coordination would limit the effectiveness of reconstruction aid. Sri Lanka's low rate of aid utilization continues to be a problem, with significant bottlenecks in the implementation process, including deficient procurement procedures, a lack of counterpart funding, inadequate coordination and implementation, and weaknesses in project monitoring. There are doubts as to whether the large volumes of aid pledged can be effectively delivered to their intended targets. Indeed, a report in the *Gulf Times* on September 30, 2006, suggested that only 13% of the promised aid had been used, with the renewed civil conflict in the north and east being blamed for some blockages to the delivery of the aid.

Of course, the physical impacts of the tsunami were just the most visible, and in many ways they were the easiest to address. Despite the lack of preparation for such a disaster, the country rallied and huge donations of international aid—cash, boats, tents, bicycles, small-scale infrastructure, and more—came pouring in to help the victims get back on their feet. However, we will argue in this chapter that some of the decisions made in the immediate aftermath of the disaster will have negative long-term social consequences; the emotional wounds may never be fully healed; and a general failure of political leadership has seriously impeded the long-term recovery.

Much of the early aid from Colombo went to the south rather than the east, despite the fact that the greatest damage occurred in places along the east coast, from Ampara up to Jaffna. This was partly a result of the fact that news of the damage came much more quickly from the south than the east but was also a result of the long-standing conflict between the national government and the movement fighting for independence for the Tamil-dominated northeast. Areas along the east coast were under the control of the military wing of the Liberation Tigers of Tamil Eelam (LTTE), and distribution of aid to such areas quickly became a new source of tension between the government and the LTTE. The politicization of issues relating to tsunami relief was not a surprise, but what did come as a surprise to many Sri Lankans was the strength of the mood for peace that came in the immediate aftermath of the disaster. Television debates and newspaper articles were full of impassioned appeals to put aside past differences and turn the fragile ceasefire between the government and the LTTE into a meaningful peace agreement. Unfortunately, as we shall see, this opportunity was lost as politicians from both sides engaged in point scoring and brinkmanship. A golden opportunity was frittered away, and within a year of the tsunami the ceasefire was all but dead.

The Scope of the Problem

The tsunami affected a 1,000 km stretch of land from Jaffna in the north to Colombo in the southwest. Although the tsunami waves impacted nearly 65% of Sri Lanka's coastline, the local impacts varied considerably depending on landforms and the presence or otherwise of natural features—such as mangrove clusters—that could mitigate the damage. The worst destruction occurred in the northern and eastern provinces, which accounted for two-thirds of deaths and 60% of those displaced. One-third of the total deaths occurred in the eastern district of Ampara, where a large strip of flat land meets the sea.

Damage in the south and southwest was generally more moderate, with some protection provided by headlands, dunes, and steep coastal gradients. While there were pockets of acute damage in the southern districts of Galle and Hambantota, it is estimated that only 20% of the southern coastal population was affected, by comparison with up to 80% in the eastern districts of Ampara and Mullaitivu.

Initial predictions that the tsunami would shave more than a percentage point from GDP growth proved excessively pessimistic, and in fact GDP growth increased from 5.4% in 2004 to 6% in 2005 (Central Bank of Sri Lanka 2006). The relatively limited economic impact is due to the fact that the sectors that experienced the most extensive damage, fisheries and tourism, are relatively minor contributors to the national economy, and losses in these sectors were offset by a post-tsunami construction boom and strong growth in the manufacturing and inland plantation agriculture sectors, which were unaffected by the tsunami.

While the macroeconomic impact of the tsunami was limited, the localized effects were severe. Catastrophic human and asset losses and disruption to markets and social networks have sharply reduced employment and output.

Table 11.1. Estimated economic losses caused by the tsunami ($ millions)

Sector	Asset losses	Output losses	
Housing	340	—	65,275 houses destroyed; 38,261 houses damaged
Transport infrastructure	75	—	415 km of roads damaged; southern railway line damaged
Water and sanitation	42	—	Damage to pipelines, wells, and coastal irrigation facilities
Education and health	86	—	100 hospitals and clinics and 182 schools damaged or destroyed
Fisheries	97	200	20,000 fishing vessels damaged or destroyed
Tourism	250	130	58 of the country's 242 registered hotels damaged or destroyed
Other	110	—	
Total	1,000	330	

Sources: Asian Development Bank 2005; Central Bank of Sri Lanka 2006.

Human suffering was exacerbated by delays, inequities, and inefficiencies in housing and livelihood rehabilitation processes that have increased poverty and threatened social stability. As is usually the case with disasters in developing countries, impacts fell disproportionately among the poorest and most vulnerable population groups: fishing communities, shanty dwellers, and those living in the northern and eastern provinces, which prior to the tsunami had been ravaged by two decades of civil war.

Environmental Impacts

The most obvious environmental impacts came from the massive intrusion of saltwater into estuaries and freshwater systems adjacent to the coast and problems caused by new deposits of sand. Some coastal vegetation, which helped reduce the impacts of the waves on houses and other infrastructure, was damaged, although the trees generally withstood the impacts better than buildings. Anecdotal evidence suggests that most animals got themselves out of harm's way (seemingly sensing the approaching waves). Sri Lankan government figures suggest that 9,380 ha (23,449 acres) of cultivated land was badly affected by the waves and saltwater intrusions, including 3,600 ha (9,000 acres) of rice paddy, while some 60,000 wells were also contaminated with saltwater.[3] No figures are available on the saltwater contamination of coastal lagoons and wetlands, but there can be no doubt that such contamination had a bad impact on the coastal freshwater ecology. New sandbars cut some estuaries off from the sea, and dredging to create new connecting channels was a fairly low priority for local government. Less obvious environmental impacts include the sucking back into the sea of considerable debris—including some hazardous and toxic materials; the spread of weeds (notably prickly pear) in areas that were impacted by the waves; and damage to coral reefs from the coast of Sri Lanka out into the Indian Ocean and the Andaman Sea. The U.S.-based Nature Conservancy sent a team of experts to Sri Lanka within weeks of the disaster and it highlighted the likely impact on ecosystems of debris (2005). However, the team reported that damage to coral reefs had been less than many feared. The picture is complicated by the fact that inappropriate human developments were having negative impacts on coastal and marine environments long before the tsunami arrived. This included the clearing of coastal vegetation and the removal of sand dunes; a lack of meaningful control over the impact of fishing and harvesting on the stock of fish and other marine animals; and the mining of coral reefs—especially near Hikkaduwa—for lime. The problem in knowing the real extent of environmental damage is the lack of baseline data about what existed before the tsunami and a lack of capacity for monitoring any recovery. Environmental monitoring has never been a high priority in Sri Lanka, and the picture regarding the environmental impacts of the tsunami remained murky until the United Nations Environment Program sent in a team of thirty international experts in May 2005 to assess the situation. However, it also struggled with the lack of adequate baseline data to make any significant comparisons (2005).

Social Impacts

Sri Lanka had no inkling that it was vulnerable to such a disaster coming from the sea—although there are references to an earlier tsunami in mythology dating back about 2,000 years. The coastal communities could not have been less prepared for such a disaster; indeed a joke that quickly did the rounds suggested that when a minor official in the prime minister's department got a phone call warning that "Tsunami" was on its way from Indonesia, he sent a welcoming party to the airport to greet the Indonesian guest (whoever he might be). There were no local or regional disaster plans in place, and, indeed, when the approaching tsunami waves sucked back the shoreline by more than

1 km, many people ran *to* the beaches to see what was happening! The only thing that prevented a far greater death toll was the fact that the tsunami struck on a Sunday, which also happened to be a public holiday and a Buddhist religious day. Many schools within meters of the sea were empty, and significant numbers of people were visiting temples away from the coast.

The most obvious social impacts came from the loss of lives and the permanent injuries suffered by many survivors. Government figures suggest that the disaster left some 40,000 people needing long-term financial assistance.[4] This included women who lost their husbands, children who lost their parents, elderly people who lost younger family members, people who suffered severe injuries, and disabled people who lost their family support. The grief of the survivors was compounded by the fact that it sometimes took days or weeks for parents to relocate missing children, and thousands of people were simply declared "missing" for up to a year after the disaster. The government followed a policy of trying to place the new orphans with members of their extended families, but in many cases there were very few family members left alive.

According to an Oxfam report (MacDonald 2005), four times as many women as men died in the tsunami. Along the east coast the killer waves hit at a time when many women were taking their daily sea bath, and, in many areas, men and boys had much more experience than women and girls in climbing trees. Sri Lankan men and boys are much more likely to be able to swim than women and girls. Of course, this meant that many surviving children lost their mothers, and this loss compounded the fact that for many Sri Lankan households it is the women more than the men who leave to take up work in the Middle East and some Western countries. A growing number of Sri Lankan children are growing up without meaningful contact with their mothers.

Once the survivors got into temporary shelter, reports began to circulate of sexual violence committed against women and girls in the chaos that immediately followed the disaster (Fisher 2005). Sexual abuse and harassment of women appears to have continued in the emergency shelter camps (ibid.)— especially with many more male survivors than female—and conditions in the camps were very difficult for pregnant women and nursing mothers. The surviving women were left with even greater responsibility for caring for their own children or the children of missing relatives. While the men went out of the temporary camps to find what work they could, the women had to make their shelters into some kind of home and make sure that their children were safe in an unfamiliar environment. Furthermore, many of the surviving children had been traumatized by their experiences during the tsunami and its aftermath, and the responsibility for looking after their emotional needs fell mainly on the women.

There was also some division across Sri Lanka about how best to remember the dead. In the wake of the tsunami much attention focused on the fact that around 1,000 people died in a train that was hit by the waves at a place called Peraliya, near Hikkaduwa, north of Galle, and four of the battered carriages of that "ghost train" were left in place for a year as a kind of memorial. Of course, most of those who died in the train were not local to the area, and locals began to resent the constant stream of visitors to the wrecked carriages. On the eve of the first anniversary of the disaster the carriages were removed, and President Rajapakse attended a ceremony at the site. He announced that a more suitable permanent memorial would be built nearby. But of course the disaster was so widespread that a single national memorial seems quite inappropriate, and as the first anniversary approached many of the people in the south who had lost relatives told one of the authors that they were hoping for a modest local, religious ceremony to honor the dead in a dignified way. The anniversary led to repeat television showings of footage from the disaster, and this only reminded the victims of the horrors they had experienced. Local ceremonies were, on the whole, subdued and low-key, as the survivors wished. However, the problem of how best to remember the victims of the disaster—dead and living—will not subside with the passing of the years.

Governance Issues in the Reconstruction Process

The reconstruction process was impeded by deficiencies in governance at all levels. There were criticisms of policy design and implementation processes, worsened by a lack of clarity in objectives and costly policy shifts and reversals. The subjugation of the national interest to the personal interests of those in power is an entrenched feature of Sri Lankan politics. The pervasive politicization of the bureaucracy hampered the ability of government agencies to manage programs in a consistent and transparent manner, and corruption and political interference have influenced the distribution of aid resources. Within the bureaucracy deficiencies in technical and management capacity are exacerbated by poorly defined organizational structures—with a multiplicity of government agencies having overlapping functions—and poor coordination between levels of government and with the nongovernment sector. Political uncertainty, exacerbated by the civil conflict and the tendency of incoming governments to overturn the arrangements of their predecessors, has contributed to a poor investment climate, which has further slowed the reconstruction process. In view of the long-standing tensions between the Tamil northeast and the Sinhalese southwest, observers emphasized the importance of conflict-sensitive recovery strategies that should be manifestly fair and equitable, decentralized (to strengthen local institutions), pro-poor, and consciously designed to enhance the peace process (Uyangoda 2005). However, a combination of political opportunism and bad policy resulted in the blocking of reconstruction aid to the worst-affected northern and eastern provinces, contributing to the resumption of the decades-old civil conflict between the government and the LTTE.

Reconstruction was hampered by poor interagency coordination and a heavily centralized power structure. The propensity of incoming governments to establish new ministries on top of existing structures led to a proliferation of government agencies with overlapping policy responsibilities.[5] In the absence of effective policy coordination mechanisms, agencies tend to act in isolation, creating confusion and inhibiting the development of unified frameworks (Wanasinghe 2004). In the wake of the tsunami several ministries established relief and reconstruction schemes with little or no consultation or coordination with other agencies (Institute of Policy Studies 2005). In the past, decentralization initiatives have met with limited success due to partisan rivalries and a lack of bureaucratic and political will. As a result, responsibilities are poorly demarcated between central and local levels of government, policy making remains driven from the center with little regional input, and local agencies charged with the delivery of public goods and services are underfunded and poorly equipped to perform their tasks (Porter 2004). The exclusion of local authorities from reconstruction planning deprived policy makers of essential local knowledge and contributed to unsuitable or impractical policies (Uyangoda 2005; Centre for Policy Alternatives 2006).

The Civil Conflict: A Failure of Leadership

In the days following the tsunami there were encouraging signs of a rapprochement between the major Sinhalese political parties, and between the government and LTTE, in their response to a disaster that had devastated Sinhalese and Tamil communities alike. As mentioned above, an initial groundswell of sentiment across Sri Lanka for finding a permanent solution to long-standing civil conflict over demands for independence for the Tamil-dominated northeast province was reflected in television debates and opinion pieces in the newspapers. Not long afterward, Rajasingham-Senanayake wrote (2005, 18): "The post-tsunami response of individuals and groups to the suffering of 'other' communities of diverse linguistic and religious persuasion demonstrated beyond doubt that the so-called ethnic conflict . . . was largely a product and sustained by power struggles among politicians, presidents and armed actors."

At the time the tsunami hit, a rather fragile "ceasefire agreement" between the national government and the Tamil Tigers—brokered by Norway—had been in place for more than two years, and there now seemed to be a new opportunity to turn it into more serious peace negotiations. In the early stages of tsunami recovery the government, led by President Chandrika Kumaratunga, and the LTTE managed to negotiate an agreement on the relief effort that was called the Post-tsunami Operation Mechanism Structures (P-TOMS). Yet on both sides the political leaders continued with divisive rhetoric, and no new proposals were put on the table to strengthen the peace talks. Allegations quickly emerged that the government had favored the Sinhalese southwestern regions over the Tamil northeast in the distribution of aid resources, and these put considerable strain on the peace process (Shanmugaratnam 2005; Sirisena 2005).

President Kumaratunga reached the end of her maximum term in 2005 and the governing party—Sri Lanka Freedom Party (SLFP)—nominated the man who had been her prime minister, Mahinda Rajapakse, as its presidential candidate. The LTTE was suspicious of Rajapakse's attitude toward the nationalistic Janatha Vimukthi Peramuna (JVP), whose stronghold was in the same southern region in which Rajapakse's electorate was located. The JVP had opposed the 2002 ceasefire agreement and continued to oppose the involvement of Norway in brokering peace talks. It had also attempted to block the implementation of P-TOMS by taking action in the Supreme Court (Silva 2005), and the group held a balance of power in the national parliament. The LTTE called for a boycott of the presidential poll. Ironically, this favored Rajapakse over the more politically pragmatic leader of the United National Party, Ranil Wickremasinghe. The JVP welcomed the election of Rajapakse and demanded a much harder line against the LTTE in any future peace negotiations. Although Rajapakse rejected JVP calls to sack Norway as the mediator of peace talks, he ratcheted up the nationalistic rhetoric, and the LTTE leaders responded with their own sharpened rhetoric.

Soon after Rajapakse was elected, LTTE militants began a series of small-scale violations of the ceasefire agreement, which they said were in response to ongoing harassment by the Sri Lankan Army based in the north.[6] The LTTE also accused the Sri Lankan government of being behind the 2005 defection of former LTTE colonel Karuna and 5,000 militants who remained loyal to him in the Batticaloa disrtrict. As the violence began to escalate both sides threatened to withdraw from formal ceasefire talks, and when delayed talks were held in Geneva in late February they made little progress. A further round of peace talks had been scheduled for April 2006, but the LTTE withdrew as violence escalated in the north. The biggest battle in the renewed conflict took place in

July over a dispute about the provision of drinking water to a housing estate near Trincomalee. Soon after that seventeen Tamil aid workers employed by the French agency Action against Hunger were murdered in the town of Muttur, and each side in the conflict accused the other of being responsible. On August 10 the Consortium of Humanitarian Agencies told the government that renewed fighting was preventing aid from reaching people in need. Yet the situation got even worse when an attack by the Sri Lankan Air Force killed nineteen Tamil schoolgirls in what the military claimed was an attack on a guerrilla training center.

At the end of September the U.N.'s deputy special envoy for tsunami recovery, Eric Schwartz, visited the conflict zone and announced, "In parts of the north and east the tsunami recovery process ground to a halt and significant investments in reconstruction, so generously supported by donors around the world, are now imperilled."[7] The next day a report in the *Gulf Times* estimated that as many as 200,000 people had been displaced by the renewed fighting, and less than a week later the Sri Lankan government announced an increase of 32% in the projected military budget for 2006/2007. This announcement of an increase in military spending came just after a Sri Lankan government audit had found that only 13% of the promised foreign aid for tsunami recovery had actually been used.[8] While much of the promised aid had simply not arrived, this disappointing performance was also due to the renewed conflict in the north and east and a slow pace of reconstruction in the south. The slow pace of rebuilding was, in turn, partly due to shortages of skilled labor and to delays in getting access to suitable land for permanent new settlements (see Steele 2005).

By the latter part of 2006 the renewed conflict was also causing other economic problems for Sri Lanka. A report from Reuters India in early October reported that around $23 billion in new investments had been canceled because of the fighting. Rising oil prices were also causing problems, and the monthly inflation rate for September rose to a high of 11.2%.

Poor economic performances may have been largely responsible for a significant political shift that took place in Sri Lanka in October 2006. The SLFP announced that it was ending its agreement with the JVP and would cooperate with the opposition United National Party (UNP) to get ceasefire talks back on track (Francis 2006). Government representatives attended mediated talks with LTTE leaders in Geneva in late October and surprisingly put a new proposal for a federal structure—giving a degree of autonomy to the northeast province—on the table. Prior to this, Rajapakse had rejected UNP calls for federalism, insisting that the unitary state was the only thing preventing the breakup of the nation. Unfortunately, the lead-up to the talks at the end of October was marred by a Tamil Tiger attack on a bus carrying Sri Lankan soldiers in the town of Habarana, which also resulted in the deaths of many civilians. The Tigers also launched a daring raid intended to sink a Sri Lankan Navy boat in Galle Harbor. The raid was foiled when the three fishing vessels carrying the Tiger militants were destroyed before reaching their target, and Sinhalese residents of Galle vented their anger by attacking businesses owned by local Tamils. Escalating military activity by the LTTE outside the northeastern province resulted in the collapse of a second promising peace initiative. Soon the government, led by President Rajapakse, announced the formal ending of the stalled peace negotiations, and the Sri Lankan Army began the buildup to the military campaign that eventually resulted in defeat for the Tamil Tigers in 2009.

Many thousands of people died during the military campaign to seize control of former strongholds of the Tamil Tigers in 2008 and 2009, although accurate figures were not available at the time of writing. By the time the final intense battle reached its bloody conclusion, more than 200,000 civilians had been evacuated into hastily constructed refugee camps, and the impact on people living along a narrow coastal strip surrounding the town of Mullaitivu had been worse than the impact of the tsunami, which had affected 80% of people living in this area. Of course, the Tamil Tigers were largely responsible for the collapse of the peace negotiations, yet it also needs to be remembered that the Sri Lankan governments of President Kumaratunga and President Rajapakse had missed major opportunities to isolate the LTTE leadership politically. Military defeat for the Tamil Tigers has done nothing to reduce ethnic divisions in Sri Lanka. The nation is badly divided.

Housing: The Policy Response

The human costs of the tsunami were tragically exacerbated by extensive unregulated coastal development, and within days of the disaster the national government announced that it would impose a buffer zone to prevent residential rebuilding within 100 m of the sea in the southwestern districts and 200 m in the eastern districts. To planners in Colombo, the tragedy of the tsunami had one positive consequence in that it created the opportunity to address the chronic problem of unplanned and inappropriate coastal development. Unfortunately, this came as a second blow to families that had lost their homes and possessions in what had now become the buffer zone. The legislation was widely criticized nationally and internationally, the Asian Development Bank noting, "While there is wide consensus that a buffer zone may be necessary to reduce potential coastal risks, there is no scientific and consultative basis for the proposed zones" (2005, 16). The absence of a convincing rationale for the buffer zone policy and lack of any serious attempt to rally public and donor support behind it were significant failures given its potentially enormous social and economic impacts, and the clumsy handling of policy in the immediate aftermath of the disaster seriously damaged the prospects for more meaningful controls over inappropriate coastal development—a lost opportunity. The exemption of undamaged houses led to charges of inconsistency, with critics pointing out that whether public safety or environmental rehabilitation is the rationale for the buffer zone, it should be uniformly applied (Institute of Policy Studies 2005). A lack of consultation with local government and planning authorities was apparent in the creation of arbitrary setback limits without reference to local topography. The exemption of hotels from the ban on building in the buffer zone led to charges that policy making had been captured by vested interests and that the true purpose of the buffer zone was the relocation of poor fishing families and squatter communities to the invisible hinterland to serve an elite vision of coastal beautification and to make way for tourism development (Uyangoda 2005; Bastian 2005).

Domestic and international criticism of the buffer zone, together with mounting evidence of its impracticality, led to its effective repeal at the end of 2005. The mandatory 100 and 200 m setbacks were abandoned in favor of a reversion to the provisions of the national coastal zone management plan (CZMP), proclaimed in 1997 but never enforced. The CZMP specifies area-specific setback zones ranging from 35 to 125 m depending on local physical conditions, and it allows for exemptions, to be decided by local government authorities in consultation with the Coastal Conservation Department. The new regulations are generally agreed to be an improvement, providing the flexibility to accommodate planning requirements to local conditions (Centre for Policy Alternatives 2006).

The creation of the controversial buffer zone resulted in the development of two separate policy frameworks governing housing assistance: one for families outside the setback limit, who were allowed to rebuild in situ; and one for those inside it who, under the terms of the legislation, would need to be relocated. The former were provided with government grants to rebuild their houses, with some additional assistance from aid agencies, while the latter were to be resettled in new housing projects (NHPs), funded and constructed by donors, primarily international NGOs, with a smaller number of local institutions, individuals, and commercial contractors. Donors were also responsible for the provision of water, power, and sewerage services. The government retained nominal responsibility for identification and acquisition of land, development of design regulations and approval of building plans, and authentication of beneficiary eligibility. A lack of communication and overlapping of responsibilities led to complex approval and management processes for NHPs, involving several separate government agencies (TAFREN 2005).

With the concentration of human settlement within 50 m of the coast in most tsunami-affected areas, the creation of the buffer zone generated massive displacement. Around 51,000 families were relocated to inland transitional shelters to wait for permanent houses to be built for them within the NHPs. More than a year after the tsunami many thousands were still there (Centre for Policy Alternatives 2005, 17). Hazardous conditions in these transitional camps were reported, with problems of overcrowding, poor sanitation and lack of drinking water, and high levels of alcoholism, domestic violence, and sexual abuse (Weinstein 2005). Camp residents in the conflict-affected northeast faced additional hazards of harassment from both government security forces and the LTTE, with reports of the use of tsunami internally displaced people (IDP) camps as bases for LTTE military operations (Amnesty International 2006).

Land scarcity proved a significant obstacle, particularly in the densely populated coastal regions of the southern and western provinces. The government's preference was to site NHPs on public land. Although the government owns more than 80% of Sri Lanka's land, most of it is unavailable for resettlement, being occupied by national parks and water catchment areas or given over to long-term agricultural leases (Centre for Policy Alternatives 2005). The scarcity of public land led to the siting of some NHPs in hazard-prone or remote areas up to 5 km from the coast. Private acquisitions, the only option in areas where public land is very limited, are associated with delays and price inflation. In some regions land prices outside the buffer zone escalated five- or tenfold (Institute of Policy Studies 2005, 45). Long delays in the acquisition process led many NGOs to engage in private negotiations with landholders.

The government contracted with various donors for the construction of 34,000 housing units on more than 300 sites; however, actual construction lagged. By April 2006 only 6,000 houses had been completed, and 10,000 were under construction. Delays in construction were particularly marked in the eastern and northern regions, where more than one year after the tsunami, the building of transitional shelters and rehabilitation of some schools and hospitals had not been completed. With the shifting of the buffer zone boundaries, an estimated 11,000 of the 51,000 households in the original buffer zone are now outside it. These households were given the option of resettling in the NHPs or returning to their land to rebuild in situ. Due to long delays in NHP construction, which have forced many households into protracted stays in transitional shelters, and misgivings regarding the location of their proposed new homes, most are opting to rebuild. While the reversion to the CZMP setbacks reduces the NHP housing requirement, the majority will still be relocated, so the fundamental policy remains unchanged.

Livelihood Rebuilding: The Policy Response

After housing, livelihoods restoration was the second major focus of post-tsunami aid, attracting $126 million in donor funds in 2005. At least eight ministries and over 100 national and international agencies were involved in livelihoods-related projects in 2005 (Kapadia 2005). With the massive destruction of assets and infrastructure, loss of human capital, and collapse of markets, and without ready access to alternative occupations, coastal households faced severe economic stress in the months after the tsunami. During the first six months a combination of government relief payments, aid, and temporary cash-for-work programs operated by aid agencies was generally effective in addressing immediate welfare needs, although the implementation of government relief measures was partial and uneven. Welfare transfers to families who had lost their houses were paid for two months but were then delayed for more than four months while eligibility criteria were changed to exclude those who maintained independent income sources after the tsunami. The four-month delay caused considerable hardship, particularly among families who had lost breadwinners and were unable to participate in work programs, and led to demonstrations in several districts. Payments to 234,000 families recommenced in June 2005.

In tsunami-affected areas an estimated three-quarters of families depended on the informal sector for their livelihoods, which typically include a mix of fishing, tourism, roadside trading, cottage industry, and wage labor. An estimated one-third of affected households earned their primary incomes from fishing or fisheries-related activities such as net making. Livelihood interventions have focused heavily on asset replacement in the fisheries sector, while other occupations, particularly those in which women predominate, have received substantially less attention (Kapadia 2005). In these sectors, which are under intense pressure in the post-tsunami environment, well-intentioned donor interventions have in some cases exacerbated their problems. Post-tsunami activity in the construction sector did little to support a hoped-for recovery in construction-related occupations as the aid agencies responsible for new housing programs tend to employ contractors from Colombo rather than local brick makers and carpenters. The female-dominated food-production and garment sectors have had to contend with competition from a well-intentioned influx of local and international aid goods. Low barriers to entry into women's occupations have attracted new entrants seeking to offset the loss of other income sources. Problems of market saturation were compounded by poorly planned asset replacement initiatives that have little regard for market conditions or the capacity and experience of recipients. At a time when depopulation and a precipitous decline in household incomes were exerting severe downward pressure on demand, more households than ever were in possession of sewing machines, coir-making machines, and fish boxes for mobile trade, including many who had never previously engaged in these occupations (Kapadia 2005; Haug and Weerackody 2005).

Given the difficulties of promoting alternative occupations to traumatized and asset-depleted populations, it is not surprising that many development agencies have focused on restoring traditional, well-understood occupations. A narrow focus on restoring fisheries entails longer-term risks, however, with growing awareness that the sector in its pre-tsunami form is economically and environmentally unsustainable and is associated with high poverty incidence. The modernization of fisheries and the development of downstream and ancillary value-adding activities such as food processing and packaging and the servicing of boats and equipment, together with the promotion of growth sectors such as local manufacturing, tourism, and services, are important considerations in longer-term livelihood planning. Although observers have for several years been keenly aware of the declining ability of traditional livelihood activities to provide sustainable rural employment, there were few coordinated attempts to address the problem, due to a combination of policy inertia and lack of economic and technical resources. The post-tsunami environment provides a rare conjunction of incentive and resources for the promotion of more sustainable, higher-income livelihood options, an opportunity that is in danger of being wasted by the focus on restoring the pre-tsunami status quo.

The Role of Donors and Nongovernment Actors

Since the tsunami the number of international NGOs working in Sri Lanka has increased from 50 prior to the tsunami to more than 150 (Centre for Policy Alternatives 2006), and government agencies were faced with the challenge of managing an enormous influx of resources and NGOs with varying degrees of experience and resources. Due to pressures on local public sector capacity, governments in the affected countries have contracted the construction of NHPs to multilateral and bilateral donors and NGOs, retaining a coordination and regulatory role. Implementation is complicated by limited state capacity to manage politically and technically complex problems of land availability, valuation, boundary establishment, and attribution of title. There are concerns regarding the experience and competence of some NGOs, with claims of competition for "clients," duplication of activities, and poorly designed interventions. Aid agencies and governments are under pressure to show immediate results, overriding consultative processes and contributing to hasty policy decisions. Questions were raised regarding the motivations and activities of nonstate agencies, with allegations that some are pursuing business interests or religious proselytization agendas, or acting as fronts for political parties (Wickramasinghe 2005). Government officials have found it difficult to distinguish between established professional NGOs and a plethora of newly constituted agencies, some of which likely were formed opportunistically in response to the presence of aid funds (Weinstein 2005). The efficiency and quality of NGO programs has been compromised by lack of experience and pressure for quick results (Haug and Weerackody 2005, 28). Some international NGOs simply arrived in local communities and started handing out cash, boats, bicycles, and sewing machines on demand. Projects that enable the fast disbursement of large volumes of funds and can be attractively presented to constituencies in donor countries, such as the establishment of orphanages and the replacement of fishing boats, which could be publicly handed over to grateful recipients, were sought after by international NGOs at the expense of less photogenic interventions (Korf 2006). The apparent simplicity and media-attractiveness of such programs attracted several agencies and individuals with little or no experience in fisheries (Creech 2005).

Deficiencies were reported in procurement and targeting practices, duplication of efforts, and competition between agencies for "clients" (Haug and Weerackody 2005). A year after the tsunami, Sri Lanka's Task Force for the Rebuilding the Nation (TAFREN) estimated that the influx of international aid meant that there were now more fishing boats in the south than there had been before the tsunami and that the danger of overfishing had increased.[9] There were complaints regarding the "crowding out" of local aid agencies by large international NGOs and the propensity of foreign agencies to employ highly paid foreign consultants with limited local knowledge rather than making use of local expertise (Uyangoda 2005; Institute of Policy Studies 2005). The poaching of local NGO staff by international NGOs offering vastly higher salaries was a matter of concern, while for their part Sri Lankan NGOs were criticized for poor project management and politicization (Haug and Weerackody 2005, 28).

Community Consultation and Participation

The absence of formal communication and consultation mechanisms and a lack of strong civil society institutions to exercise countervailing pressures have contributed to a lack of transparency and participation, and affected communities have had limited input in reconstruction planning and implementation (Uyangoda 2005; Weinstein 2005; Weligamage et al. 2005). The importance of broad consultative processes is an idea that made little headway in Sri Lanka's bureaucratic culture, with a commonly held view among government officials that public participation in policy making is more an inconvenience than a useful input, causing distractions and delays, and that the opinions of "beneficiaries" are of little value as they lack technical expertise. An official "top-down" approach is reported in some cases to extend to a failure to keep survivors informed of progress with resettlement plans.[10] At the same time, there is widespread disquiet among the prospective occupants of the NHPs regarding the quality and location of their new homes, with many voicing concerns regarding access to their livelihoods and the loss of links with their traditional neighborhoods. The failure to allow affected communities a say in the reconstruction process has led to public expressions of frustration through demonstrations. Failures to take specific measures to inform all members of communities about their programs led to the exclusion of poorer, more socially isolated families from aid beneficiary lists, while extended families with social and political resources were able to use multiple strategies for accessing aid (Haug and Weerackody 2005, 23).

A lack of consultation with affected communities was apparent in planning and design rules, which were drawn up in Colombo with little regard for local family arrangements and housing practices. Concerns were voiced regarding the layout and design of the new projects, which vary significantly in terms of attractiveness, building quality, and sensitivity to community practices. The design specifications drawn up by TAFREN include a minimum floor area of 46.45 m^2 (500 sq. feet): a size that is arguably suitable for very small families, but represents a substantial reduction for many relocated households. Some contractors have interpreted the specified minimum floor area as a standard, making no allowance for variations in household size. With customs of extended family cohabitation in coastal regions, it is common for a single household to include seven to ten members, a pattern that has likely intensified with the post-tsunami integration of extended families. Moreover, fishing villages have traditionally consisted of groups of discrete hamlets or family compounds of up to ten houses each. Rather than incorporating a variety of dwellings suitable for various household sizes and configurations, some newly built NHPs consist of barracks-like rows of identical small buildings. The adoption of inappropriate layout plans is a concern, with approvals having been given for multistory high-density developments in coastal towns, a design form hitherto confined to major urban centres. There are concerns regarding the design quality of some NHPs, with warnings that they may become a euphemism for substandard, low-cost housing (Philips 2005).

A lack of local expertise among international aid agency staff coupled with a failure to consult with local experts was noted (Uyangoda 2005). The use of Colombo-based architects, with little or no local knowledge and limited consultation with end-users, to prepare site plans has raised concerns regarding inappropriate design features—for example, the design of inadequate ventilation systems based on an erroneous assumption that gas fuel will be used for cooking, despite estimates that around 75% of households in affected districts use cheaper biomass fuels such as wood and paddy husks (Institute of Policy Studies 2005). Other design problems are raised by lack of space and include insufficient separation between wells and septic tanks. Quality concerns were raised by the high cost of construction materials, due in part to Sri Lanka's congested and dilapidated regional road network, coupled with an acute labor and skills shortage, with reports that untrained contractors are using inappropriate materials and methods (ibid.).

Politicization and Corruption

The reconstruction process operates in a highly politicized context. Successive governments have allowed partisan political considerations to distort policy and administrative processes, a practice that was accelerated by the progressive erosion of public service neutrality since the 1970s, when a series of constitutional amendments strengthened political control of the bureaucracy by transferring control of public service appointments to politicians. Appointments based on patronage rather than merit have reduced the quality of public servants and enabled political interference in the allocation of public resources (Porter 2004). Hand in hand with the problem of political interference is the problem of petty corruption, which is embedded in a wide range of official transactions, including the delivery of welfare goods and services.

There is abundant evidence that political considerations have affected the allocation of post-tsunami aid resources at all levels of government. At the central level, political factors are evident in significant regional disparities in resource allocation and the failure to implement the P-TOMS agreement. Almost all of the construction commenced by mid-2005 was in the southern districts, which account for less than a quarter of total housing losses, while in the severely affected eastern districts of Ampara, Batticaloa, and Trincomalee, there was little or no progress with reconstruction. Hambantota district, the constituency of former prime minister and now president Mahinda Rajapakse, was singled out for favorable attention, with the establishment of a special "Helping Hambantota" office by the prime minister in addition to the standard district-level organizational structures set up to manage recovery (Weligamage et al. 2005). In Hambantota the number of new houses under construction exceeds the estimated requirement by nearly 2,000 (Centre for Policy Alternatives 2006).

At the local level, the use of state resources to reward political support has long been a feature of Sri Lankan politics, and there is widespread evidence of political interference in beneficiary selection and the distribution of aid resources. Considerable discretionary power is exercised by the village chief (*Grama Nilidari*), who is appointed by the local member of Parliament. The Grama Nilidari is a key gatekeeper of access to government resources, as his approval is required for welfare payments, asset replacements, housing, and a variety of other government benefits. In addition, the Grama Nilidari indirectly controls access to nongovernment benefits, as most NGOs rely on beneficiary lists provided by government sources. There is widespread evidence of the misallocation of benefits by local officials, including the taking of bribes and political partisanship in the compilation of beneficiary lists. As well, politicians have directly engaged in the misallocation of aid resources to their own supporters or electorates, in some cases to nonaffected inland communities. During the 2005 presidential election campaign, it is alleged, one local politician handed out some thirty fishing boats to win support for his party. Corruption is not restricted to the state sector, with evidence of diversion of aid funds by NGO officials and by community-based organizations, with allegations that valuable goods such as boats are distributed to the relatives and friends of committee members (Haug and Weerackody 2005).

Failures of coordination and mistargeting have created serious inequities and inefficiencies in asset replacement in the fisheries sector. In one example, in a southern village in which only twenty-three boats had been damaged, seven or eight agencies were operating boat replacement programs, and in many districts the number of fishing craft replaced exceeds the estimated number destroyed by wide margins (Haug and Weerackody 2005). Stories proliferated of households that managed to obtain multiple boats and other equipment while others missed out completely. Some men who had never been to sea were given brand-new fishing boats, and some of these were then sold at profit to those who could use them; others who had lost their boats did not receive replacements (Creech 2005). The use of fishermen's cooperatives, traditionally an avenue for the dispensation of political patronage, as conduits for aid distribution was criticized, with reports of mistargeting and the denial of assistance to nonmembers (ibid.).

Administrative Inefficiencies

Duplication and lack of coordination between government agencies created considerable confusion, with as many as four ministries issuing various buffer zone regulations during 2005. Confusion regarding the demarcation of responsibilities contributed to delays. In Thiraimadu in the Batticaloa district, for example, an area of public land designated as an NHP site was found to be flood-prone and required dredging and filling prior to construction. Disagreement between the Ministry for Urban Development and the Tsunami Housing Reconstruction Unit ensued, with each claiming that the other was responsible for making the land suitable for building. The government pledged in August 2005 to contribute half of the dredging costs, but by March 2006 the Treasury had still not released the funds and no works had commenced (Centre for Policy Alternatives 2006). As a result of poor communication between the center and provinces, local officials are often unaware of policy developments, leading to the inconsistent application of regulations. In some areas, the buffer zone legislation was strictly enforced, with reports of residents being forcibly removed by police when they attempted to rebuild their homes and of NGOs being instructed to remove emergency tents in which people were staying, while in other areas, local authorities were allowing rebuilding within the buffer zone (Weinstein 2005). Directives regarding the revision of buffer zone rules took several months to be issued to local authorities in Hambantota and Batticaloa districts, who in March 2006 were continuing to apply the original legislation, a factor that contributed to the excess of NHP construction in Hambantota (Centre for Policy Alternatives 2006).

Obstructive administrative practices have created obstacles in service delivery, exacerbating a sense of helplessness and anger among survivors. Many of the tsunami survivors lost all their possessions, including any documents that could establish their identities. Many could not access existing bank accounts or prove that they had indeed owned houses that were destroyed or damaged. A year after the tsunami, volunteer lawyers were still helping people to re-create necessary documentation. In some areas local officials insisted that only those whose names were on the electoral roll prior to the tsunami were eligible for assistance. There were reports of survivors being turned away from banks distributing relief funds because they had lost their identification documents or because there were minor mistakes in the replacement documents provided by local government officials (Weinstein 2005).

The eligibility criteria for government relief schemes were often very broad and provided substantial discretion to local government officials, leading to inconsistencies in interpretation, delays, and appeals. Mistargeting created inefficiencies in the allocation of food rations, with evidence that around 10% of ration cards were issued to nonaffected individuals (Institute of Policy Studies 2005). Poor targeting contributed to social tensions. Perceptions that some have unduly benefited from tsunami aid while the genuinely affected have not received their fair share have fueled resentment (Haug and Weerackody 2005; Weligamage et al. 2005). The fisheries sector was relatively well served by livelihood programs, while other livelihood activities have received less attention, leading to tensions between fishing families and others who feel that their needs were neglected. Tensions also exist between the new "tsunami poor" and long-term poor families who were not affected by the tsunami, as many of the latter are excluded from post-tsunami aid programs. Families displaced by the civil conflict, many of whom were living in camps for many years, remain ineligible for the housing and welfare benefits directed to tsunami survivors. The earmarking of donor funds for tsunami relief led NGOs to focus on tsunami work to the neglect of other equally disadvantaged groups, notably households displaced by the civil conflict, exacerbating intracommunal tensions. Although NGOs acknowledge this problem, most claim to be limited by funding arrangements that restrict their activities to tsunami rehabilitation (Kapadia 2005).

A grant of 250,000 rupees was made available for houses outside the buffer zone deemed to be "fully damaged"—damage amounting to more than 40% of total value—and 100,000 rupees for houses deemed to be partly damaged. The fixing of payments at arbitrary levels without reference to actual reconstruction costs created inequities and inefficiencies. Households that successfully utilized their grants were eligible for further low-interest loans of up to 500,000 rupees, administered by the state banks, if they could demonstrate repayment capacity and provide collateral, thereby discriminating against low-income households. Women in some districts experienced difficulties in accessing the housing grants, which are issued in the name of the male household head, with reports that the banks that administered the payments were insisting that female property owners sign their land over to their husbands in order to qualify for the payment (ActionAid International 2006).

The high-profile state-led *Susahana* credit program that was set up to assist microentrepreneurs to rebuild their assets and expand their businesses after the tsunami has had little impact in practice, and by mid-2005 fewer than 10,000 applicants had taken loans under the scheme. The limited outreach is due to highly restrictive loan conditions that impact poorer borrowers disproportionately. In a departure from standard microfinance practice, loan applicants under the Susahana scheme are required to provide both collateral and guarantors above a certain income level, conditions that many tsunami survivors are unable to meet. In addition, loans are given only for businesses registered before the tsunami—thereby excluding the vast majority of microenterprises that operate in the informal sector and are unregistered, as well as those seeking to take up new livelihoods in response to changed post-tsunami circumstances such as the loss of an income earner.

Conclusion

While the tsunami crisis created an opportunity for Sri Lanka to rethink important aspects of its physical and social development—such as the prior lack of strategic planning in regard to coastal development and an overreliance on industries that fail to provide sustainable livelihoods for the poor—inherent weaknesses in regard to governance and the development and implementation of public policy have meant that this opportunity was largely lost. Even worse, the opportunity to deepen the dialogue for peace that grew in the aftermath of the tsunami was also frittered away by politicians on both sides of the civil divide, who quickly returned to their divisive rhetoric. The results of the 2005 presidential elections deepened the political crisis, and the Sri Lankan government was far too slow in putting a proposal for federalism on the negotiating table. The virtual collapse of the fragile ceasefire that existed at the time the tsunami arrived ensured that the impact of the natural disaster was compounded by the worsening human disaster (the conflict)—especially in the areas worst affected by the tsunami.

What should never be forgotten, however, is that Sri Lankans responded generously to each other in the face of such a crisis and that the world community tried to respond quickly, effectively, and generously as well. This was the first natural disaster to affect so many countries at the same time, and, in the context of global climate change, it may not be the last. There are still many lessons to be learned about the successes, as well as the failures, and it is never too late for Sri Lanka to address the ongoing weaknesses that have seriously undermined the recovery effort to date.

Notes

1. Figures compiled by the Sri Lankan government were made available through the U.N. Office of the Special Envoy for Tsunami Recovery, www.tsunamispecialenvoy.org.

2. Azmi Thassim discussed his memories of the tsunami recovery effort in Hambantota in an interview with Martin Mulligan conducted in Hambantota in December 2005.

3. Figures on environmental impacts are from official Sri Lankan government statistics made available through the U.N. Office of the Special Envoy for Tsunami Recovery, www.tsunamispecialenvoy.org.

4. According to Sri Lankan government figures reported by the U.N. Office of the Special Envoy for Tsunami Recovery, www.tsunamispecialenvoy.org/country/srilanka.asap.

5. These included the Task Force for Rebuilding the Nation (TAFREN), Task Force for Relief (TAFOR), and Tsunami Housing Reconstruction Unit (THRU).

6. The following account of renewed conflict in Sri Lanka is taken from a range of online newspaper and magazine reports, cross-referenced to ensure accuracy.

7. Eric Schwartz, as cited in a news release from the U.N. News Centre, "Deputy UN envoy for tsunami recovery deplores rising bloodshed in Sri Lanka," www.un.org/apps/news/story/asp?NewsID=20085&Cr=tsunami&Cr1=.

8. According to a report carried by the *Gulf Times*, Qatar, on September 30, 2006.

9. According to the Galle district livelihood coordinator for TAFREN, Dr. A. D. Nanayakarra, who was interviewed by Martin Mulligan in December 2005.

10. In 2004 Sri Lanka had thirty-five ministries headed by a cabinet minister, with an additional twenty-one headed by ministers of noncabinet rank. Policy responsibilities in key sectors such as agriculture, industry, and education are divided between several ministries (Porter 2004, 4).

References

ActionAid International. 2006. *Tsunami response: A human rights assessment.* New Delhi: ActionAid International.

Amnesty International. 2006. *Tsunami response: A human rights assessment.* New Delhi: Amnesty International.

Asian Development Bank. 2005. *Sri Lanka: Post-tsunami recovery program: Preliminary damage and needs assessment.* Manila: Asian Development Bank.

Bastian, Sunil. 2005. Limits of aid. *Polity* (Social Scientists' Association, Colombo) 2 (3).

Central Bank of Sri Lanka. 2006. *Annual report 2005.* Colombo: Central Bank.

Centre for Policy Alternatives. 2005. *Landless and land rights in post-tsunami Sri Lanka.* Colombo: Centre for Policy Alternatives.

———. 2006. *Reflections on the tsunami one year on: Lessons to be learnt.* Colombo: Centre for Policy Alternatives.

Creech, Steve. 2005. Tsunami issues affecting fishing communities and the challenges to be addressed if "build back better" is to contribute toward sustainable livelihood development. In *Livelihoods in post-tsunami Sri Lanka: "Building back better"?* ed. Paul Steele, 43–63. Colombo: Institute of Policy Studies.

Fisher, Sarah. 2005. Gender based violence in Sri Lanka in the after-math of the 2004 tsunami crisis. MA thesis, University of Leeds, UK.

Francis, Krishnan. 2006. Report on Sri Lanka. *Forbes Magazine.* www.forbes.com.

Haug, Marit, and Chamindra Weerackody. 2005. Delivery of tsunami aid for livelihood development at the community level. In *Livelihoods in post-tsunami Sri Lanka: "Building back better?"* ed. Paul Steele, 19–33. Colombo: Institute of Policy Studies.

Institute of Policy Studies. 2005. *Sri Lanka: State of the economy 2005.* Colombo: Institute of Policy Studies.

Kapadia, Kamal. 2005. Reviving livelihoods after the tsunami: Identifying gaps in existing programmes. In *Livelihoods in post-tsunami Sri Lanka: "Building back better?"* ed. Paul Steele, 1–18. Colombo: Institute of Policy Studies.

Korf, Benedikt. 2006. Disasters, generosity and the other. *Geographical Journal* 172 (3): 245–47.

MacDonald, Rhona. 2005. *How women were affected by the tsunami: Perspective from Oxfam.* http://medical.plosjournals.org.

Nature Conservancy. 2005. *Report of early assessment of environmental damage.* www.natureorg/pressroom/press/press1797.html.

Philips, Rajan. 2005. After the tsunami: A plea for responsible reconstruction. *Polity* (Social Scientists' Association, Colombo) 2 (3).

Porter, Doug. 2004. *Review of governance and public management for Sri Lanka.* Manila: Asian Development Bank.

Rajasingham-Senanayake, Darini. 2005. After the tsunami: Reconstruction, deconstruction and social analysis. *Polity* (Social Scientists' Association, Colombo) 2 (5–6): 17–26.

Shanmugaratnam, N. 2005. The spectre of a "second tsunami" in Sri Lanka: What can we do to prevent a human-made disaster? *Polity* (Social Scientists' Association, Colombo) 2 (3).

Silva, Sarath N. 2005. Supreme Court judgement of P-TOMS. *Polity* (Social Scientists' Association, Colombo) 2 (5).

Sirisena, Mihirini. 2005. Old habits die hard: Nationhood in the aftermath of tsunami. *Polity* (Social Scientists' Association, Colombo) 2 (4).

Steele, Paul. 2005. Phoenix from the ashes? Economic policy challenges and opportunities for post-tsunami Sri Lanka. Research Studies Working Paper 7, Institute for Policy Studies, Colombo.

TAFREN. 2005. *Housing and township development: Assistance policy and implementation guidelines.* Colombo: TAFREN.

United Nations Environment Program. 2005. *Report on tsunami damage in Sri Lanka.* www.unep.org/Tsunami/reports/Sri_Lanka_Report_2005.

Uyangoda, Jayadeva. 2005. Post-tsunami recovery in Sri Lanka. *Polity* (Social Scientists' Association, Colombo) 2 (3).

Wanasinghe, Shelton. 2004. *Governance issues in poverty reduction in Sri Lanka.* Colombo: Institute of Policy Studies.

Weinstein, Harvey M. 2005. Sri Lanka. In *After the tsunami: Human rights of vulnerable populations,* ed. Laurel E. Fletcher, Eric Stover, and Harvey M. Weinstein, 57–73. Berkeley: University of California Press.

Weligamage, Parakrama, Markandu Aṇputhas, Ranjith Ariyaratne, Nilantha Gamage, Priyantha Jayakody, K. Jinapala, P. G. Somaratna, Neelanga Weragala, and Deeptha Wijerathna. 2005. *Bringing Hambantota back to normal: A post-tsunami needs assessment of Hambantota district in southern Sri Lanka.* International Water Management Institute, www.iwmi.org.

Wickramasinghe, Anoja. 2005. Tsunami: Rebuilding the nation through reciprocity while reconstructing the affected areas in Sri Lanka. *Local Environment* 10 (5): 543–49.

12

Improving Governance Structures for Natural Disaster Response

Lessons from the Indian Ocean Tsunami

Miranda A. Schreurs

The December 26, 2004, great Sumatra-Andaman Earthquake and resulting tsunamis were among the most destructive natural disasters of recent times. The death toll from the tsunami was staggering, reaching close to a quarter of a million people, although the exact number will never be known. Beyond this, another estimated 1.7 million people were displaced.[1] The scenes of coastal devastation and shattered lives that the media broadcast around the world led to the single largest outpouring of international natural disaster assistance ever seen. It also resulted in major reevaluations of national and international disaster preparedness, governance structures, and information tools.

The December tsunami is an example of how catastrophes can open the door for deep policy change. Thomas Birkland defines catastrophes as "more profound than disasters because they affect a much broader area, render local and neighboring governments unable to respond because they, too, are affected, and therefore require considerable assistance from regional and national governments or from international or nongovernmental relief organizations." He goes on to note that catastrophes are "the events most likely to trigger policy change."[2] In the wake of one of the world's worst natural disasters, natural disaster management laws have been introduced, tsunami regional warning systems established, and new natural disaster response programs formed.

There has also been much reflection on the successes and failures of the disaster recovery operations. While there are still many sovereignty and national security concerns that have limited the willingness of governments to fully integrate early warning systems or establish a supranational regional disaster relief center, there have been important steps taken toward greater regional and global cooperation.

What are the governance lessons the international community has learned and can learn from the tsunami? What kinds of institutional mechanisms have been created so that the next time a tsunami or other natural disaster hits, the international community can respond more effectively and efficiently? What kinds of preventative measures have been introduced to better protect coastal communities?

This chapter examines the governance responses of national governments, the Association of Southeast Asian Nations (ASEAN), and the international community to the tsunami along several dimensions: the development of a tsunami warning system for the Indian Ocean; changes to national disaster management legislation and institutional structures; the strengthening of regional and global institutions and mechanisms for disaster reduction and prevention; strengthened coordination of international humanitarian assistance; and environmental and development planning lessons.

The International Community's Response to the Tsunami

Early responders at the national and international level had to prevent a second humanitarian disaster in the tsunami-affected regions from malnutrition, dehydration, and disease. They needed to provide food, clean water, and shelter to survivors. They had to take on the gruesome task of rapidly burying or cremating thousands of tsunami victims. It was a heroic effort that most observers agree worked remarkably well considering the scale of the disaster—its huge geographical impact, the large number of communities affected, and the high death toll.[3]

Many affected areas were remote and difficult to access. Others were already suffering economies, like the Seychelles, Sri Lanka, the Maldives, and Sumatra. Yet others were in conflict-stricken regions, such as Somalia, where up to forty villages were affected by the tsunami. This complicated the work of national and international aid teams trying to bring in medical assistance, water, food supplies, clothing, temporary shelters (e.g., tents and tarpaulins), cooking equipment, generators, and sanitation equipment. Militaries from around the world were sent to the region to aid in emergency response. In Sri Lanka alone forty-three militaries were deployed for emergency assistance.[4] International search and rescue teams were sent in. Governments from around the world sent in medical teams to assist in emergency medical relief.

Once the emergency phase of the relief efforts began winding down, the multiyear process of reconstruction commenced. The tsunami left behind huge amounts of waste and debris. It caused coastal erosion and destroyed farmlands. It destroyed industries that contained hazardous materials. It contaminated groundwater supplies. Homes, schools, and hospitals needed to be rebuilt. For the many people who lost their means of making a livelihood, new opportunities were required. Legal issues—including the ownership of land—needed to be addressed. These kinds of problems required the development of long-term recovery and reconstruction programs that extended long beyond the immediate emergency response period. In early 2005, the World Bank estimated it would take at least four years to reconstruct the infrastructure—the roads, bridges, water supply, sewers, hospitals, electric systems, etc.—that had been washed away by the tsunami.[5]

The United Nations Development Programme described the tsunami as an exceptional event, one that occurs only about once in every 200 years.[6] In the first several months after the tsunami hit, the World Bank estimated that damage costs to the four worst-hit countries—Indonesia, India, Sri Lanka, and the Maldives—was on the order of U.S.$6.9 billion. The loss of life was highest in Indonesia, Sri Lanka, Thailand, and India, but there was severe damage in many other regions as well. Damage in the Maldives equaled an estimated 62% of that country's GDP. Some islands were simply abandoned, damage was so complete.[7] Because of its enormous impact, the tsunami has forced governments, international disaster and humanitarian aid agencies, and civil society to reflect on how planning and governance can be improved to limit the extent of death, illness, and damage from future tsunamis and other natural disasters. It has also been an impetus for strengthening national, regional, and international cooperation in disaster preparedness and response.

The United Nations Indian Ocean Tsunami Flash Appeal

The scale of the disaster required an almost immediate assessment of aid priorities that could then be communicated to donor nations and groups. On January 6, 2005, the United Nations Office for the Coordination of Humanitarian Affairs reacted by issuing a "flash appeal." A consolidated flash appeal is one way the U.N. responds to sudden, large-scale humanitarian crises requiring an extended emergency response and recovery. The flash appeal, which is modified as new information comes in, presents to the international community a unified assessment of needs and priorities. It is not a channel for funds, but rather a process for identifying needs, coordinating a strategic response, publicizing funding needs, and inventorying relief and early recovery projects.[8]

In its first phase, the Indian Ocean Tsunami Flash Appeal called for $977 million to fund the work of some forty U.N. agencies and nongovernmental organizations in addressing the survival and recovery needs of an estimated 5 million people. In April a revised requirement was issued, totaling $1,086 billion. The appeal addressed financial, technical, supply, and project needs in the agriculture, education, health, food, shelter, water, and sanitation sectors in the countries directly impacted by the tsunami. The flash appeal focused on the work of the U.N. Children's Fund (UNICEF), the World Food Program (WFP), the Food and Agricultural Organization (FAO), the U.N. Population Fund (UNPF), the U.N. Development Programme (UNDP), Islamic Relief Indonesia, Save the Children, CARE, Catholic Relief Services, and the International Rescue Committee, among many others.

The Donor Response

It was not immediately clear in the hours after the earthquake and tsunami waves struck just how much death and destruction the Indian Ocean Tsunami had caused. As the enormity of the damage came to be understood, the international community mobilized in an unprecedented fashion. Financial assistance poured in from individuals, school groups, corporations, community organizations, and governments. One year after the crisis, the British Red Cross reported that its Asia Earthquake and Flood Appeal had brought in an unprecedented 26 million pounds, including 3.5 million pounds from the British government. An additional 372 million pounds was raised by the Disasters Emergency Committee Appeal.[9] The American Red Cross reported that as of May 31, 2007, it had received over $581 million to assist affected communities.[10] As of mid-February, 2005, the United Nations had coordinated food relief to over 1.2 million people and fresh water to 500,000. It also estimated that $5.5 billion had been spent in humanitarian assistance.[11] The Asian Development Bank reported that as of June 30, 2007, it had approved assistance and cofinanced funds for the tsunami-affected countries to the tune of $892 million.[12] The European Commission situated itself as the top donor in the tsunami response, pledging 137 million euros for humanitarian aid in 2005 and 350 million euros for reconstruction support in 2005 and 2006.[13] The United Nations Office for the Coordination of Humanitarian Affairs has tracked commitments, contributions, and pledges from the international community. As of January 24, 2008, it had recorded over $6 billion in donations coming from governments and NGOs around the world. The list of commitments is 124 pages long![14]

With so much aid flowing in and so many urgent relief and reconstruction needs, numerous efforts were made to improve coordination among donors, aid agencies, and NGOs. In March 2005, for example, the Asian Development Bank organized a high-level coordination meeting on rehabilitation and reconstruction assistance among world governments and private donors in Manila. The meeting was intended to provide a comprehensive overview of recovery efforts, address coordination needs and mechanisms, and consider lessons learned.[15] The United Nations established a Web site for tracking expenditures coming in under the flash appeal. The Web site presents an overview of the assistance provided to the affected countries to help donors, implementers, governments, and the public understand the flow of funds.[16]

Long-term Post-disaster Reconstruction Financing

Efforts were launched almost from the beginning to make sure that aid did not dry up once the emergency phase of the post-disaster response transitioned to the recovery, reconstruction, and rehabilitation phases. To this end, former U.S. president William Clinton was appointed by the United Nations as special envoy for the tsunami response in order to keep world attention focused on tsunami-recovery needs and to coordinate country-level aid donations.[17] In late February 2005, former president George H. W. Bush joined Clinton on a tour of the region. They pointed out that while some $7 billion had already been committed to tsunami relief in Asia, another $4 billion would be needed for long-term reconstruction efforts.[18]

Strengthening National, Regional, and International Governance Mechanisms for Natural Disaster Preparedness and Response

The high number of deaths and injuries and the extent of coastal damage across Southeast and South Asia initiated serious discussion in the region about the lack of adequate tsunami disaster preparedness and contingency plans at the local and national levels. Even though Asia is the region of the world that regularly suffers the largest number of deaths from natural disasters, including floods, hurricanes, earthquakes, and landslides, the region's national disaster preparedness and response capacity were seriously underdeveloped.

Developing a Tsunami Early Warning System

Perhaps the single biggest failure of governments around the region was that they had never established an Indian Ocean Tsunami warning system. The magnitude 9 earthquake sent tsunami waves traveling at hundreds of kilometers per hour across the Indian Ocean. In some places, tsunami waves estimated to be 10 m (30 feet) in height crashed onto coastal shorelines. There was no regional tsunami warning system in the Indian Ocean. As a result, unsuspecting coastal communities across East and South Asia had no idea that the massive tsunami waves were approaching.

In all fairness, a large percentage of the deaths caused by the tsunami waves were most certainly unavoidable.[19] The series of tsunami waves that hit Aceh province, Indonesia, just some forty minutes after the earthquake occurred in the waters off the northwestern tip of Sumatra came too quickly and were too large and forceful. Even had a tsunami warning system been in place, it is doubtful that much of the populace of Aceh would have had sufficient time to flee the calamity.

Yet, the tsunami waves caused death and damage in a dozen countries, stretching from Indonesia all the way to the eastern shores of Africa. The death tolls were particularly high in Indonesia, Sri Lanka, India, and Thailand. Entire towns in the Maldives, a chain of islands that were directly in the tsunami's path, were wiped out by the waves.

Whereas the tsunami waves hit Indonesia just a short time after the earthquake struck, it took over two hours before the first wave hit Phuket, Thailand, and another one and a half hours before they hit the Bay of Bengal. Had a coordinated international tsunami warning system been in place, probably thousands and maybe even tens of thousands of people could have been saved. The governments of the region and the international community had failed utterly in this important aspect of disaster prevention. As a result, almost immediately after the disaster struck, international efforts began on the introduction of tsunami alert systems not only for the Indian Ocean but also for other regions and at the global level as well.[20]

It is a great tragedy that earlier tsunami lessons had not been brought to the Southeast Asian region. The development of the Pacific Tsunami Warning System began in 1949 after the 1946 Aleutian Island earthquake devastated Hilo, Hawaii. After the 1960 Chilean earthquake and tsunami killed dozens in Hawaii and around 200 in Japan, the littoral states of the Pacific Ocean decided to coordinate efforts to prevent such a loss of life from ocean-crossing tsunamis. The United Nations Intergovernmental Oceanographic Commission then formed a body that was to become the Pacific Tsunami Warning System in 1968. A separate West Coast and Alaska Tsunami Warning Center was established in 1967.[21] No tsunami warning systems, however, had been set up in the Indian Ocean.

Discussions of an early warning system progressed rapidly. On January 6, 2005, a special leaders' meeting of the Association of Southeast Asian Nations,

"The Aftermath of the Earthquake and Tsunamis" agreed to establish a regional early warning system. As a follow-up, the Thai government convened a ministerial meeting, "Regional Cooperation on Tsunami Early Warning Arrangements," in Phuket on January 28–29. One month later, UNESCO's Intergovernmental Oceanographic Commission organized the "International Coordination Meeting for the Development of a Tsunami Warning and Mitigation System for the Indian Ocean within a Global Framework." UNESCO director-general Koichiro Matsuura made it clear that he saw the development of an Indian Ocean early warning system as an important step toward the eventual development of a global tsunami warning system.[22]

Parallel efforts began at the national level as well. A special workshop between ASEAN and China on earthquakes and tsunamis held in January 2005 led to an action plan for the formulation of an early warning system.[23] In April 2005, Indonesia hosted a tsunami early warning system workshop with the goal of establishing a national early warning system that could then be integrated into a regional and eventually a global system.

Various donor countries stepped in to provide technical and capacity-building support. Japan offered lessons from its own tsunami experiences. China offered training and equipment for earthquake and natural disaster management.[24] The United States Geological Survey and National Oceanic and Atmospheric Administration offered assistance in the development of an early warning system, and the Pacific Tsunami Warning System became the interim warning center for the Indian Ocean.[25] The German federal Ministry of Education and Research and the Indonesian government signed a cooperation agreement for the development of the German-Indonesian Tsunami Early Warning System, which was to become the main part of the UNESCO/Intergovernmental Oceanographic Commission Indian Ocean Tsunami Warning System. The German federal Ministry of Education and Research commissioned the Helmholtz Association of National Research Centres to coordinate the activities of several scientific organizations for this purpose.[26]

Importantly, other regions of the world, including the Caribbean and the Mediterranean, have also learned from the December 2004 tsunami experience and are working on the development of regional tsunami warning systems as well.

Evaluating National and Local Government Disaster Management Capacity

Many governments, both at the national and local levels, were caught "totally off-guard" by the tsunami disaster.[27] This was especially true for Sri Lanka and in Aceh, Indonesia. In the case of Sri Lanka, a Tsunami Coalition Evaluation commission found that the National Disaster Management Center was woefully understaffed, and, because the government had not passed into law the Disaster Counter Measures bill that had been put together by a previous administration, the legal and institutional structure for handling a major disaster was not in place. The Sri Lankan government did rapidly respond to the disaster by setting up a number of national bodies to run the official response to the tsunami disaster, but the capacity of these new offices to oversee and coordinate the relief efforts across the thirteen districts that were affected by the tsunami was deemed inadequate. This complicated international aid agencies' ability to provide assistance to devastated regions.[28]

In Indonesia, the Tsunami Coalition Evaluation commission found that while the National Disaster Management Board had an ad hoc disaster management system that included special boards at provincial and district levels, there were no contingency plans in place. The long-standing conflict between the Indonesian government and the armed separatist Free Aceh Movement had led to the imposition of martial law in Aceh and a retreat by most international nongovernmental organizations. Aceh, moreover, was one of Indonesia's poorest regions. When the tsunami struck there was little capacity on the ground to deal with the disaster.[29] It took aid workers between one day (Banda Aceh) and ten days (Krueng Sabee) to reach affected communities. In the wake of the tsunami, in April 2005 the Indonesian government established a high-level Rehabilitation and Reconstruction Agency for Aceh and Nias with a four-year mandate. This became the main governmental body overseeing reconstruction efforts. Nevertheless, governmental coordination efforts remained fragmented, leading to many problems on the ground.

In several affected countries, international agencies stepped in to assist with the coordination of donor assistance. The World Bank's International Development Association (IDA), which serves the world's poorest countries, became the trustee and administrator of a multidonor trust fund (MDTF) for Aceh and North Sumatra. The MDTF steering committee became the main mechanism for donor coordination and policy dialogue with the government.[30] In the Maldives, the World Bank and the Asian Development Bank set up temporary offices to assist in the coordination of donor assistance with the Maldive government's national reconstruction program.

Capacity problems were less pressing in India and Thailand. The Indian government refused offers of external assistance in the first, emergency phase of the post-disaster relief, as it felt it had sufficient domestic governmental and NGO capacity to address the crisis. A briefing report prepared for William Clinton prior to his tsunami tour in India noted the strong governmental response there: "The Government of India, in association with the States/ Union Territories, mounted massive relief and rescue operations. For example, the Central Government mobilized around 11,000 metric tons of relief goods and 2,400 civil servants/volunteers to the affected areas. . . . Civil society and NGOs have also extended substantial support to the affected people, supported through financial donations to public/private funds."[31] The Indian government did, however, approve assistance from the World Bank, Asian Development Bank, and U.N. agencies for long-term reconstruction.[32] The U.N. system, thus, expanded its existing programs to support the Indian government's relief efforts. UNICEF led the humanitarian efforts.

The Thai government activated the 1979 Civil Defence Act in response to the tsunami and "executed an efficient immediate emergency and early recovery response. It included the prompt provision of health services, a major forensic operation, construction of temporary shelters and permanent houses, compensating survivors, the use of military assets to support recovery and mobilizing public funds and attention to disaster management."[33] Thailand refused financial assistance, but did accept technical assistance.

Lesson Learning

In the aftermath of the tsunami, the governments of the region held emergency sessions and high-level governmental meetings to coordinate the assistance that was pouring into the region. In subsequent months, efforts began to assess responses to the tsunami, reflect upon governance successes and failures, and consider future plans of action. Similar initiatives were held at the regional level by ASEAN and between ASEAN and other governments (e.g., Japan, China, the United States, and Europe). International aid and disaster response agencies also took the opportunity to debate their own roles and actions. These efforts were intended both to smooth the dispersal of aid to the region for post-tsunami reconstruction and to provide lessons for improving responses to future disasters.

In May 2005, for example, the Indonesian government, in cooperation with the United Nations, held a workshop on the theme of lessons learned. The expert participants at the workshop pointed to several capacity and management problems, but also some positive lessons learned. Reflecting the outcomes of the Second World Conference on Disaster Reduction, one problematic area pointed to was the lack of awareness among communities living in vulnerable areas of the threats posed by tsunamis and the warning signs of an approaching tsunami, such as receding sea levels on the coastline. The Indonesia workshop pointed to the importance of publication education and awareness and early warning for saving lives.[34]

Workshop participants also pointed to shortcomings in the national and local legal frameworks for disaster response and problems in coordination within the national government and among the government, nongovernmental organizations, and the United Nations. The workshop led to several recommendations. First among them was the rapid passing into law of a draft bill, National Disaster Management. A second was enhancing coordination among international militaries in emergency response preparedness and training in working together with civilian humanitarian response groups.[35]

A positive lesson learned was the effectiveness of an open-skies policy that waived visa requirements for aid workers and customs duties for relief commodities. It is also significant that in Aceh province, which was by far the worst hit of all tsunami-affected regions, the need to deal with the suffering caused by the tsunami appears to have contributed to a peace-building process that led to the signing of a peace agreement in August 2005, ending a thirty-year conflict. The tsunami shifted the population's attention from the conflict to efforts to rebuild communities. It also forced the central government to provide support to a region that had long been neglected as a result of the conflict and brought international aid organizations back into the area.

A similar workshop was held in Colombo, Sri Lanka, by the Sri Lankan government and the United Nations. Many of the lessons learned were similar to those in Indonesia: the need for disaster risk management legislation and institutions with trained emergency response staff; early warning systems; risk awareness education; coordination agencies at each level of government; and better linkage and command and control structures among different governmental bodies. It was found that the lack of adequate command and control structures led to delay in mobilization and utilization of resources. Interestingly, both workshops also had much to praise about the rapid international disaster relief and humanitarian aid response.[36]

Disaster Preparedness and Response Education

Many NGOs and international agencies share the assessment that there was insufficient disaster prevention and preparedness education in the region. Had communities had sufficient disaster training, some of the suffering, destruction, injury, and death could have been mitigated or prevented. There are several examples of communities that survived the tsunami with less devastating destruction than others. In Mombasa, Kenya, there was an evacuation of people along the coast in response to the tsunami wave making its way across the Indian

Ocean.[37] Villagers in Samiyarpettai, India, who had previously received training under a United Nations Development Programme–funded Government Disaster and Management Mitigation Program, which included survival skills, the development of emergency rescue teams, and disaster awareness training, suffered considerably less loss of life than neighboring Pudukkupam, which had not received such training.[38] In Simeulue, Indonesia, where local villagers had passed down over the generations ancient knowledge of tsunamis, people sought refuge on higher ground, thereby reducing the number of deaths. In Meulaboh, Indonesia, the army reacted to early indications and began evacuating people.[39] In most places, however, there had been no disaster preparedness training.

Since the tsunami, efforts have been introduced around the region to improve disaster preparedness. In December 2005, Thailand held its first official test of its tsunami warning system and evacuation plans.[40] Sri Lanka established a Disaster Management Centre in response to the tsunami that has as part of its mandate public education and training and rehearsals for disaster preparedness.[41] The U.N./ International Strategy for Disaster Reduction (ISDR) Asia and Pacific launched a "Disaster Reduction Begins at School" campaign in 2006.[42]

Improving Coordination of Disaster Assistance and Building Local Capacity

While the general assessment of the international response has been largely positive, many lessons have been learned in this realm as well. Although the United Nations and national governments tried to coordinate the aid drive and to channel aid disbursement through national governments, there was such an overwhelming response to the disaster that coordination efforts sometimes bogged down. There were hundreds of different aid agencies, nongovernmental and private organizations, and volunteers working on the ground. Alex Irwan of the Indonesian Tifa Foundation remarked, "The international NGOs are all over Aceh. Everybody's doing their own thing, running their own relief services. There has been some effort by the Indonesian government to make NGOs report to it, but they aren't complying with that." Another aid worker, Andrew Harding, noted: "In the first weeks I saw aid agencies just throwing stuff in and taking pot luck, seeing whether they could charter a helicopter for a few hours, land somewhere, and more often than not someone had arrived just before and dumped a whole lot of aid, so actually it was a wasted trip."[43]

There is no doubt that much of this assistance was critical, saving many lives and helping many communities. Yet, despite the many efforts to coordinate NGO activities, many groups made independent assessments of where funds and supplies were most needed. The result was that while some communities were overwhelmed with assistance, others were underserviced or neglected. There were not sufficient governmental disaster management structures, capacity, or know-how at the national or local levels in many affected communities to deal with the collection and disbursement of the large amounts of assistance coming from so many different groups.

Many challenges accompanied the influx of relief funds. Local communities did not always have the capacity to cope with the huge sums of aid money, to monitor reconstruction efforts, and prevent corruption. Many of the worst-hit areas did not have offices or staff to handle the rapid influx of money or to disperse it to the individuals and communities most in need of help. There were many problems in making sure that funds were equitably and transparently spent.[44]

At the same time, as the damage was not only to public but also and primarily to private assets, it was necessary to develop mechanisms to support individuals and small-scale entrepreneurs so that they could rebuild their lives. Determining what kind of assistance was the most appropriate was a challenge that faced the many providers of aid funds. Traditionally, in-kind assistance, including the provision of food aid, shelter materials, and fishing equipment, has been supplied in post-disaster situations.

Lack of coordination among donors, however, meant that at times there was too much provision of a particular kind of assistance. One widely noted example is the large number of fishing boats that were supplied to affected coastal regions. The United States Agency for International Development (USAID) noted that more fishing boats were replaced than were lost, "swelling fishing fleets to a size greater than they were before the disaster." This threatened the ability of communities to maintain age-old practices that ensured sustainable livelihoods.[45]

A key conclusion of post-tsunami relief effort evaluations has been the need to include affected populations in recovery planning and build local capacity. In its evaluation, the United Nations Development Programme pointed to the importance of combining initial recovery activities with the rapid introduction of reconstruction programs involving those affected by the disaster. An example it provided was of local populations in some areas being involved in rubble removal and in helping displaced populations move from tents to temporary shelters. "Cash for work" programs were set up to help with reconstruction and to address the psychological stresses the impacted communities faced.[46]

Many NGOs, including CARE, Oxfam, Save the Children, Mercy Corps International, and Goal, began to experiment with cash-based interventions to support livelihood recovery. These included cash for work programs (such as providing cash for assistance with recovery work) and voucher systems. Doing this, however, also required developing standards, programming guidelines, and training local staff to be able to design, manage, and monitor cash approaches.[47]

In December 2006, a new U.N./ISDR project, "Building Resilience to Tsunamis in the Indian Ocean," was approved, with funding from the European Community. It builds on the Tsunami Flash Appeal and is a three-year initiative with the goal of heightening the resilience of communities and nations to disasters. This is to be done through the strengthening of institutional capacity building in disaster risk reduction and management; public awareness enhancement; education as a component of early warning and disaster risk reduction; and community-based approaches to support preparedness, mitigation, and response capacity of local communities. Also central to the project is completion of implantation plans for an early warning core system and coordination of research development and risk assessment in high-risk areas. The initiative focuses on India, Indonesia, the Maldives, and Sri Lanka.[48]

Environmental and Development Planning Lessons

The destructive power of the tsunami waves was aggravated by the damage that had been done to coastal regions as a result of increased population pressures, poorly planned development, the tourist industry, and agriculture and fisheries. Environmentally destructive coastal development was a contributing factor both in the high death toll and in the destruction of coastal towns and villages. In many areas that were affected the most severely by the tsunami, coastal areas had been cleared of forests, either for farming purposes or to develop resorts and other buildings.[49] The widespread destruction of mangrove forests and coral reefs for shrimp and fish farms, to clear land for farming, and to develop resorts and coastal communities throughout much of Southeast Asia has removed natural buffer zones that protect coastlines from the full strength of the ocean. In areas where mangrove swamps, coral reefs, sand dunes, and other coastal ecosystems remained, there were fewer deaths and less damage.[50] Recognizing this, the Indonesian government announced plans to replant 30,000 ha (74,132 acres) with mangrove trees along the coast of Sumatra to serve as a buffer against future tsunamis.[51]

Another central lesson stemming from the tsunami is that post-disaster development reconstruction must take risk considerations into account in determining where to build hospitals and schools, the types of materials to use in construction, and approaches to land development. The importance of environmental buffer zones and no-build zones is a significant component of this.

Enhancing Regional Cooperation for Disaster Response and Risk Reduction: ASEAN

Another central finding was the need for coordination mechanisms within and between governments and between governments and civil society at the regional level. Just two weeks after the tsunami, in an effort to take stock of the situation and determine priorities, an ASEAN leaders' special summit was held, bringing in leaders of the affected countries and heads of international organizations, including the Asian Development Bank, the World Bank, the International Monetary Fund, and the United Nations. The summit participants focused attention on three major disaster management issues: emergency relief, rehabilitation and reconstruction, and prevention and mitigation. The president of Indonesia also called for a strengthening of the ASEAN Regional Program on Disaster Management that was launched just months before the disaster struck, in May 2004, and the drafting of an action plan for the establishment of an ASEAN Security Community to provide for coordinated use of military and logistics in rescue and relief operations.[52] In a declaration of action, the ASEAN heads of state and government agreed on the importance of deepening cooperation in disaster mitigation and response. They specifically highlighted their support for ASEAN's development of an ASEAN Humanitarian Assistance Centre, an ASEAN Disaster Information Sharing and Communication Network, and a Regional Tsunami Early Warning Center, among other items.[53]

To this end, in July 2005 the ASEAN Agreement on Disaster Management and Emergency Response was formulated. The agreement established the ASEAN Coordinating Centre for Humanitarian Assistance on Disaster Management. This center has been charged with, among other things, coordinating emergency response assistance offered by ASEAN parties in cases of disasters.[54]

Building Capacity at the Global Level: The Second World Conference on Disaster Reduction and the Indian Ocean Tsunami

It was a coincidence that the Second World Conference on Disaster Reduction, organized on the ten-year anniversary of the Yokohama Conference on Disaster Reduction of 1994 was held in Kobe, Japan, January 18–22, 2005, just weeks after the tsunami. One hundred and sixty-eight countries and multilateral organizations participated. The timing of the conference so soon after the tsunami gave it a momentum it would otherwise likely not have had. The resulting Hyogo Framework for Action 2005–15, endorsed by the United Nations General Assembly Resolution 60/195, is the primary international agreement for disaster reduction.

It called for: "The substantial reduction of disaster losses, in lives and in the social, economic and environmental assets of communities and countries." To reach this goal, the conference called for more effective integration of disaster risk considerations into sustainable development policies and planning; the development and strengthening of institutions, mechanisms, and capacities; and the systematic incorporation of risk reduction approaches into the design and implementation of emergency preparedness, response, and recovery programs.[55] In a special statement, delegates pledged their support for the creation of a regional tsunami early warning system and emphasized "the importance of regional cooperation and coordination in disaster reduction, including enhanced institutional arrangements, technical cooperation based on most effective technical equipment and capacity building to effectively address the impact of natural disasters . . . [as well as] the urgent need . . . to strengthen national systems and to expand existing mechanisms for sharing of information and best practices in disaster detection, early warning, prevention, and assessment of natural disasters and for disaster relief, post-disaster rehabilitation and reconstruction."[56]

Since the tsunami disaster and the Kobe meeting, 39 countries have established Hyogo Framework focal points, and over 100 have developed national platforms for disaster risk reduction; they share this information on an Internet platform of the U.N. International Strategy for Disaster Reduction.[57]

The Hyogo Framework for Action also called for a strengthening of the ISDR. The ISDR was adopted by the U.N. General Assembly in January 2000 as a follow-on to the U.N. International Decade for Natural Disaster Reduction. The goal of the ISDR was to facilitate the implementation of disaster reduction globally.

Efforts to document and share information related to disaster prevention and recovery have intensified. In May 2005, the United Nations Development Programme and other U.N. agencies established the International Recovery Platform (IRP) to act as a repository of knowledge and clearinghouse mechanism for recovery to avoid the fragmented, isolated, and uncoordinated interventions that have characterized recovery efforts in recent disasters. The idea behind the IRP is to put in place a post-disaster needs assessment methodology, along the lines of the UNDP–World Bank Post-conflict Needs Assessment, to help coordinate the activities of all stakeholders.[58]

There have also been numerous efforts to strengthen the ISDR. In 2006, in partnership with the ISDR, the World Bank launched the Global Facility for Disaster Reduction and Recovery (GFDRR). The idea behind GFDRR is to enable low- and middle-income countries to mainstream disaster reduction in national development strategies and plans to achieve the Millennium Development Goals. The goal is to reduce disaster losses by 2015.[59]

There are also now calls for the development of a Global Platform for Disaster Risk Reduction. The goal is to empower the ISDR system at the regional and subregional levels to coordinate disaster risk reduction efforts.[60]

Conclusion

The magnitude of the death and destruction caused by the Indian Ocean earthquake and tsunami is almost unfathomable. The sheer geographical scope of the tsunami damage and the huge numbers of lost lives will leave a long-lasting scar on the region. To the extent that any silver lining can be found in such a disaster, the tsunami has forced governments, NGOs, and international organizations to take stock and reflect on their own disaster preparedness readiness and know-how. It has produced significant changes in local, national, regional, and international disaster response programs and institutions. Perhaps no other international natural disaster response has been as scrutinized as that for the Indian Ocean Tsunami.

In reaction to the tsunami catastrophe, governments around the region have introduced and strengthened national disaster management institutions and laws. They have also joined forces with the international community in the development of an Indian Ocean Tsunami Early Warning System and emergency evacuation and recovery plans. Many steps have been taken to enhance disaster management coordination and communication capacities between national and local governments and between governments and NGOs in the region. Various local capacity-building programs have been undertaken.

There is no doubt that there are still many significant capacity problems. The extent to which disaster risk reduction is being incorporated into planning can be questioned. Whether emergency disaster, evacuation, and recovery training is adequate is questionable. Aid to the tsunami-affected regions began to dry up within a few years of the disaster, and certainly not all of the assistance that was pledged ended up where it was intended. There have been many allegations of fraud, corruption, and funds gone missing.

Still, there are many reasons to believe that the region is now better prepared to handle disasters when they strike. The disaster may also have played a small role in pushing the states of Southeast Asia one step closer to the development of an Asian regional community.

Notes

1. American Red Cross, *Tsunami Strategic Plan,* http://www.oregonredcross.org/pdf/FundamentalPrinciples.pdf.

2. Thomas A. Birkland, *Lessons of Disaster: Policy Change after Catastrophic Events* (Washington, DC: Georgetown University Press, 2006), 4.

3. Emma Bath, "Tsunami Response Was World's Best—UN," *Reuters,* December 19, 2005, http://www.alertnet.org/thefacts/reliefresources/113777913049.htm.

4. Government of Sri Lanka and United Nations, *National Post-tsunami Lessons Learned and Best Practices Workshop Report,* June 8–9, 2005, Colombo, Tsuri Sri Lanka, http://www.preventionweb.net/files/2176_VL323138.pdf.

5. World Bank, *Update on the World Bank Response to the Tsunami Disaster,* April 22, 2005, http://siteresources.worldbank.org/INTTSUNAMI/Resources/tsunamireport-042205.pdf.

6. United Nations Development Programme Bureau for Crisis Prevention and Recovery, "The Post-tsunami Recovery in the Indian Ocean: Lessons Learned, Successes, Challenges, and Future Action," April 2005.

7. World Bank, "Update on the World Bank Response to the Tsunami Disaster."

8. United Nations Office of Humanitarian Assistance, *What Is a Flash Appeal?* January 6, 2005, http://ocha.unog.ch/ets/Default.aspx?ContentType=FixedContent&ContentID=3#.

9. British Red Cross, *One Year On Tsunami Report,* December 16, 2005, URL: http://ocha-gwapps1.unog.ch/rw/rwb.nsf/db900sid/DPAS-6K5DJR?Open Document.

10. American Red Cross, *Tsunami Strategic Plan.*

11. United Nations Foundation, *United Nations Coordinates International Response to Tsunami,* February 14, 2005, http://www.unfoundation.org/files/pdf/2005/UNroleintsunamirelief.pdf.

12. Asian Development Bank, *Tsunami Response: Three Years On: Lives and Communities Being Rebuilt,* September 23, 2009, http://www.adb.org/Tsunami/default.asp.

13. Silvia Hidalgo, Ricardo Sole, and Kim Wuyts, *The International Community's Funding of the Tsunami Emergency and Relief: Government Funding, European Commission* (London: Tsunami Evaluation Coalition, 2006).

14. United Nations Office for the Coordination of Humanitarian Affairs, *Indian Ocean—Earthquake/Tsunami—December 2004, Table A: List of all commitments/contributions and pledges as of 03-July-2010,* http://ocha.unog.ch/fts/reports/daily/ocha_R10_E14794_asof___1007030209.pdf (table ref: R10).

15. Asian Development Bank, *High-level Coordination Meeting on Rehabilitation and Reconstruction Assistance to Tsunami-affected Countries,* Manila, Philippines, March 18, 2005, http://www.adb.org/Documents/Events/2005/Rehabilitation-Reconstruction/default.asp.

16. *Indian Ocean Earthquake-Tsunami Flash Appeal Expenditure Tracking,* http://ocha.unog.ch/ets/Default.aspx?ContentType=FixedContent&ContentID=1.

17. "Clinton Made UN's Tsunami Envoy," *BBC News,* February 1, 2005.

18. "Bush and Clinton, in Thailand, Start Tour of Tsunami Region," *New York Times,* February 20, 2005.

19. Scientists argue that many of the deaths could have been prevented had an

early warning system been in place. Martin Williams, "Tsunami: The Wave That Shook the World," *NOVA* (Boston: NONVVWGBH Educational Foundation, 2005) (documentary video).

20. Richard Stone and Richard A. Kerr, "Indian Ocean Tsunami: Girding for the Next Killer Wave," *Science,* December 9, 2005, 1602–5.

21. National Oceanic and Atmospheric Association, Pacific Tsunami Warning Center, *Pacific Tsunami Warning Center History,* November 25, 2009, http://www.weather .gov/ptwc/history.php.

22. Address by Koichiro Matsuura, director-general of the United Nations Educational, Scientific and Cultural Organization (UNESCO) on the occasion of the opening of the "International Coordination Meeting for the Development of a Tsunami Warning and Mitigation System for the Indian Ocean within a Global Framework," UNESCO, March 3, 2005, http://ioc3.unesco.org/indotsunami/UNESCO_DG_speech_ tsunami_paris_0305.htm.

23. ASEAN, "Action Plan to Formulate a Technology Platform for Earthquake-Generated Tsunami Warning," China-ASEAN Workshop on Earthquake-Generated Tsunami Warning, Beijing, January 25–26, 2005, http://www.aseansec.org/17249.htm.

24. United States Embassy, *Jakarta: Tsunami Early Warning System Workshop,* n.d., http://jakarta.usembassy.gov/econ/EWS%20Workshop_Website%20Version.pdf.

25. National Oceanic and Atmospheric Association, *Pacific Tsunami Warning Center History.* See also United Nations Educational, Cultural and Scientific Organization, *Towards the Establishment of a Tsunami Warning and Mitigation System for the Indian Ocean,* n.d., http;//ioc3.unesco.org/indotsunami/.

26. Bundesministerium für Bildung und Forschung, *Tsunami Early Warning System (TEWS): The German-Indonesian Contribution,* February 2, 2010, http://www.bgr .bund.de/nn_324952/EN/Themen/TZ/TechnZusammenarb/Projekte/Abgeschlossen/ Asien/indonesien__gitews__en.html.

27. Jon Bennett, William Bertrand, Clare Harkin, Stanley Samarasinghe, and Hemantha Wickramatillake (members of NGOs in Sri Lanka), *Coordination of International Humanitarian Assistance in Tsunami-Affected Countries: Evaluation Findings; Sri Lanka* (London: Tsunami Evaluation Coalition, 2006), http:// www.tsunami-evaluation.org/NR/rdonlyres/6A1C7C4D-D99C-4ECE-A207– 99589C212E78/0/coordination_sri_lanka.pdf.

28. Ibid.

29. Elisabeth Scheper, Arjuna Parakrama, and Smruti Patel, with contributions from Tony Vaux, *Impact of the Tsunami Response on Local and National Capacities,* (London: Tsunami Evaluation Coalition, 2006).

30. World Bank, "Update on the World Bank Response to the Tsunami Disaster."

31. U.N. Resident/Humanitarian Coordinators, *Briefing Note for President Clinton, Special Envoy for Tsunami Response: Key Trends and Issues regarding Relief and Recovery for India, Indonesia, Maldives, Sri-Lanka and Thailand,* February 9, 2005, ftp://ftp.fao .org/FI/DOCUMENT/tsunamis_05/NEWS/Keycountryissues9Feb05.pdf.

32. United Nations, *Country Status Report: UN Tsunami Recovery India,* April 2006, http://www.un.org.in/untrs/reports/Tsunami_UN_Status_report_India_Apr06.doc.

33. Elisabeth Scheper, with contributions from Smruti Patel, *The Impact of The Tsunami Response on Local and National Capacities: Thailand Country Report* (London: Tsunami Evaluation Coalition, 2006), http://www.alnap.org/pool/files/capacities-thailand.pdf.

34. Traditional knowledge in some regions led people to evacuate to higher grounds before the tsunami hit. In one case, a ten-year-old British girl's geography lesson led her to recognize the signs of the impending tsunami and she was able to save other tourists in Phuket with her knowledge.

35. Government of Indonesia and United Nations, "Post-tsunami Lessons Learned and Best Practices Workshop: Report and Working Groups Output," May 16–17, 2005, Jakarta, Indonesia.

36. Government of Sri Lanka and United Nations, "National Post-tsunami Lessons Learned and Best Practices Workshop Report," June 8–9, 2005, Colombo, Tsuri, Sri Lanka.

37. Sálvano Briceño, "10 Lessons Learned from the South Asia Tsunami of 26 December 2004," Inter-agency Secretariat of the International Strategy for Disaster Reduction, January 7, 2005, www.unisdr.org.

38. United Nations Development Programme Bureau for Crisis Prevention and Recovery, "The Post-tsunami Recovery in the Indian Ocean."

39. Government of Indonesia and United Nations, "Post-tsunami Lessons Learned and Best Practices Workshop: Report and Working Groups Output," May 16–17, 2005, Jakarta, Indonesia.

40. Pennapa Hongthong, "Tsunami: One Year On," *Nation,* December 25, 2005, http://www.nationmultimedia.com/specials/tsunami/25dec3.php.

41. Disaster Management Centre, Ministry of Disaster Management for Safer Communities and Sustainable Management in Sri Lanka, http://www.dmc.gov.lk/index_english.htm.

42. http://www.unisdr.org/asiapacific/ap-highlights/2006/march06.htm.

43. "After the Tsunami—Build Local Capacity: Interview with Mathew Cherian, Alex Irwan and Andrew Harding," *Alliance Extra,* February 25, 2005, http://www.allavida.org/alliance/axfeb05b.html.

44. World Bank, "Update on the World Bank Response to the Tsunami Disaster."

45. USAID/Asia, "Lessons Learned in Recovery: Post-tsunami Relief and Reconstruction for Sustainable Coastal Development," proceedings report from a workshop hosted by the USAID Post-tsunami Sustainable Coastal Livelihoods Program in collaboration with the U.S. government Indian Ocean Tsunami Warning System Program (IOTWS), March 28, 2006. See also Bath, "Tsunami Response Was World's Best."

46. United Nations Development Programme Bureau for Crisis Prevention and Recovery, "The Post-tsunami Recovery in the Indian Ocean."

47. Paul Harvey, *Cash-based Responses in Emergencies* (London: Overseas Development Institute, 2007), http://www.odi.org.uk/resources/download/229.pdf.

48. United Nations, International Strategy for Disaster Reduction, Platform for the Promotion of Early Warning, http://www.unisdr.org/ppew/ppew-index.htm.

49. United Nations Environment Programme, press release IHA/1055, UNEP/283,

"UNEP Post-tsunami Assessment Finds Environmental Impacts in Maldives," June 17, 2005, http://www.un.org/News/Press/docs/2005/iha1055.doc.htm.

50. Nirmal Ghosh, "Destroyed Mangroves Could Have Saved Lives," *Straight Times, Singapore,* January 8, 2005, http://www.ecologyasia.com/news-archives/2005/jan-05/st_050108_1.htm; Hari Srinivas, "The Indian Ocean Tsunami and its Environmental Impacts," *A Global Development Research Center Special Feature on Environmental Management and Risk Reduction,* n.d., http://www.gdrc.org/uem/disasters/disenvi/index.html.

51. Andrew Quinn, "Indonesia to Replant Mangroves in Tsunami Defense," *Reuters,* January 18, 2005, http://www.forestsandtradeasia.org/posting/Indonesia/English/287.

52. Asian Development Bank, *Briefing Paper: The ASEAN Leaders' Special Summit Earthquake and Tsunami Disaster, January 6, 2005, Jakarta and Aceh, Indonesia,* http://www.adb.org/Documents/Papers/Tsunami/asean-earthquake-tsunami.pdf.

53. ASEAN, "Declaration on Action to Strengthen Emergency Relief, Rehabilitation, Reconstruction, and Prevention on the Aftermath of Earthquake and Tsunami Disaster of 26 December," Special ASEAN Leaders' Meeting on Aftermath of Earthquake and Tsunami, January 6, 2005, Jakarta, Indonesia, http://www.aseansec.org/17066.htm.

54. ASEAN Agreement on Disaster Management and Emergency Response, Vientiane, July 26, 2005, http://www.aseansec.org/17579.htm.

55. International Strategy for Disaster Reduction, *Hyogo Framework for Action 2005–15: Building the Resilience of Nations and Communities to Disasters* (extract from the final report of the World Conference on Disaster Reduction, A/CONF.206/6), http://www.unisdr.org/eng/hfa/hfa.htm.

56. International Strategy for Disaster Reduction, *Common Statement of the Special Session on the Indian Ocean Disaster: Risk Reduction for a Safer Future* (extract from the final report of the World Conference on Disaster Reduction, A/CONF.206/6), http://www.unisdr.org/wcdr/intergover/official-doc/L-docs/special-session-indian-ocean.pdf.

57. http://www.unisdr.org/.

58. United Nations Development Programme Bureau for Crisis Prevention and Recovery, "The Post-tsunami Recovery in the Indian Ocean."

59. Global Facility for Disaster Reduction and Recovery, *Reducing Vulnerability to Natural Disasters,* October 2007, http://gfdrr.org/docs/GFDRR_Brochure_At_a_glance.pdf.

60. Global Platform for Disaster Reduction, First Session, June 5–7, 2007, Geneva, Switzerland, http://www.preventionweb.net/globalplatform/gp-abouth.html.

Part 3

Geopolitical Perspective

13

Transnational Geopolitical Competition and Natural Disasters

Lessons from the Indian Ocean Tsunami

Christopher Jasparro and Jonathan Taylor

The shock and magnitude of the Indian Ocean Tsunami triggered the largest international relief operation in history (Tang 2007, 1). The massive outpouring of aid from countries, multilateral organizations, nongovernmental organizations, and individual donors produced a phenomenon that came to be described as "competitive compassion" (Bindra 2005, 181).

In the days and weeks following the tsunami, all the major powers with geostrategic interests in Southeast Asia—China, India, Japan, and the United States—donated to the relief effort. Within two days of the tsunami strike, Japan announced a $30 million aid package, double the initial U.S. pledge. The United States then raised its offer to $350 million, while China pledged $63 million. Japan responded by increasing its offer to $500 million (Tamamoto 2005). Thailand and India, also hit by the tsunami, asserted their regional positions by giving aid to smaller neighbors while themselves rejecting most outside assistance (Greenhough, Jazeel, and Massey 2005, 370).

A similar pattern of "competitive compassion" emerged in the aftermath of the massive 2005 Pakistan earthquake. The major state donors to the relief effort were the United States and the Arab countries of Saudi Arabia, Kuwait, and the United Arab Emirates (all of which had taken considerable criticism for their limited assistance to Indonesia following the tsunami). India also played a major role in the relief effort.

It is therefore not a stretch, or even novel, to argue that aid in the wake of mega-disasters is an arena for geopolitical competition. However, today's "competitive compassion" is not merely an extension of interstate geopolitics as usual, but rather one dimension of a wider playing field where the international system's "legitimate" actors—states, on one hand, and international civil society (e.g., multilateral organizations, NGOs, the private sector), on the other—are in competition with the denizens of globalization's underside: such as transnational criminals and terrorist/extremist groups.[1] According to *Foreign Policy* editor Moises Naim, through the dynamic of globalization, global criminal networks have amassed enormous profits and become powerful political forces while those fighting them have been correspondingly weakened (2005, 12–13). Transnational terrorist organizations and networks have also emerged as powerful challengers to the traditional international system. Not surprisingly, both sets of actors have become players in disaster geopolitics.

The chaos created by natural disasters increases the risk of money laundering and terrorist financing. With their well-established networks and sophisticated technology, criminal groups are flexible, ready, and able to exploit any opportunities to launder their illegal proceeds (McKenzie and Bryant 2006, 198–99). In the aftermath of a disaster, trade, charities, and remittance services are vulnerable to exploitation by those wishing to finance terrorism (ibid., 200; Napoleoni 2003). Disaster relief is likewise a field for ideological competition between transnational terrorist groups and their opponents. For example, following the 2005 Pakistan earthquake, Ayman al-Zwahiri (Al-Qaeda's second in command) appeared in a broadcast saying, "I am appealing to all Muslims in general, and the Islamic charity organizations in particular, to move to Pakistan to extend relief to their brothers in Pakistan, and to rush to do that, and to consider all the hardships and harm they face in that to be for the sake of God. We all are aware of the extent of the raging US war against Islamic charity work" (Al-Jazirah 2005).

Samson (2003) describes this emerging geopolitical situation as a triangle between "states," "project" society (e.g., civil society and other actors with resources and relief or development missions), and "mafia" (organized crime, warlords, etc.). The sides of the triangle may act antagonistically toward each as well as in concert, but the relationship is mediated by state-centered coalitions (ibid., 337–38). This geopolitics of compassion, as well as the relationship and motivations between different actors, is, according to Hyndman, driven by fear, which becomes securitized. Fear is employed to instigate "political demands for protection from ill-defined geographically diffuse threats: disease, asylum seekers, transnational crime, terrorism" (2007, 367). Consequently, humanitarian and development assistance is "increasingly being linked with issues of (in)security and (in)stability," while states may cooperate in the face of shared fears (ibid.). Disaster relief thus has become (at least in part) an exercise in geopolitics and security.

Events in the aftermath of the Asian tsunami vividly illustrate how disasters have become a new front for this type of geopolitical competition and interplay among state and nonstate actors. The tsunami did not just unleash a wave of physical death and destruction, but also created and exacerbated fears and vulnerabilities that nonstate criminals and extremists (not just states or humanitarian agencies) could potentially exploit. In this case, we see a loose coalition of states and project (or international civil) society acting against criminal and extremist organizations (albeit with some crossover between state actors and criminals/extremists), attempting to exploit post-disaster conditions along the lines just described. On the other hand, opportunities also opened for states and the international community to counterattack—providing some useful lessons for strategists and disaster planners as well as questions for scholars to ponder.

Nonstate Transnational Threats in Southeast Asia: Definitions and Regional Vulnerability

Nonstate transnational security (also commonly referred to as nontraditional or "gray area") threats are nonmilitary threats that cross borders and threaten either the political and social integrity of a state or the health and quality of life of its inhabitants (Smith 2000, 78). As such, they operate at the intersection of often competing notions of human security and more traditional understandings of state/national security. Commonly cited examples of such threats include organized crime, terrorism, illicit trafficking (in drugs, wildlife, humans, arms, etc.), piracy, infectious disease and pandemics, and illegal migration flows (ibid., 77–78).

Southeast Asia is particularly vulnerable to transnational threats because of its crossroads location for trade, transport, and finance; rapid economic growth coupled with intense poverty and inequalities; high levels of government corruption in many states; severe environmental degradation; the historic importance and occurrence of low-intensity conflict and high level of organized crime and piracy; ethnic diversity; and location along major natural hazard belts. These threats are clearly increasing and intensifying in potential and scope (Tan and Boutin 2001; Chalk 2000).

Transnational Threats and Tsunami: Indonesia

Several nonstate threats manifested themselves in northern Sumatra in the weeks after the tsunami struck. Terrorism and human trafficking both received considerable media attention and will be the main focus of this chapter. Concerns over piracy, environmental crime, and financial cyber crime also emerged as the tsunami's waters receded. Therefore, these issues will also be addressed because they offer some interesting questions and lessons learned.

Terrorism

Soon after the tsunami struck, a complex web of extremist and/or terrorist-affiliated organizations began to weave itself into the fabric of the stricken zone. Four organizations with extremist ties quickly deployed personnel to Aceh. The Majelis Mujahidin Indonesia (MMI—Indonesia Mujahidin Council), an Islamist extremist umbrella group with a paramilitary wing (van Bruinessen 2002) founded in 2000 by Abu Bakar Ba'asyir (Barton 2004, 114), is thought to have moved around seventy members into Aceh by early January 2004 (Kurniawan 2005). Laskar Mujahidin (LM), an Islamist jihadi militia (Barton 2004, 114), as well as the Medical Emergency Relief Charity (MER-C), which has been linked to Jemaah Islamiah (JI) and Al-Qaeda personnel (Abuza 2003, 144), also sent personnel. The fourth group to enter was the Islamic Defenders Front (more commonly known by its Bahasa acronym FPI). The FPI, known for vandalizing bars and discos as well as for encouraging volunteers to fight against U.S. forces in Iraq (Harvey 2003), also sent 200 volunteers to Sumatra. They later threatened violence against Christian aid groups providing tsunami relief (Associated Press 2005).

Another group, Committee for Crisis Response (abbreviated as KOMPAK in Bahasa), channeled seventeen tons of medicine donated by Hungarian Muslims into Aceh and northern Sumatra that were to be distributed by the cigarette company PT Djarum as well as MER-C (Indonesia Relief 2005a). KOMPAK is the charity arm of the Dewaan Dakwah Islam Indonesia (DDII) or Islam Propagation Council of Indonesia. DDII itself has helped funnel 6.5 billion rupees of relief supplies and cash into Sumatra as well as built sixty houses, rebuilt four mosques, and donated scholarships for orphans (ibid.).

However, DDII has had ties to JI personnel going back to the 1970s (International Crisis Group 2004).[2] KOMPAK earned notoriety as a conduit for funding arms, propaganda, and jihadi activities in Ambon—reportedly in concert with Al-Qaeda members (ibid., 4). KOMPAK's former head, Agus Dwikarna, arrested in Manila in March 2002, has also served as MMI secretary (International Crisis Group 2002, 20). Prior to Dwikarna's arrest, he revealed in an interview how KOMPAK had worked with other charities including al-Haramain and the International Islamic Relief Organization (IIRO) (International Crisis Group

2004). Both of these organizations have had ties to terrorist financing (Krause 2006; Kohlmann 2004, 41–42; Gunaratna 2002, 68).

According to the Tsunami Relief Database (Indonesia Relief 2005b), al-Haramain and the IIRO have also been active in the tsunami zone, although al-Haramain had supposedly been dissolved by the Saudi government before the tsunami. The IIRO Philippine branch office was founded by Muhammad Jamal Khalifah, a senior member of Al-Qaeda and brother-in-law of Osama bin Laden, while the IIRO Indonesia branch is suspected of helping direct funds to JI-affiliated organizations. In August 2006 the U.S. Department of the Treasury "designated the Philippine and Indonesian branch offices of the Saudi Arabia–based International Islamic Relief Organization (IIRO) as entities that have assisted the fundraising efforts of al-Qaeda and related terrorist groups" (Krause 2006). Abd Al Hamid Sulaiman Al-Mujil, the executive director of the Eastern Province Branch of IIRO in Saudi Arabia, has also been designated as a terrorist financier for allegedly helping finance Al-Qaeda activities in Southeast Asia (ibid.). The United States and Saudi Arabia have jointly designated eleven branches of al-Haramain as front organizations for terrorist activities and have asked the U.N. to add the branches to its consolidated list of terrorists tied to Al-Qaeda and the Taliban (Prados and Blanchard 2004, 17).

In addition to attempting relief work, several of these extremist or terrorist-affiliated organizations quickly launched information campaigns to counter what they feared were Western and U.S. attempts to spread Christianity or establish a military presence in yet another Muslim country under the guise of disaster relief. For instance, the MMI's head of information, Fauzan Al-Anshari, cautioned that foreign intelligence agents might ride along with humanitarian aid missions (quote given to Indonesian newspaper *Jakarta Rakyat Merdeka* 2005, 1). The MMI also questioned the Indonesian government's legitimacy, accusing it of catering to foreign aid groups over local volunteers and arguing that indigenous efforts would have ultimately been sufficient. The FPI warned relief workers against engaging in un-Islamic behavior in public (Kingsbury 2005), while FPI's Aceh chief, Hilmy Bakar Almascaty, pronounced, "So far, America has come here like an angel, but if it turns into a Satan as it did in Afghanistan and Iraq, we must fight it" (Tayler 2005, 15).

Several observers and analysts also speculated that militants may have intended to directly exploit tsunami-induced disorder to engage in or incite violence against foreign military and relief personnel or Acehnese separatists (with whom they have a history of animosity and ideological difference). Alternatively, others suggested that the movement of militants to Aceh was facilitated by the Indonesian Army (Brummitt 2005). Among the reasons cited for this move are use of militants as paramilitary proxies (as has been the case in other areas of sectarian conflict), incompetence or inexperience among some generals, political battles within the army, or to counter foreign influences and domestic charges of favoritism to foreign relief agencies (Abuza and Smith 2005; Kingsbury 2005).

Some Western media outlets also raised the specter of extremist groups infiltrating international aid efforts or appropriating international assistance for their own purposes. The large media, military, government, and international scrutiny focused upon the relief effort largely prevented these fears from being realized. The MMI did indeed manage to slip under the radar and sign a contract with the U.N. World Food Program and even received ninety-five tons of food to distribute to tsunami victims. However, the U.N. canceled the contract under pressure from the Australian government (Australian Broadcasting Corporation 2006).[3]

Two years after the tsunami struck, groups such as the FPI and suspect charities such as MER-C still maintained a presence in the impacted area. To date, outside militant groups have not conducted any terrorist operations and do not appear to have had much political effect in Aceh. Meanwhile, both the U.S. and international aid efforts received widespread and positive press in Indonesia. The combination of international media scrutiny, the tremendous resources and capacity of the international relief effort, and the traditional antipathy of the Free Aceh Movement (Gerakan Aceh Merdeka, or GAM) toward outside militant groups seems to have constrained their impact (Jasparro 2005). Although their presence has been tolerated by the army and GAM, their room for maneuver has remained limited.

In fact, the international response to the tsunami seems to have weakened support for militant Islamist groups and anti-Americanism within Indonesia as a whole, at least temporarily. The first poll taken in Indonesia after the tsunami showed that 65% of respondents viewed the United States positively. Some 23% showed support for Osama bin Laden versus 58% in 2003, while a plurality regarded U.S. antiterrorism activities favorably ("Indonesian Poll" 2005). Similarly, anecdotal evidence, such as media interviews with earthquake survivors in parts of Pakistan, suggests that American and Western assistance may also have temporarily improved local images of the United States and other Western countries (Rhode 2005).

Simultaneously, however, Al-Qaeda and likeminded groups seemed to have learned a lesson from the tsunami and appear determined not to again so easily cede the high ground of compassion to the United States or the international community. After the 2005 Pakistan earthquake, charities associated with militant groups responded to the disaster much as they had earlier in Indonesia. These groups included the al-Rashid Trust, which has been accused of helping fund Al-Qaeda and which is banned by the U.N. Security Council and is listed on Pakistan's terrorism watch list (Clarke 2006). Crossover between international aid donors and groups with extremist ties was also a problem following the Pakistan earthquake. According to a BBC investigation, U.N. relief aid was actually delivered to al-Rashid camps while U.N. agencies also worked with Jamaat ud-Dawa, a charity with suspected links to Lashkar-e-Toiba (LeT) (ibid.). The LeT is thought to have close links with Al-Qaeda and has surfaced in the investigations of the 7/11 London subway bombings and other transnational terrorist plots.

Unlike the case of the tsunami, unfulfilled aid pledges have meant that earthquake relief operations in Pakistan are still largely underfunded (Inderfurth, Fabryky, and Cohen 2005), thus enabling militants to better compete for influence against the international community. The persistence of extremist groups in both Indonesia and Pakistan suggests that gains achieved by states and the international community might not always be sustainable if donor fatigue sets in and media attention dissipates.

Human Trafficking

In 2003 the Indonesia government estimated that around a million of the country's women and children had been trafficked. Aceh province had been singled out as a major trafficking node where women and girls affected by the conflict and/or poverty were forced into prostitution and trafficked to brothels in Banda Aceh and Mualaboh ("Trading in People" 2005). Neighboring North Sumatra province is also a known sending, transit, and receiving area for trafficking in sex and domestic workers, child labor, and illegal adoption (Agustinanto 2003, 174). Traffickers target children by going to rural villages and persuading parents to let their children go with promises of good jobs. In urban areas street children are similarly targeted with promises of employment. Child laborers are trafficked locally, to other parts of Indonesia, and internationally to Malaysia (ibid.). To date, little is known about the organizational structure of domestic and transnational trafficking rings operating out of the northern half of Sumatra.

In the immediate post-disaster period, Indonesian officials estimated that 35,000 Acehnese children were orphaned. Given the existing child trafficking threat in the region, it is not surprising that within days reports surfaced of human traffickers attempting to prey upon the thousands of orphaned and unregistered children. According to National Police general Suyitno Landung, trafficking rings employed three scams to target orphans or displaced children: posing as NGO representatives, claiming to be family members, or pretending to be foster parents. UNICEF confirmed its first case of child trafficking by January 7 (Nishiyama 2005). According to a study conducted by the Indonesian NGO PKPA, traffickers promised parents on the tsunami-devastated island of Nias that their children would be adopted by rich people in Medan and continue their schooling, but several parents lost all contact with their children and never saw them again (Agustinanto 2003, 75).

Fortunately an effective and rapid international and Indonesian government response was mounted. The Indonesian government moved fast to prohibit the movement of children out of impacted areas. Among the antitrafficking measures implemented were:

- A moratorium on adoptions from Aceh;
- A ban on Acehnese children under sixteen leaving the country;
- Increased surveillance at airports and seaports in North Sumatra and Aceh;
- The placement of children in Sumatran orphanages or with Acehnese families under a temporary foster care scheme;
- The opening of twenty centers for unaccompanied children in displaced persons camps;
- The registration of children;
- Priority given to Acehnese residents once adoptions were allowed to proceed (Margesson 2005).

UNICEF and other international agencies quickly began monitoring orphan registration efforts. The U.S. State Department's Office to Monitor and Combat Trafficking in Persons immediately established communication with NGOs and provided advice on how to reduce opportunities for child exploitation, including identification and registration of children in refugee camps and educating camp workers on trafficking (Human Trafficking.Org 2005).

Unique interagency and international partnerships formed to help counter the threat. For example, the United Kingdom's Metropolitan Police set up an intelligence unit to investigate trafficking cases in support of UNICEF, the U.K.'s Foreign Office, Commonwealth Office, and Home Office, INTERPOL, EUROPOL, the International Organisation for Migration (IOM), and NGOs such as End Child Prostitution and Trafficking, the National Missing Persons Helpline, and Save the Children. These efforts, combined with intensive international media scrutiny, quickly limited and shut down opportunistic trafficking ("Police to Protect Tsunami Orphans" 2005). By February 2005 John Miller, director of the U.S. State Department's Office to Monitor and Combat Trafficking in Persons, was able to report that "there has been virtually no increase in verified incidents of human trafficking in countries hit by the Indian Ocean tsunami" (Human Trafficking.Org 2005).

In the years following the tsunami there has been no significant reporting of sustained upsurges in human trafficking activities. Meanwhile, new international initiatives for countering victims' longer-term vulnerability have been implemented in conjunction with existing programs. The IOM, for example, had been providing women with training in various cottage industries in order to reduce their trafficking risk before the tsunami. It has now added animal husbandry programs focused on women in tsunami-stricken areas (International Organisation for Migration 2005).

It is difficult to ascertain what the longer-term effects of the tsunami on human trafficking in Indonesia might be. Sustained long-term antitrafficking and vulnerability reduction efforts could have far-reaching effects. On the other hand, if recovery rates in affected areas are slow, additional migration push factors will emerge that may also act as disincentives for displaced persons to return home. Since legal channels for migration in Asia are limited, there is a risk that the tsunami may contribute to an increase in "irregular migration" (Laczko and Collett 2005).

The limited information available at the moment provides a mixed picture. New antitrafficking initiatives have been forthcoming in Indonesia. Recently, for example, Australia announced an A$21 million regional initiative that would help Indonesia's criminal justice system enhance regional efforts to stem human trafficking (Khalik 2007). The Indonesian government has made significant strides in addressing the issue of human trafficking as well, in key areas from prevention to enforcement to legal reform. Law enforcement efforts, for instance, are improving, with arrests up 29%, from 110 to 142, and prosecutions up 87%, from 30 to 56, between 2005 and 2006 (U.S. State Department 2007). The Indonesian House of Representatives has passed a bill, with the full support of all major political factions and signed into law by the president in April 2007, criminalizing human trafficking and related activities (including illegal foreign adoption) that metes out punishments including maximum fifteen-year jail sentences and fines of up to 5 billion rupees. The bill subjects ordinary people as well as public officials, corporations, and syndicates to sanction (Sijabat 2007; U.S. State Department 2007). Yet, Indonesia still has Southeast Asia's largest trafficking problem. Indonesian noncompliance with minimum antitrafficking standards is considerable, and the country has yet to sign the 2000 U.N. Convention on Trafficking in Persons (U.S. State Department 2007).

Piracy and Environmental Crime

Immediately following the tsunami, the presence of groups with JI and/or Al-Qaeda links near the entrance to one of the world's most important sea-lanes fueled the ongoing debate between maritime security experts as to whether Southeast Asia's high incidence of piracy portends an increasing maritime terrorism threat. The LM, for example, is believed to have experience in small boat operations, while JI has attempted maritime operations in the past.

However, pirate activity ceased completely off Aceh following the tsunami. No pirate attacks were reported in the Straits of Malacca for a full two months after the tsunami struck (International Maritime Bureau 2006, 15). This appears to be a result of tsunami-induced deaths among pirates, damage to pirate bases and equipment, possible changes in water depth, and the high level of military activity in the area during relief operations ("Constant Tsunamis" 2005; Shrader 2005).

This respite was short-lived. According to International Maritime Bureau (IMB) figures, piracy has recommenced off of Aceh and in the Malacca Straits (2006). Along with a renewal of piracy off the waters of Sumatra, some indications of a nexus between post-tsunami events and individual pirate attacks have emerged. In July 2006, the Indonesian Navy arrested three former GAM rebels for pirating ships carrying tsunami aid into western Aceh ("Indonesia Navy" 2006). Relief supplies and ships may thus have become a tempting target for former rebels who have managed to keep their arms, but perhaps not secured other employment. All in all, however, there is little to suggest that the tsunami has had much of a long-term effect on the piracy situation.

The tsunami has also generated opportunities for organized environmental crime. Illegal logging has long been a complicated phenomenon in Aceh, guided by the interests of a diverse set of actors (McCarthy 2002, 2006). The projected timber demand for rebuilding in Indonesia is between 4 and 8 million m^3 of logs higher than what can be harvested legally and sustainably from within Indonesia. Between just February and March 2005, lumber prices soared by at least 20% in Banda Aceh (Montlake 2005). This has raised fears that illegal logging will increase both in natural areas (such as the Gunung Leuser ecosystem) close to the impact zone as well as further afield (UNEP 2005, 27). Indeed, a field survey conducted by the independent NGO Greenomics Indonesia has found that around 850,000 m^3 of illegal logs have been used in Aceh reconstruction projects, and several local and international NGOs and agencies are believed to have unwittingly used illegally procured timber (Renner 2007; Casey 2006).

Since the tsunami, most of the illegal logging seems to have been conducted by criminals and desperate residents. During pre-tsunami conflict days, elements of both GAM and the Indonesia military were widely suspected of involvement in illegal logging. Some of those accused of cutting illegal timber are now unemployed former members of GAM. It is unclear to what extent Indonesian military personnel are now involved in illegal logging in Aceh. President Yudhoyono has taken steps against illegal logging by government forces. Some also claim the high profile of Aceh since the tsunami is having a deterrent effect. According to Alwi Shihab, coordinating minister for public welfare, "Military and police won't dare to do such a thing [in Aceh], because the president is watching this closely" (Montlake 2005).

Cyber Crime

Within hours of the tsunami fraudulent scams soliciting relief "donations" began appearing online around the world (Keizer 2005). Most scams were purported to have been launched by individuals. For instance, only several weeks after the tsunami, on January 20, a U.S. federal grand jury indicted American Matthew Schmieder for wire and e-mail fraud. He is accused of distributing more than 800,000 e-mails soliciting donations for a fake charity (U.S. Department of Justice 2005). Others, however, according to Vincent Weaver of the computer security company Symantec, "appear to have been part of a growing problem of Internet fraud by organized-crime groups and other cyber crooks in Eastern Europe, West Africa, Asia and the USA . . . scams [that] increase after every major disaster" (Iwata and Kasindorf 2005).

Responses to the scams appeared nearly as fast as the scams themselves. The U.S. Federal Bureau of Investigation (FBI) and the U.K. National Criminal Investigative Service had issued anti-scam warnings as early as January 1, 2005 (FBI and NCIS 2005). Nonprofit antifraud groups such as ScamBusters.org, Fraudaid, and DOSHELP.org (Fraudaid/DOSHELP/ScamBusters 2005) also quickly jumped into the act, posting Internet warnings and setting up reporting sites for tsunami-related fraud. Media coverage of the scams followed quickly on the heels of government and nongovernment warnings.

Internet security companies also offered assistance and capitalized on the opportunity for publicity. Cloudmark, Inc., for example, a company that delivers e-mail immune systems, launched an educational campaign to help protect tsunami relief organizations and individual donors from online "phishing" scams along with offering free fraud protection to donors and relief organizations (Cloudmark 2005). Ad hoc partnerships such as those formed to combat human trafficking also took shape. The FBI, for instance, partnered with various private industries to identify approximately 850 fraudulent tsunami Web sites and online schemes (FBI 2005).

Unfortunately, accurate and conclusive data are not available on how much money these scams generated or on the effectiveness of the rapidly generated counter-responses. It is clear, however, that the tsunami created a nearly instantaneous cyber battlefield between organized and individual criminals on one side and law enforcement, NGOs, and private business on the other.

Conclusion

There are four conclusions (or perhaps inferences) that can be drawn from this study. First, it is clear that large-scale disasters are arenas for "nontraditional" geopolitical competition in which criminals, terrorists, and other illicit networks compete for profit and influence against states and myriad other actors in the international system. Extremist and terrorist affiliates clearly tried to exert influence (and possibly raise funds) in the tsunami's aftermath, while criminals attempted to profit from the disorder on the ground as well as from the sympathy of donors.

Second, the minimal impact that extremist groups and criminals had in the wake of the tsunami suggests these groups may be, at least in this particular circumstance, more limited in their power and capabilities than is often feared. Furthermore, it appears possible that when states, NGOs, international organizations, and private sector actors focus their attention and work together, nonstate threats can be thwarted or at least managed. Indeed, factors that are often cited as enablers of transnational "bad" actors, such as the media, Internet, and networks, can be effectively employed against criminals, terrorists, and extremists.

Third, it is unclear how long post-disaster management or mitigation of nonstate threats can be sustained as time passes and attention shifts elsewhere. In spite of various shortcomings, the tsunami relief effort is atypical in the amount of attention and fulfilled aid pledges it was able to garner. Eleven months after the disaster, 84% of the financial needs of the U.N. tsunami appeal had been met, whereas the twenty-five other U.N.-consolidated appeals for 2005 were funded at an average of only 50% (Inderfurth, Fabryky, and Cohen 2005). Fourth, there is certainly a lack of in-depth and comprehensive data and field-based analysis of the topics discussed in this chapter.

From these four conclusions at least two issues of practical and scholarly significance may be drawn. First, from a purely practical point of view, consideration of nonstate, transnational threats should become part of the standard four-part emergency management cycle of preparedness, response, recovery, and mitigation by state, NGO, and private sector actors.[4] Such awareness and training may have to extend beyond actors traditionally involved in disaster relief. Financial institutions, for example, should reevaluate policies and procedures to counter the potential for criminal groups to exploit disasters in order to gain access to financial systems (McKenzie and Bryant 2006, 202). Key to this will be education and training. Particular attention should be paid to raising awareness of potential "nontraditional" threats (and how they operate and manifest themselves) among responders during the prevention/preparedness phases and then among the public, media, and international community during the response and mitigation phases. On the other hand, care must be taken to contextualize and avoid abusive articulation of such threats because the production of fear and crisis can generate mistrust and discrimination as well as be used to justify violence (Hyndman 2007, 369).

Second, there is a dearth of concrete data and comprehensive in-depth analysis upon which the aforementioned consideration can be based and applied. There is a need to develop and refine conceptual frameworks that can be applied to analyze and study the geopolitics of nontraditional, post-disaster competition. There is also a particular need for research into four other areas: the activities and operations of criminals and extremists in the wake of disasters, along with the local and international effects (or lack thereof) of their actions; the formation of ad hoc networks, how they function, and their effectiveness (i.e., the operationalization of Samson's triangle); the impact and effect of information activities undertaken to counter things such as extremist propaganda, cyber crime, and illicit trafficking; and assessment of the extent to which prior preparation and training helped disaster responders counter criminal, terrorist, and extremist activity.

Notes

1. There is some historic precedent for militants attempting to exploit the aftermath of disasters in Indonesia during an earlier era of globalization. In 1883, an impressive relief effort was mounted by the international community and Dutch colonial government in northern Java and southern Sumatra, following the Krakatoa eruption, whose devastating impact included tsunamis. However, once the international spotlight shifted elsewhere and resources for long-term recovery dwindled, radical preachers (the antecedents of today's religious militants) from what are now Yemen and Saudi Arabia stepped into the breach, ultimately helping precipitate the 1888 Banten Peasants Rebellion (Winchester 2004).

2. The DDII was founded in 1967 as part of the Islamist opposition to Suharto. It became increasingly attracted to Saudi-style Wahhabism as well as a beneficiary of Saudi Arabian funds (Ramakrishna 2004, 6).

3. In May 2007 Australian police arrested two leaders of Melbourne's Sri Lankan community for allegedly funneling aid money to the Tamil Tigers (Oakes, Medew, and Jackson 2007).

4. There are numerous articulations of this cycle in use around the world, but they are essentially merely variations on a theme. The U.S. Federal Emergency Management Administration (FEMA), for instance, now uses a five-component emergency management spectrum: prevention, preparedness, response, recovery, and mitigation (2006, 9.3).

References

Abuza, Zachary. 2003. *Militant Islam in Southeast Asia.* Boulder, CO: Lynne Rienner.

Abuza, Zachary (Simmons College), and Anthony Smith (Asia-Pacific Center for Security Studies). 2005. Personal communication, January.

Agustinanto, F. 2003. North Sumatra. In *Trafficking of women and children in Indonesia,* ed. R. Rosenberg, 174–77. Jakarta: USAID.

Al-Jazirah. 2005. Al-Zawahiri urges Muslims to aid Pakistan earthquake victims. October 23. Federal Broadcast Information Servicetranslation.

Associated Press. 2005. Tsunami aid workers suspected of trying to convert Muslims. January 21. http//www.foxnews.com/story/0,2933,145049,00.html.

Australian Broadcasting Corporation. 2006. UN cancels aid contract over Bashir links. June 15. http://www.abc.net.au/news/stories/ 2006/06/15/1664180.htm.

Barton, Greg. 2004. *Jemaah Islamiyah.* Singapore: Singapore University Press.

Bindra, Satindar. 2005. *Tsunami: 7 hours that shook the world.* Colombo: Vijitha Yapa.

Brummitt, C. 2005. Radical group aiding relief cause. *Associated Press Asia,* January 7.

Casey, Michael 2006. Tsunami boosts illegal logging. Associated Press, August 7. http://dsc.discovery.com/news/2006/08/07/logging_pla.html?category=travel&guid=20060807163030.

Chalk, Peter. 2000. *Grey area phenomena in Southeast Asia: Piracy, drug trafficking, and political terrorism.* Canberra: Strategic and Defence Studies Centre, Australian National University.

Clarke, K. 2006. UN aid went to extremists. *BBC News,* October 5.

Cloudmark, Inc. 2005. Cloudmark to help tsunami relief donors "catch" fraudulent emails. January 25. http://www.cloudmark.com/press/releases/?release=2005–01–25.

Constant tsunamis are called for to end the scourge of maritime piracy! Tsunamis end Malacca Straits piracy: Official. 2005. *AFP,* January 10.

FBI. 2005. Remarks by Grant D. Ashley, executive assistant director, Federal Bureau of Investigation Merchant Risk Council. March 9. http://www.fbi.gov/pressrel/speeches/ashley03092005.htm.

FBI and NCIS. 2005. "Tsunami Disaster Relief Fraud Alert! Don't be scammed." http://www.fbi.gov/page2/jan05/tsunamiscam010505.htm and http://cms.met.police

.uk/news/ppeals/robbery/fraud_alert_warning_bogus_charity_ messages_ for_tsunami_relief.

Fraudaid/DOSHELP/ScamBusters. 2005. http://www.fraudaid.com/tsunami_frauds/ index.htm, http://www.doshelp.com/SOHO/index.html, www.scambusters.org.

Greenhough, H., T. Jazeel, and D. Massey. 2005. Introduction: Geographical encounters with the Indian Ocean Tsunami. *Geographical Journal* 171 (4): 369–71.

Gunaratna, Rohan. 2002. *Inside Al-Qaeda.* New York: Columbia University Press.

Harvey, R. 2003. Spotlight on Indonesia's Islamic schools. *BBC News,* September 3.

Human Trafficking.Org. 2005. Few reports of increased human trafficking in tsunami-hit nations. February. http://www.humantrafficking.org/updates/88.

Hyndman, Jennifer. 2007. The securitization of fear in post-tsunami Sri Lanka. *Annals of the Association of American Geographers* 97 (2): 361–72.

Inderfurth, K., D. Fabryky, and S. Cohen. 2005. The tsunami report card. *Foreign Policy* (December). http://www.foreignpolicy.com/story/cms.php?story_id=3314.

Indonesia navy arrests tsunami aid pirates in Aceh. 2006. *Shipping Times,* July 26. http://www.kabar-irian.com/pipermail/kabar—indonesia/2006-July/002378.html.

Indonesian poll finds tsunami aid boosts US support. 2005. *Reuters,* March 4. http:// www.alertnet.org/thenews/newsdesk/N04624899.htm.

Indonesia Relief. 2005a. Hungarian Muslims sent 17 tons of medicine to Aceh. *Jakarta Republika,* July 7. http://www.indonesia—relief.org/mod=publisher&op =viewarticle&cid=4&artid=1378.

———. 2005b. *Indonesia relief portal tsunami database.* http://www.indonesia-relief. org/mod.php?mod=bank&op=infobank&bankid=23).

International Crisis Group. 2002. *Al-Qaeda in Southeast Asia: The case of the "Ngruki network" in Indonesia.* Jakarta: ICG.

———. 2004. *Indonesia backgrounder: Jihad in Central Sulawesi.* ICG Asia Report 74. Jakarta/Brussels: International Crisis Group.

International Maritime Bureau. 2006. *ICC International Maritime Bureau piracy and armed robbery against ships annual report.* Barking, UK: IMB.

International Organisation for Migration. 2005. Human trafficking: Animal husbandry part of IOM counter trafficking initiative in Indonesia. *IOM Press Briefing Notes,* April 22 (updated September). http://www.iom.int/en/news/PBN220405 .shtml#item4.

Iwata, Edward, and Martin Kasindorf. 2005. Crooks faking Web sites to bilk unwitting donors. *USA Today,* January 10. http://www.usatoday.com/news/world/2005-01-10-scams-tsunami_x.htm.

Jakarta Rakyat Merdeka. 2005. January 2. http://www.rakyatmerdeka.co.id/.

Jasparro, Christopher. 2005. Old threats, new opportunities in the tsunami's wake. *Yale Global Online* (March). http://yaleglobal.yale.edu/display.article?id=546123.

Keizer, Gregg. 2005. Groups warn of tsunami scams. *ITnews.com.au,* January 10. www .crime-research.org/news/10.01.2005/887/.

Khalik, Abdul. 2007. Australia gives aid to slave trade fight. *Jakarta Post,* August 28. http://www.thejakartapost.com/detailheadlines.asp?fileid=20070828.@01&irec=0.

Kingsbury, Damian. 2005. Growing doubts on Aceh's relief effort. *The Australian,* January 12. www.theaustralian.news.com.au/common/story_page/0,5744,11914 044%255E7583,00.html.

Kohlmann, Evan. 2004. *Al-Qaida's jihad in Europe.* Oxford: Berg.

Krause, Susan. 2006. Saudi charity in Indonesia, Philippines tied to terrorist funding. U.S. State Department USINFO.State.Gov, August 4. http://usinfo.state.gov/ xarchives/display.html?p=washfile-english&y=2006&m=August&x=2006080410 2418ASesuarK4.920596e-02.

Kurniawan, B. 2005. 77 MMI members sent to Aceh to provide spiritual guidance. *Jakarta Detikcom (WWW-Text),* January 4.

Laczko, F., and E. Collett. 2005. Assessing the tsunami's effects on migration. *Migration Information Source,* April 1. http://www.migrationinformation.org/feature/ display.cfm?id=299.

Margesson, Rhoda. 2005. *CRS report—Indian Ocean earthquake and tsunami: Humanitarian assistance and relief operations.* Washington, DC: Congressional Research Service.

McCarthy, John. 2002. Turning in circles: District governance, illegal logging, and environmental decline in Sumatra, Indonesia. *Society and Natural Resources* 15:867–86.

———. 2006. *The fourth circle: A political ecology of Sumatra's rainforest frontier.* Stanford, CA: Stanford University Press.

McKenzie, Mark, and Kenneth Bryant. 2006. Natural disasters and money laundering risks. *Journal of Money Laundering Control* 9 (2): 198–202.

Montlake, Simon. 2005. Timber trouble in Aceh. *Christian Science Monitor,* March 9. http://search.yahoo.com/search;_ylt=A0geu9tiV9xGFGoAwjNXNyoA?p=illegal+l ogging+and+tsunami+And+army&fr=slv8-grpj.

Naim, Moises. 2005. *Illicit.* New York: Anchor Books.

Napoleoni, Loretta. 2003. *Modern jihad: Tracing the dollars behind the terror networks.* London: Pluto.

Nishiyama, George. 2005. UNICEF confirms tsunami child trafficking case. *Reuters,* January 7.

Oakes, Dan, Julia Medew, and Andra Jackson. 2007. Pair arrested over tsunami aid sent to Tamil Tigers. *The Age,* May 2., http://www.theage.com.au/news/national/pair-arrested-over-tsunami-aid-sent-to-tamil-tigers/2007/05/01/1177788141406.html.

Police to protect tsunami orphans. 2005. *BBC News,* January 11.

Prados, Alfred, and Christopher Blanchard. 2004. *CRS report—Saudi Arabia: Terrorist financing issues.* Washington, DC: Congressional Research Service.

Ramakrishna, Kumar. 2004. Constructing the Jemaah Islamiyah terrorist: A preliminary inquiry. Working paper 71, Institute of Defence and Strategic Studies, Singapore.

Renner, Michael. 2007. Illegal logging, tsunami reconstruction, biofuels, and climate change: Indonesian governors take action. Worldwatch Institute, May 15. http:// www.worldwatch.org/node/5073.

Rhode, David. 2005. For devout Pakistani Muslims, aid muddles loyalties. *New York Times,* October 26.

Samson, Scott. 2003. "Trouble spots": Projects, bandits, and state fragmentation. In

Globalization, the State, and Violence, ed. J. Friedman, 309–42. New York: Rowan and Littlefield.

Shrader, K. Pfleger. 2005. Cartographers redrawing maps after tsunami. January 5. http://www.freerepublic.com/focus/f-news/1314839/posts.

Sijabat, Ridwan Max. 2007. Legislature approves harsh bill to combat human trafficking. *Jakarta Post,* March 21. http://www.thejakartapost.com/yesterdaydetail .asp?fileid=20070321.A04.

Smith, Paul. 2000. Transnational security threats and state survival: A role for the military? *Parameters* 30:77–91.

Tamamoto, Masaru. 2005. After the tsunami, how Japan can lead. *Far Eastern Economic Review,* February 5. http://www.howardwfrench.com/cgi-bin/mt/mt—tb.cgi/169.

Tan, Andrew, and J. Boutin. 2001. *Non-traditional security issues in Southeast Asia.* Singapore: IDSS.

Tang, Catherine So-kum. 2007. Posttraumatic growth of Southeast Asian survivors with physical injuries: Six months after the 2004 Southeast Asian earthquake-tsunami. *Australasian Journal of Disaster and Trauma Studies* 2007 (1): 1–10.

Tayler, L. 2005. When relief fights belief. *Long Island Newsday,* January 23, 15.

Trading in people: The abuse and exploitation of people trafficking. 2005. *Social Justice,* September 25, 10–11. http://www.ncca.org.au/files/Archives/Kits/SJS_2005/8.pdf.

UNEP. 2005. *After the tsunami: Rapid environmental assessment.* N.p.: UNEP. http:// www.unep.org/tsunami/reports/TSUNAMI_report_complete.pdf.

U.S. Department of Justice. 2005. Tsunami relief fraud spammer indicted. January 20. http://www.usdoj.gov/usao/or/PressReleases/20050120_tsunami_relief_fraud.htm.

U.S. Federal Emergency Management Administration. 2006. *Principles of emergency management.* www.training.fema.gov.

U.S. State Department. 2007. *Trafficking in persons report.* http://www.state.gov/g/tip/ rls/tiprpt/2007/82806.htm.

van Bruinessen, Martin. 2002. The violent fringes of Indonesia's Islam. *ISIM Newsletter* (December), 7.

Winchester, Simon. 2004. *The day the world exploded.* London: Penguin.

Contributors

KOJI FUJIMA is professor in the Department of Civil and Environmental Engineering at the National Defense Academy, Yokosuka, Japan. His research focus is on tsunami hazard, coastal engineering, and wave propagation and transformation.

CHRISTOPHER JASPARRO is associate professor of national security affairs at U.S. Naval War College, Newport, Rhode Island. His primary interests are transnational and environmental security issues and the regional geography of Asia and Africa. His recent research has been published in outlets such as *Geopolitics* and *Jane's Intelligence Review*.

PRADYUMNA P. KARAN, University Research Professor in the Department of Geography, University of Kentucky, is author of several books on environment and development issues in the non-Western world.

MUTHUSAMI KUMARAN is assistant professor of nonprofit management and community organizations in the Department of Family, Youth and Community Sciences at the University of Florida. He has worked in both government and nonprofit sectors, and has assisted nonprofit organizations and NGOs in the United States and India.

J. FRANCIS LAWRENCE is professor of geology at the Presidency College, Chennai, India.

K. MANOHARAN is on the faculty of the Department of Earth Sciences, Annamalai University, Tamil Nadu, India.

M. V. MUKESH is assistant professor in the Department of Earth Sciences, Annamalai University, Tamil Nadu, India.

MARTIN MULLIGAN is director of the Globalism Research Centre at RMIT University in Melbourne, Australia. He specializes in research on the sustainability of local communities in the context of accelerating global integration, and is the author of *Decolonizing Nature: Strategies for Conservation in a Postcolonial World* (2003).

PURVAJA RAMACHANDRAN is a scientist at the Institute for Ocean Management, Anna University, Chennai, India. Her research interests include studies on trace gas emissions from mangroves and biogeochemical cycles in coastal ecosystems.

RAMESH RAMCHANDRAN is the director of the Institute for Ocean Management, Anna University, Chennai, India. His research deals with coastal zone management.

ANTONYSAMY SAGAYARAJ is lecturer in the Department of Anthropology and Philosophy at Nanzan University, Nagoya, Japan. His research interests are socioreligious movements, caste, communalism, and gender in India.

MIRANDA A. SCHREURS is director of the Environmental Policy Research Centre and professor of comparative politics at the Free University of Berlin, and dean of research in the Department of Political and Social Sciences. She serves on the German Advisory Council on the Environment.

S. RANI SENTHAMARAI is professor of geography at the Presidency College, Chennai, India.

BOJARAJAN SENTHILKUMAR is research associate at the Institute for Ocean Management, Anna University, Chennai, India.

P. SERALATHAN is professor in the Department of Marine Geology and Geophysics in the School of Marine Sciences at Cochin University of Science and Technology, Cochin, Kerala, India.

JUDITH SHAW is senior research fellow at Monash Asia Institute, Monash University, Victoria, Australia. She is the leader of the research team investigating housing resettlement projects in areas affected by the 2004 tsunami in India and Sri Lanka.

S. R. SINGARASUBRAMANIAN is associate professor in the Department of Earth Sciences at Annamalai University, Tamil Nadu, India.

S. SRINIVASALU is associate professor in the Department of Geology, Anna University, Chennai, India.

SHANMUGAM P. SUBBIAH, professor emeritus of geography at the University of Madras, Chennai, India, is editor of the *Indian Geographical Journal* and *Natural Hazards and Disasters: Essays on Impacts and Management* (2009).

SEIKO SUGIMOTO is professor of social anthropology at Kyoto Bunkyo University, with regional specialization in India, Madagascar, Mauritius, and Japan. She is the author of *Goddess, Temples and Village Networks in Kongunadu, Tamil Nadu, India* (2006).

YOSHIO SUGIMOTO, a senior faculty member in anthropology at the National Museum of Ethnology, Osaka, Japan, directs studies on the social anthropology of South Asia. His current research focus is on Christianity and popular cultures in the context of nationalism in India.

JONATHAN TAYLOR is associate professor of geography at California State University, Fullerton. He conducts research on environmental issues in Asia, particularly vulnerabilities to climate change, and has published in journals such as *Geopolitics*, *Political Geography*, and the *Geographical Review*.

TRICIA TORRIS is working with the University of Hawaii Department of Family Medicine and Community Health as program coordinator for a cooperative agreement through the Centers for Disease Control and Prevention (CDC) in the U.S.-Affiliated Pacific Islands. She has several years of experience in disaster management and humanitarian assistance. She worked with the NGOs involved in tsunami relief in Cuddalore district of Tamil Nadu, India.

MASATOMO UMITSU, professor emeritus at Nagoya University, is a professor of geography at Nara University, Japan. His research field is late Quaternary landform evolution and environmental change of coastal regions in Southeast Asia, the Ganges Delta, Japan, and Australia.

BRIGITTE URBAN is a biologist and Quaternary geoecologist. She is speaker of the research group Ecosystem Functioning and Global Change at Leuphana University, Germany.

KENJI YAMAZAKI is professor of geography at Iwate University, Morioka, Japan. He has published widely on natural hazards and disasters as well as on environmental geography.

TOMOKO YAMAZAKI is a graduate of the University of Tokyo and Harvard University. She is on the faculty of Iwate University, Morioka, Japan, and is engaged in teacher training and English education programs.

DAVID ZURICK is professor of geography at Eastern Kentucky University. He is the author of numerous books and research papers on the Himalaya.

Index

Aceh Besar, 13, 51
Aceh city, 13, 26, 51, 58, 62, 63, 66, 74, 75, 290, 292
Aceh River, 13, 25, 51, 54, 63, 65, 66, 67
Aceh West Coast Road, 60, 63
Action Aid India (AAI), 196, 197, 207
    role in tsunami relief, 198
Action for Food Production (AFPRO), 223
Adyar River, 103, 215
aid agencies
    and perception of victims' needs, 23
    See also specific organizations;
        nongovernmental organizations
Al-Qaeda, 284, 286, 287, 288, 289, 292
American Red Cross, 106, 206, 264, 276
Ampara district, Sri Lanka, 21, 238, 239, 254
Andaman and Nicobar Environmental Team, 19
Andaman Islands, 6, 7, 8, 15, 19, 113, 114
    coastal ecosystem, 18
    damage from tsunami, 8, 116
    geomorphic changes in, 117
    run-up of seawater in, 117–18
    tsunamigenic sediments in, 119–23
Andaman Sea coast, 35, 43, 114, 174, 175, 177, 181
Andaman-Sumatra subduction zone, 113, 114
Asian Development Bank, 5, 20, 24, 27, 170, 247, 264, 265, 268, 269, 274
Association of Southeast Asian Nations (ASEAN), 262, 266
    need for cooperation within, 274

Banda Aceh coastal plain, 13–15, 51

brothels in, 289
destruction in, 52–54
inundation heights, 54–56
landforms and tsunami flow in, 57
recovery and rehabilitation in, 61–62
zones of damage, 54
Bangladesh, 7
Bhumika, 185
British Red Cross, 264

Calang, 58–59, 60, 63
CARE, 185, 264, 272
Caritas India, 222
Car Nicobar, 4
    population of, 18
    run-up levels in, 118
Catholic Bishops' Conference of India, 222
Catholic Relief Services, 185, 222, 264
Chennai, 2, 15, 23, 25, 66, 67, 80, 89, 103, 116, 119, 125, 196, 197, 203, 215, 223, 224, 225, 226, 227, 228, 234
    death toll in, 101
Chidambaram, 222
Chola dynasty, 106
Christianity, 26, 219, 231, 232, 233, 235
    history in India, 224
    miracles, 226
coastal development, 247–48, 258, 273
coastal geomorphology, 84, 111, 117
coastal landforms
    impact on tsunami inundation, 9–10
Coleroon River, 16, 71, 77, 102, 217
Colombo, 2, 20, 136, 137, 155, 237, 238, 239, 247, 250, 253, 254
Committee for Crisis Response, 286
Coovum River, 103

coral islands, 128
 tsunami effect on, 86–87, 130–31
coral reef mining, 8
coral reefs, 38, 114, 116, 273
 as barriers, 68, 132
 tsunami damage in Andaman, 123–24
 tsunami damage in Maldives, 128–30, 133
 tsunami damage in Sri Lanka, 241
 tsunami damage in Thailand, 172
Cuddalore, 8, 16, 22, 66, 80, 88, 89, 94, 102,
  183, 185
 death toll in, 77, 101, 188
 devastation in, 188
 inequality in services, 199–201
 inundation in, 104
 NGOs relief in, 188–96
 reconstruction efforts in, 195
 recovery experience in, 196–97
 shelters in, 190, 198–99
cyber crime, 293

Dalit Munnurimai Koottamaippu (DMK),
  190, 197
Department of Science and Technology,
  India, 99, 124
Dewaan Dakwah Islam Indonesia (DDII),
  286
Dhan Foundation, 185
disaster management, 261
 administrative inefficiencies in, 256–58
 building local and national capacity in,
  267–69
 governance issues in, 243
 governance mechanisms in, 265
 improving coordination in, 271–72
 preparedness and education, 270–71
 role of religious institutions in, 221, 223

ECHO, 185
environmental crime, 292
environmental impact of tsunami, 5, 6
 in Andaman Islands, 19
 in Banda Aceh, 13
 in Maldives, 133
 in Sri Lanka, 240–41
 in Tamil Nadu, 70–77
Eurasian plate, 7

farmland and tsunami, 263
 in Andaman Islands, 123
 in Tamil Nadu, 218
 in Thailand, 164, 172
FEMA, 206
fishing communities, 23, 26, 208, 215, 216,
  227
fishing industry, 216, 217
fishing loss from tsunami, 17
 in Banda Aceh, 54
 in Cuddalore district, India, 188, 191,
  192, 193, 199, 201, 204
 in Maldives, 128
 in Sri Lanka, 240, 241, 248, 250, 252,
  253, 255, 257
 in Tamil Nadu, India, 69, 83, 85, 224
 in Thailand, 42, 164, 169, 171, 172, 175,
  178
Food and Agricultural Organization
  (FAO), 264
foreign tourists, 1–2, 164, 165, 173, 175, 176
Free Aceh Movement, 59, 268, 288
Fritz Institute, 187, 188

Gadillam River, 71
Galle, 21, 136, 239, 243, 247, 259
Gulf of Mannar, 68, 70, 80, 84, 102, 189
 coral ecosystem of, 86

Human Rights Forum for Dalit Liberation,
  197
Hyogo Framework for Action, 274–75

India
 coastal landscapes of, 7–8, 10
 cultural factors in developing
  rehabilitation policy, 22
 NGOs in, 183–87
 plate, 7
 reconstruction experience in, 27
 role of religious organizations in, 22–23
 southeastern coast, 15–18
Indian Air Force base, 4, 18
Indian Ocean Tsunami, 1, 4, 5, 6, 24, 88,
  123, 127, 131, 133, 163, 181, 185, 210,
  227, 261, 274, 276
 aid to areas affected by, 25, 263–64

death toll, 2
developing an early warning system,
    265–67, 276
geography of, 7
human trafficking in countries affected
    by, 291
in Kaveri delta, 99–112
lessons learned from, 193–94
militant Islamic groups, 286–89
NGO's relief efforts, 183
nonstate criminals and extremists, 285
recovery and response to, 21–22
in Sri Lanka, 135
tourism, impact on, 168, 178
See also specific locations affected;
    tsunami
Indian Red Cross, 197
    approach to tsunami relief, 203
indigenous communities, 171
    understanding of tsunami signals, 19
Indira Point, 18, 19
Indo-Global Social Service Society, 223
Indonesia, 1, 2, 5, 6, 7, 9, 10, 13, 24, 25, 26,
    27, 51, 114, 119, 127, 136, 176, 234,
    237, 241, 263, 264, 266, 267, 268, 269,
    270, 271, 273, 274, 289
    anti-Americanism in, 288
    assistance to, 283
    human trafficking in, 289, 291
    illegal logs in reconstruction projects,
        293
    militant groups in, 288
    organized crime and tsunami in, 292
    terrorism in, 286–88
    transnational threats, 285
Indonesian Tifa Foundation, 271
Integrated Coastal and Marine Area
    Management (ICMAM), India, 117
interdisciplinary group, 7
International Islamic Relief Organization
    (IIRO), 286–87
international nongovernmental
    organizations (INGOs), 186
    language problems faced by, 207
International Rescue Committee, 264
Islamic Defenders Front, 286
Islamic Relief Indonesia, 264

Jamaat ud-Dawa, 289
Janatha Vimukthi Peramuna (JVP),
    245–46
Japan Platform, 234
Jemaah Islamiah (JI), 286

Kanyakumari, 10, 16, 69, 86, 89, 192
    Christians in, 219
    communal riots in, 221
    death toll in, 101
    second attack of tsunami in, 104
Karaikal, 8, 66, 71, 92, 99, 101, 104, 222
    impact of tsunami on groundwater in,
        107–8
Katrina, Hurricane, 27
    similarities to Indian Ocean Tsunami,
        206
Kaveri delta, 18, 65, 99, 106
    death toll in, 101
    extent of inundation in, 105
    impact of inundation in, 18
    run-up and infiltration, 99–111
Kerala coast, 10, 216, 222, 230, 234
    death toll in, 185
    impact of tsunami in, 101
Khao Lak, 11, 12, 21, 22, 39, 41, 163, 164,
    174, 175, 177
    landform changes in, 45–46
    recovery from tsunami, 48
Khao Phra Thaeo Reserve, 169
Kobe-Awaji earthquake, 218–19
Kodiyakarai, 71, 83, 99, 106
Koh Phi Phi National Park, 169
Kollidam River, 104, 107
Koswari Island, 87
Krabi, 11, 21, 35, 163–64, 165, 171, 173,
    174, 176, 177, 178, 179, 180

land ownership problems
    in Sri Lanka, 257
    in Tamil Nadu, India, 197–98, 202, 214
    in Thailand, 178
Lashkar-e-Toiba, 289
Laskar Mujahidin (LM), 286
League for Education and Development,
    185
Lho'nga village, 58

Liberation Tigers of Tamil Eelam (LTTE), 239, 244–45, 247

Mahabalipuram, 80, 103
Majelis Mujahidin Indonesia (MMI), 286, 287, 288
Maldives, 4, 8–9, 10, 19–20, 104, 127
   damage to buildings and death toll in, 128
   damage to coral reefs in, 130–31
   fishing vessels, 128
   groundwater pollution, 128
   population of, 127
Male, 4, 8, 20, 127, 128, 130, 131
mangrove forest, tsunami effects on, 10–11, 13, 25, 273
   in Kaveri delta, 106
   in Thailand, 172
   in Wright Myo, Andaman, 120, 122
Marina Beach, Chennai, 2, 71, 103, 215, 227
Mata Amritanandamayi Mission, Kerala, 234
Medical Emergency Relief Charity (MER-C), 286
Meiji Great Tsunami, 149, 150
Meulaboh, Aceh, 58–59, 60, 233, 271
Muthupet lagoon, 17, 104, 106, 107

Nagapattinam, 8, 10, 16, 17, 67, 80, 89, 94, 99, 101, 104, 105, 107, 185, 192, 214–15, 223, 227, 228, 230, 231
   castes in, 218
   death toll in, 77
   economy of, 217
   fishing industry in, 216
Nam Khem coastal plain, 11–13, 41, 42, 43
   landform changes in, 45–46
Nam Khem village, 42, 49
National Disaster Management Center, Maldives, 128, 130
National Disaster Warning Center, Thailand, 178
natural disasters, 1, 4, 6, 24, 202, 214, 219, 261, 263, 275
   and global criminal networks, 284
natural hazard research, 4

and tourism, 165
   perception-adjustment paradigm, 4–5
   political ecology approach, 5
nature-society relationship, 7
Nicobar Islands, 15, 18, 19, 113, 114, 118, 223
   run-up levels, 117–18
nongovernmental organizations (NGOs), 21, 22, 27
   in Banda Aceh, 61
   experience of work with, 197
   in India, 183–87
   role in tsunami rehabilitation, 22, 27
   in Sri Lanka, 251–52
   in Thailand, 176
   See also specific organizations

Oxfam, 185, 192, 197
   approach to tsunami relief, 202
   report, 242

Pak Ko River, 43, 45
Palar River, 65–67, 103
Palk Bay, 66, 80, 83, 84
Palk Strait, 83
Palyar River, 86
Panchayat leaders, distribution of relief supplies by, 209
Pandian Island, 87
Parankippettai Islamic Ikkya Jamaat, 222
Patang Beach, 37–38, 180
Phang Nga, 35, 36, 37, 38, 39, 41, 163, 164, 173, 174, 175, 177
Phi Phi, 11, 35, 38, 163, 169, 175
Phuket, 11, 21, 26, 35, 37, 38, 163–64, 165, 173
   death toll in, 174
   geography and economy of, 168–69
   reconstruction in, 48
   recovery efforts in, 175–76, 179
pilgrim towns, 16, 218, 223, 230
Point Calimere, 17, 66–67, 80, 83, 89
Pondicherry, 66, 67, 80, 99, 185, 218, 222
   homeless in, 101
Port Blair, 19, 118, 125
Post-tsunami Operation Mechanism Structures (P-TOMS), 245
Project Concern International, 185

Pulavali, 85, 89
Pulicat lagoon, 66, 103

Rameshwaram coast, 84
    coral islands of, 86
Ramnathapuram, 104
Ranong, 35, 163
Rashtriya Swayamsevak Sangh, 232
Red Cross. See American Red Cross;
    British Red Cross; Indian Red Cross
Redskin Island, 120, 122, 123
Rishikesh Swamy Dayananda Educational
    Trust, 234

Saint Hazrath Saiyed Shahul Hameed
    Qadir Oli Dargah, 222
Saint John's Medical College Hospital, 222
Saint Thomas Mount, 224–25
Santhome Cathedral, Chennai, 223, 227
    shelter for tsunami victims, 234
Satun, 21, 35
Save the Children, 264
Seenigama village, Sri Lanka, 135–36
    coping with tsunami, 144–45
    damage from tsunami, 138–40
    interviews with survivors, 141–42
    reconstruction in, 145–46
    structure of vulnerability, 157–58
Showa Great Tsunami, 152
Sirinat National Park, 169
Social Need Education and Human
    Awareness, 185, 197
Sri Lanka, 23, 24, 26, 27, 83, 89, 95, 104,
    105, 119, 135
    casualties and damaged houses, 136
    civil conflict in, 244–45
    community participation in rebuilding,
    252–53
    corruption in reconstruction process,
    254–55
    devastation from tsunami, 8, 20–21, 176
    economic losses by tsunami, 240
    environmental impacts of tsunami, 240
    government policy, 243
    housing construction in, 249
    livelihood rebuilding, 250–51
    post-tsunami reconstruction, 237–58

reconstruction experience, 27, 243–44
restriction on building close to seashore, 144
social impacts of tsunami, 241–42
train carriages, wrecked, 243
tsunami affected areas in, 239
Sri Lanka Freedom Party (SLFP), 245, 246
Sumatra-Andaman Earthquake, 7
Sumatra Island, 51
Sunda trench, 7, 69

Tamil Nadu, India, 10, 16, 17–18, 99, 101
    changes in faunal assemblages, 93–95
    coastal geomorphic features, 67–68
    continental shelf, 65–66
    Dalits in, 197
    inundation in southern sector of coast,
    85, 104
    sedimentation in fishing harbors, 83
    sediment characteristics, 87–93
    Slum Clearance Board, 215
    Social Welfare Board, 192
    tsunami deposits in, 77–83
    tsunami inundation in, 69–77, 83
Tamil Nadu Voluntary Health Association,
    185
Taro Town, Japan, 135
    tsunami history, 148–49
    tsunami mitigation efforts, 149–50
Thailand, 1, 2, 6, 7, 11, 12, 21, 25, 35, 41,
    42, 49, 114, 127, 164, 268, 271, 283
    death toll in, 35, 266
    emergency response, 165
    foreign tourists in, 165, 176
    government relief fund, 177
    post-tsunami recovery, 26, 163, 176
    reconstruction experience, 27, 180
    tourism in, 22, 164, 173–75, 179
    tsunami damage in, 168, 171
Thirumalai Rayan Pattinam, 222
Tirunelveli, 104, 218
Trang, 35, 163
transnational terrorist organizations, 284
tsunami
    and coastal morphology, 9
    community consultation and
    participation in reconstruction,
    252–53

tsunami *(cont.)*
  countries affected by, 1, 7
  definition of, 1
  donor response, 264–65
  geopolitical aspects, 25–26
  governance for recovery, 24, 181
  how to reduce damages, 154
  impact on the Indian coast, 101
  influence of geomorphic features on
    inundation, 111
  lessons learned from, 193–95, 205,
    269–70
  local capacities, 24
  maximum inundation in southeast
    India, 17
  new construction in Thailand, 180
  reconstruction experience, 27
  relief efforts in South India, 216
  relocation of people, 204–5
  role of religious institutions in relief,
    219
  societal and economic impacts, 21
  vulnerability to, 5, 6, 21
  See also Indian Ocean Tsunami
tsunami, Indian Ocean. *See* Indian Ocean
  Tsunami
Tsunami Evaluation Coalition, 25, 26
Tsunami Nagar, Chennai, 25
Tuticorin, 86, 104

Ulee Lheue, 13, 52
United Nations Children's Fund
  (UNICEF), 264, 290

United Nations Development Programme
  (UNDP), 264
United Nations Indian Ocean Tsunami
  Flash Appeal, 263–64
United Nations Population Fund (UNPF),
  264
Uppanar River, 105

Vaigai fault, 66
Van Island, 87
Vedharanyam, 71, 80, 99, 104, 105
  coastal wetlands, 107
  fault, 66
Velanganni, 218, 223, 228, 231, 234, 235
  population of, 230
Velanganni Church, 16, 17, 221
Vellar River, 71, 77, 104, 106
Villupuram, 103
Viper Island, 124

White, Gilbert F., 4, 6
women, 2, 5, 185, 191, 242
  death toll, 227, 242
  housing grants, 257
  human trafficking in, 289
  livelihood strategies, 20, 250
  rights, 193, 202
  role of, in fishing communities, 208, 216
  sexual violence against, 289
World Food Program (WFP), 264
World Vision, 185
Wright Myo, 120, 123